Taxidermied

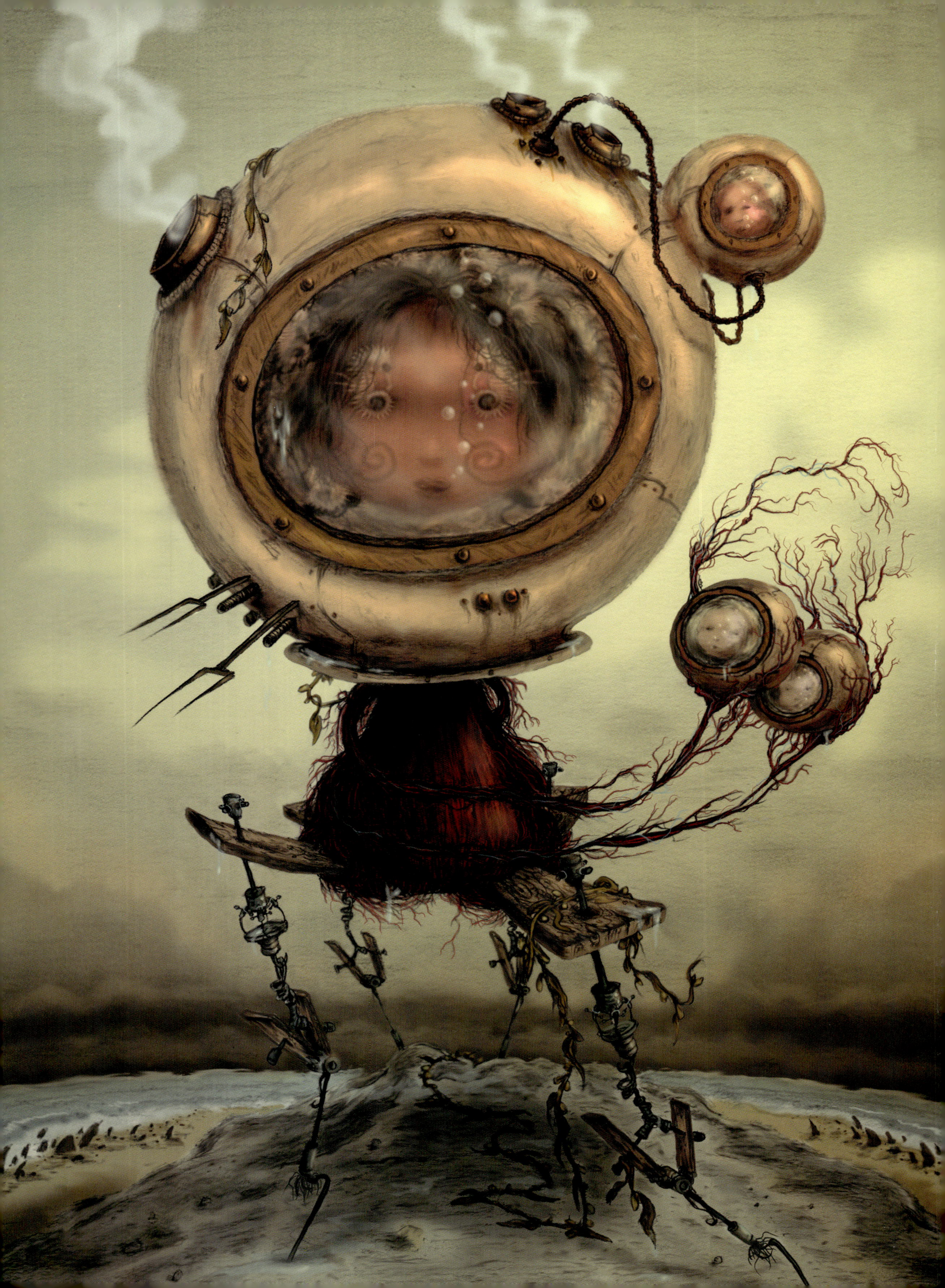

Taxidermied

The Art Of Roman Dirge

Titan Books

Taxidermied: The Art Of Roman Dirge
ISBN: 9781845769390

Published by
Titan Books
A division of Titan Publishing Group Ltd.
144 Southwark St.
London
SE1 0UP

First edition: September 2011
1 3 5 7 9 10 8 6 4 2

Front Board: "The Last Tea Party"
Frontispiece (page 2): "It Came Ashore Wanting More."

Visit our websites:
www.spookyland.com
www.titanbooks.com

What did you think of this book? We love to hear from our readers. Please e-mail us at: readerfeedback@titanemail.com or write to Reader Feedback at the above address.

A CIP catalogue record for this title is available from the British Library.

Printed and bound in China by C&C Offset Printing Co., Ltd.

Contents

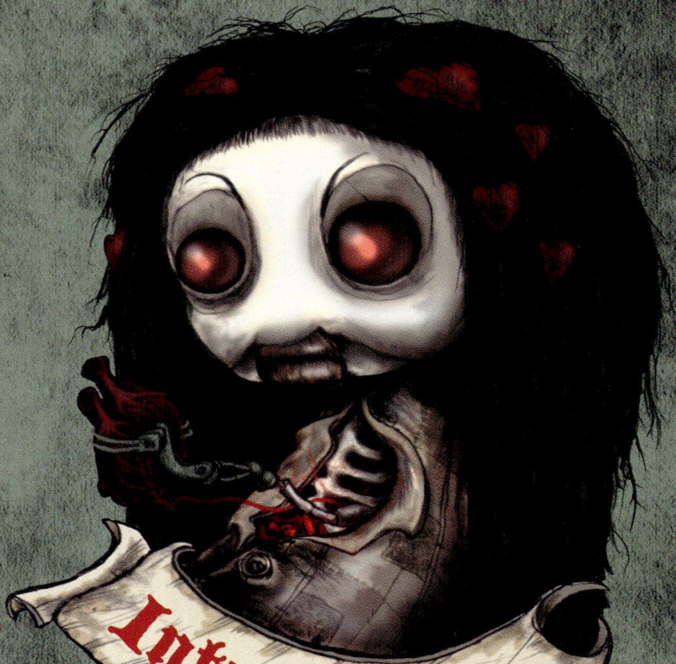

Introduction
By Roman Dirge

Greetings, salutations and booga-booga. My name is Roman Dirge and welcome to my first art book collecting pieces old and new. It's a real journey for me to see them all together like this, as some illicit, interesting, and at times horrid memories of old. As slow as I work, the next book won't come out until after I'm dead, and it will be a really boring one, just filled with lonely, blank pages. The works presented here were mainly done by way of pencil drawings and then colored electronically. By electronically I mean I have a colorist robot named Colortron 5000 that does my color-y bidding. All right, I call my hand Colortron 5000. Is that weird? It is? Oh.

My art reflects me pretty appropriately. My love of taxidermy and oddities seeps its way into pretty much everything I do. I can try to draw the simplest, most innocent of things… but I guarantee it'll end up with blood and a restraining order involved.

I'd really like to thank the fine folks at Titan Books for letting me churn out this weirdness. I've been wanting to do this for as long as I can remember, which was Tuesday.

So, flex your jaw, jiggle your page turning arms, wear something nice and come with me on a magical journey as you dance your eyeballs across the pages ahead. I won't actually be with you, but I will be there in spirit… Floating next to you… Just to the left. You really need to clean up your place. It's disgusting in here.

DIRGE!

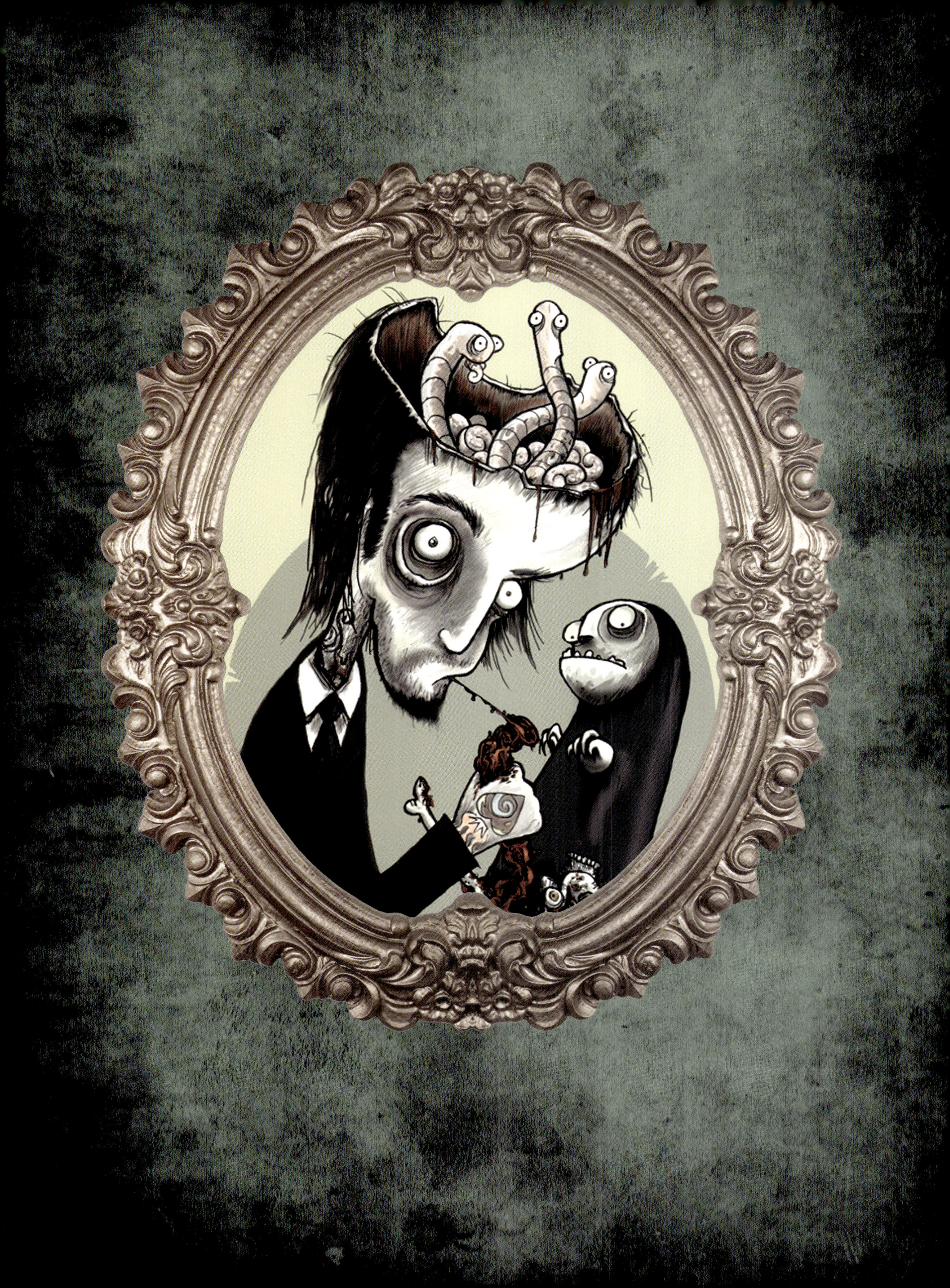

Sketches

I perused some of my old sketchbooks and found some forgotten ditties. Whoa, the spell check almost changed that sentence into something a lot more interesting! Anyhoo, not much to say about these. They're sketches. A monkey can sketch.

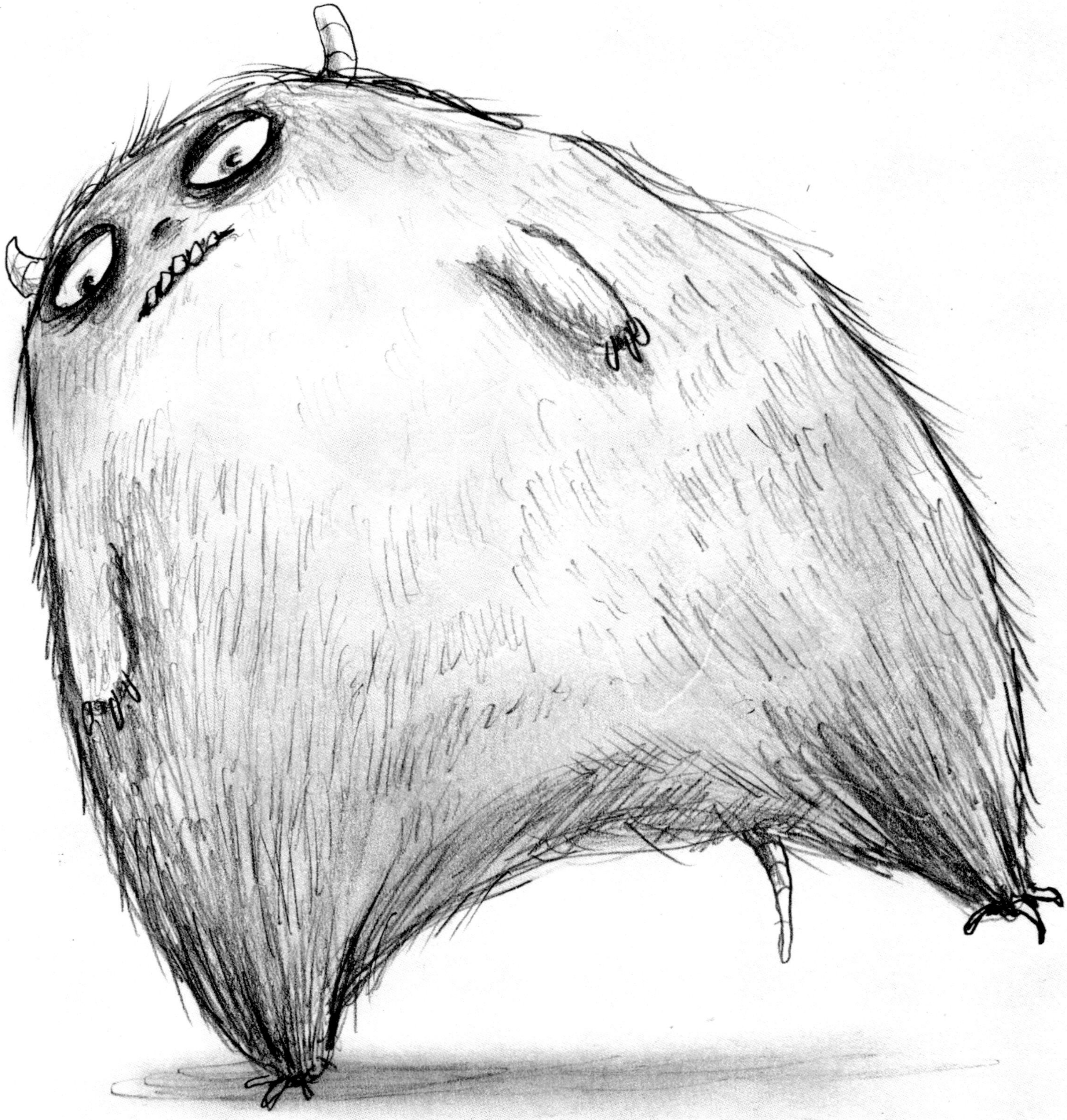

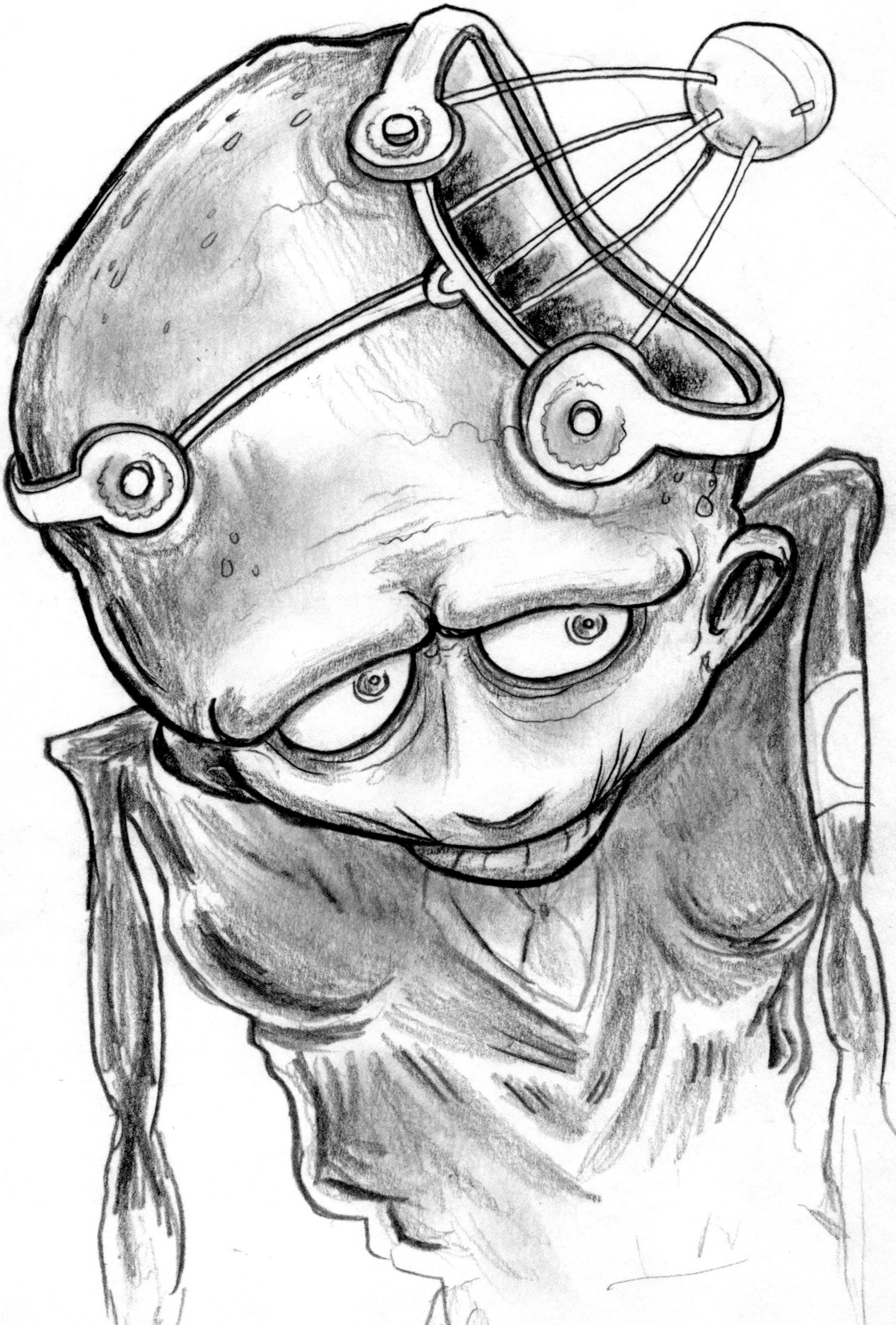

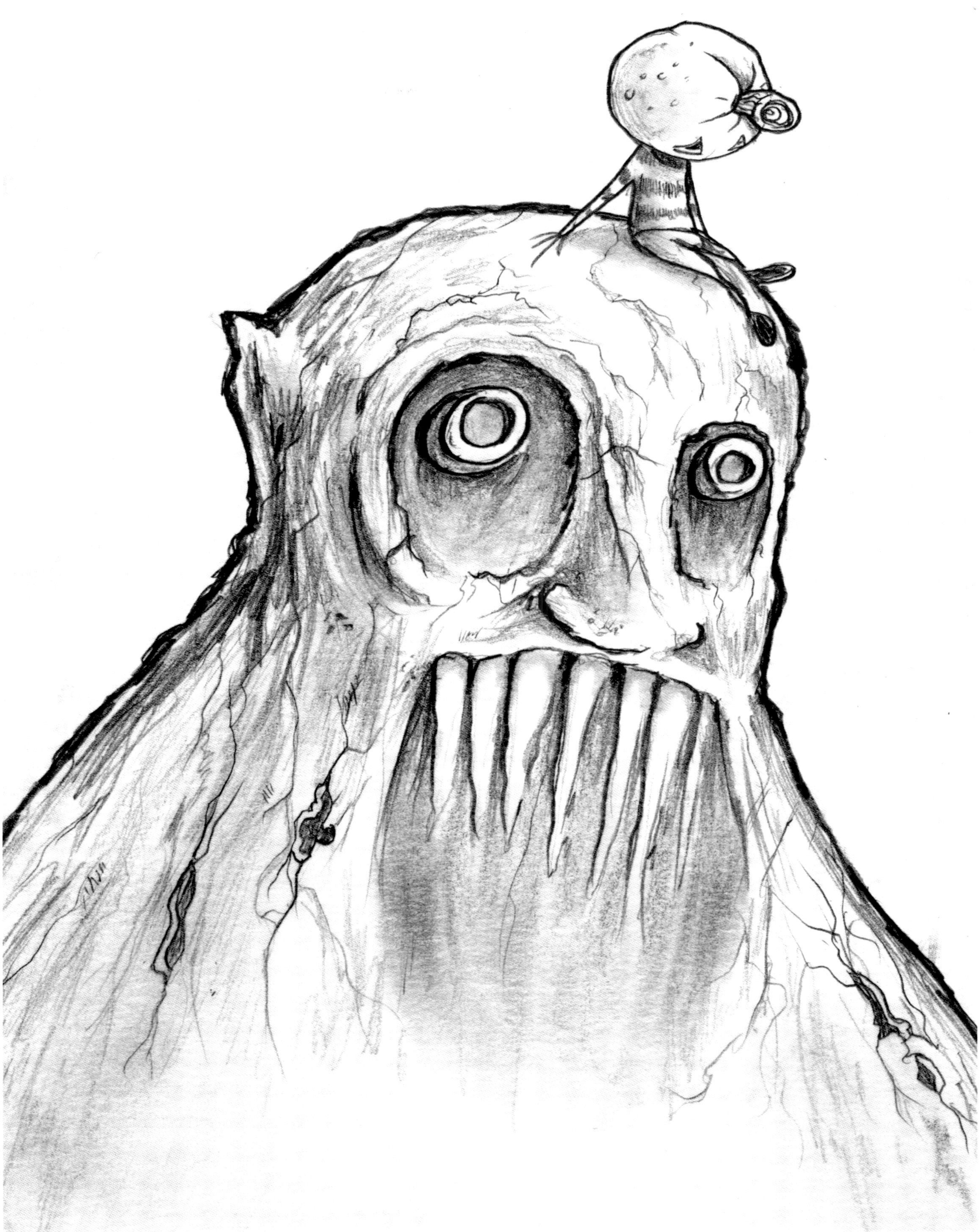

Opposite:
I vaguely remember I was doodling an old man who wanted to get satellite info beamed directly into his head. It didn't work though, 'cause he hollowed his head and just became a mindless drooler.

Above:
That little pumpkin boy is named Choobie and he's sitting on a rock monster. Pumpkin boys do that.

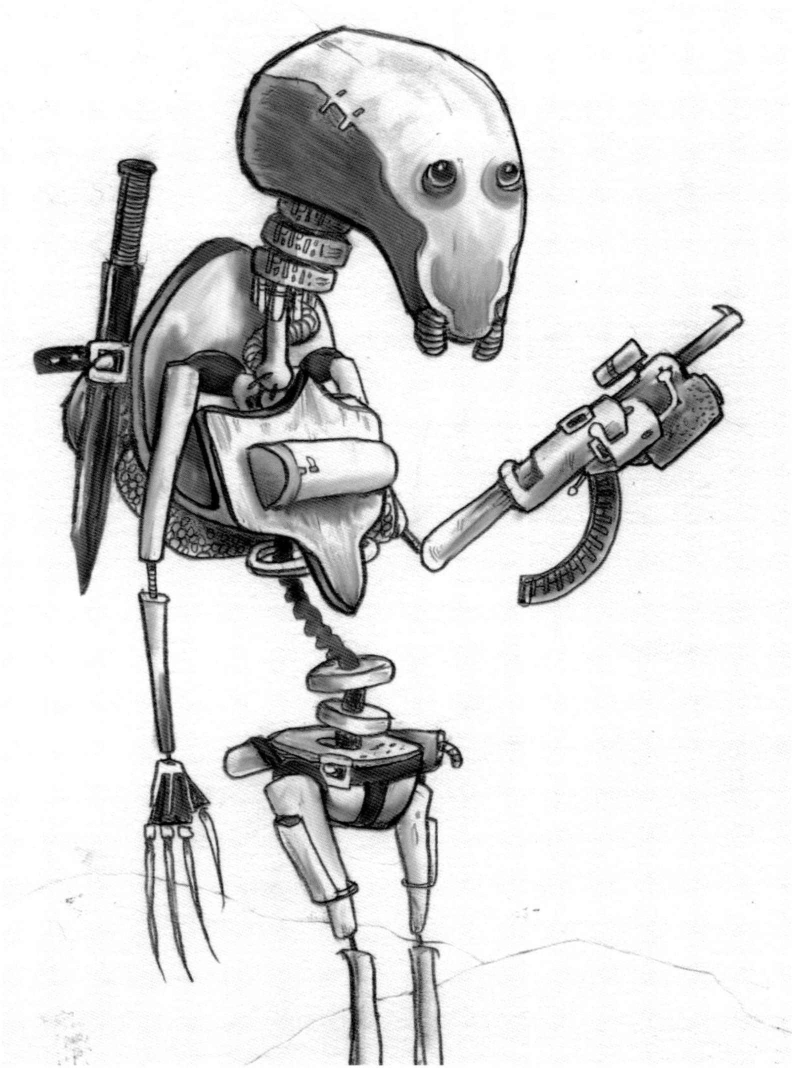

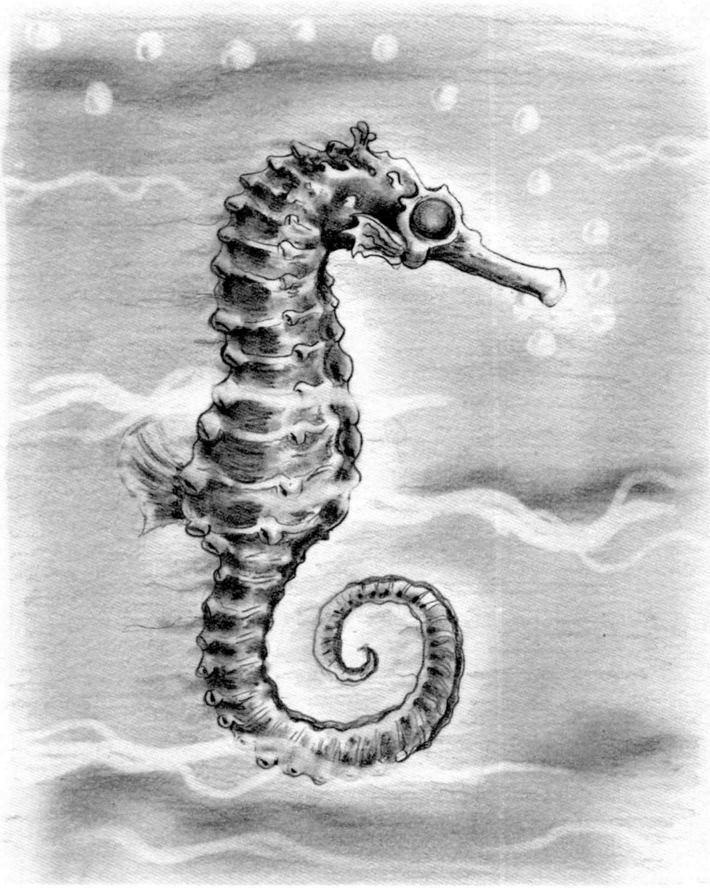

Above:
Robot. He's an oldie. I wanted a robot army to conquer the world and was toying with the basic design. I later discovered booze, subsequently ending my dream of making a robot army.

Right:
Seahorse. Little horsey of the sea sketched for an ex-girlfriend who had a seahorse fixation.

Opposite:
An elf, cleverly named "Elf." I wanted to make a short film about a demon who had escaped Hell and disguised himself as an elf who accompanied Santa only so he could secretly feed off the calcium from children's teeth. You know, that old tale. Oddly enough, that film never got finished. I played with a gaggle of elf designs, but he was my favorite.

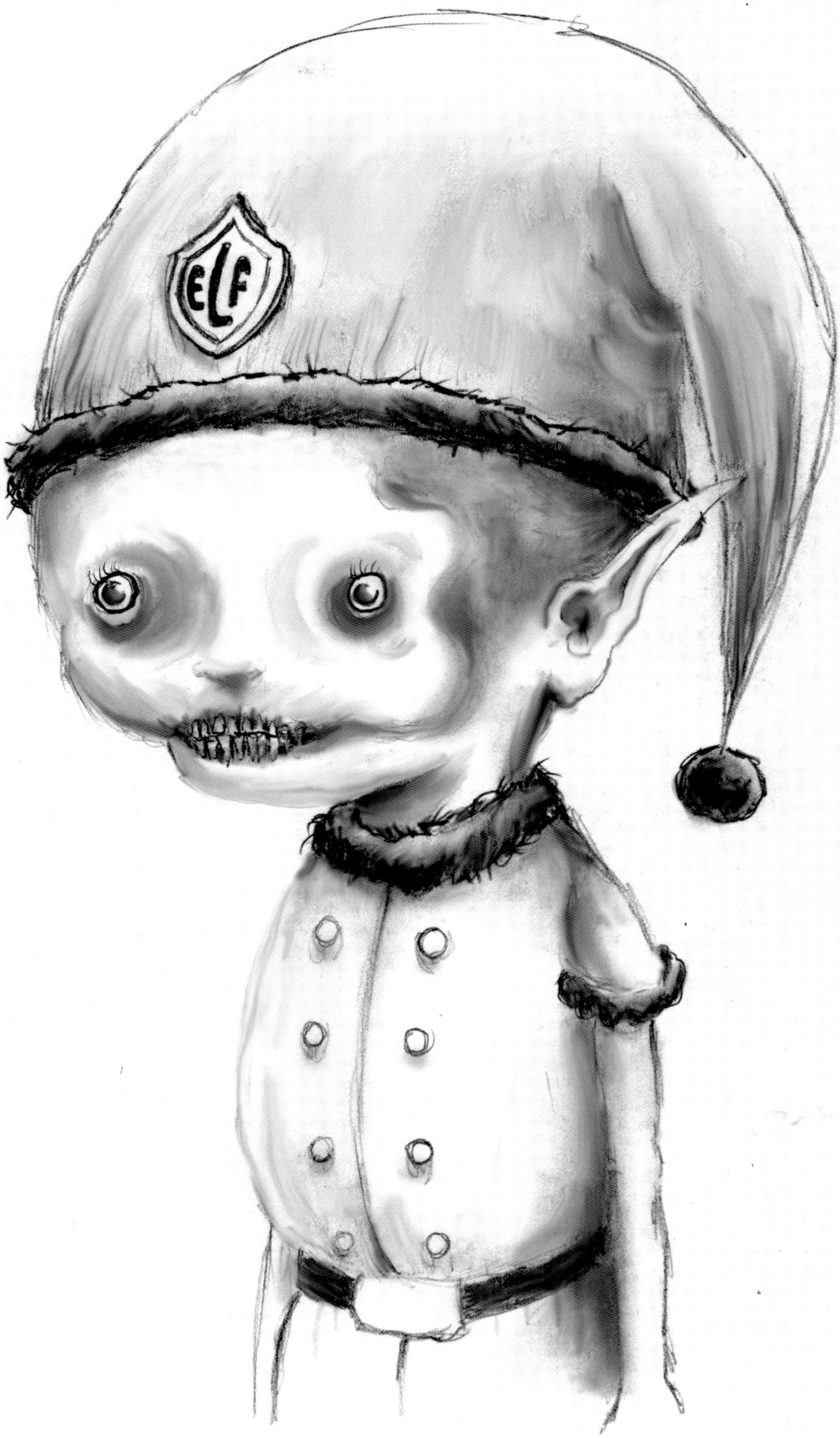
ELF

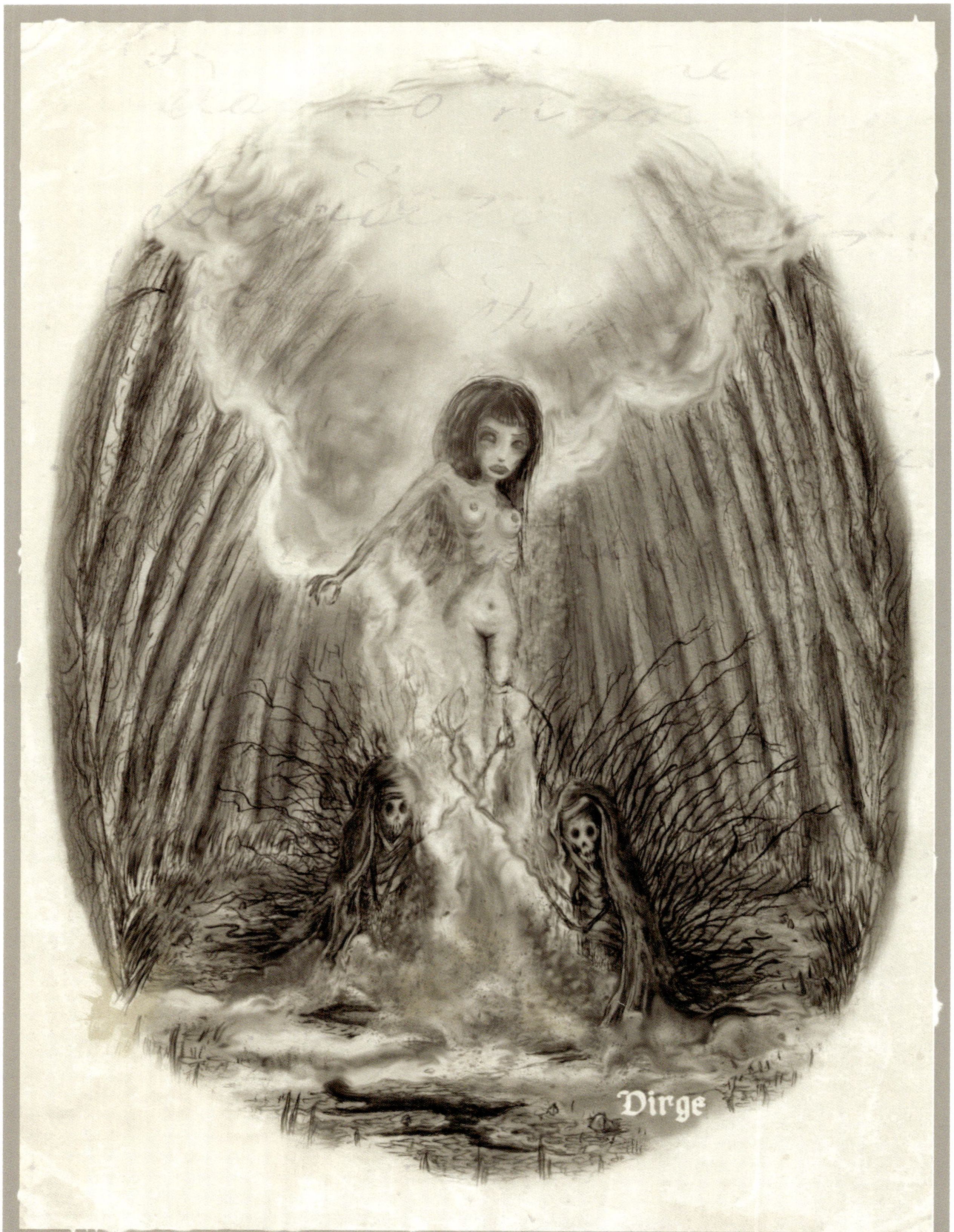

Above:
This was a weird dream I was having, so I sketched it out the second I woke up. Unfortunately, I was on a plane at the time and the floating girl was a random attractive stranger sitting next to me. She seemed flattered… or scared. Not sure. She got off the plane fast when we landed. Could have been a bathroom issue though.

Opposite: "NECKOLOPOLIS."
Drawn for an ex-girlfriend who had a serious giraffe fixation. Don't know what that was about.

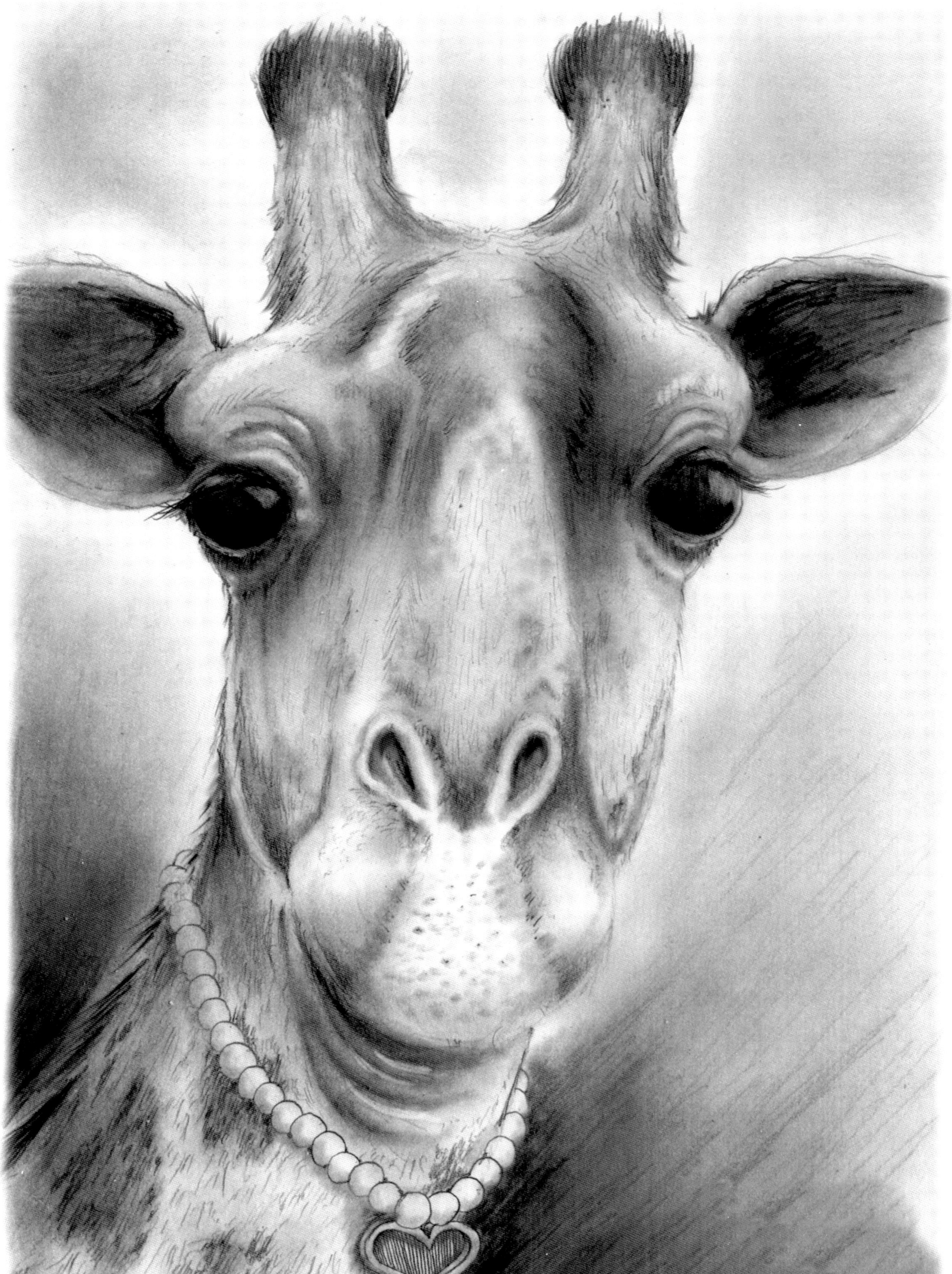

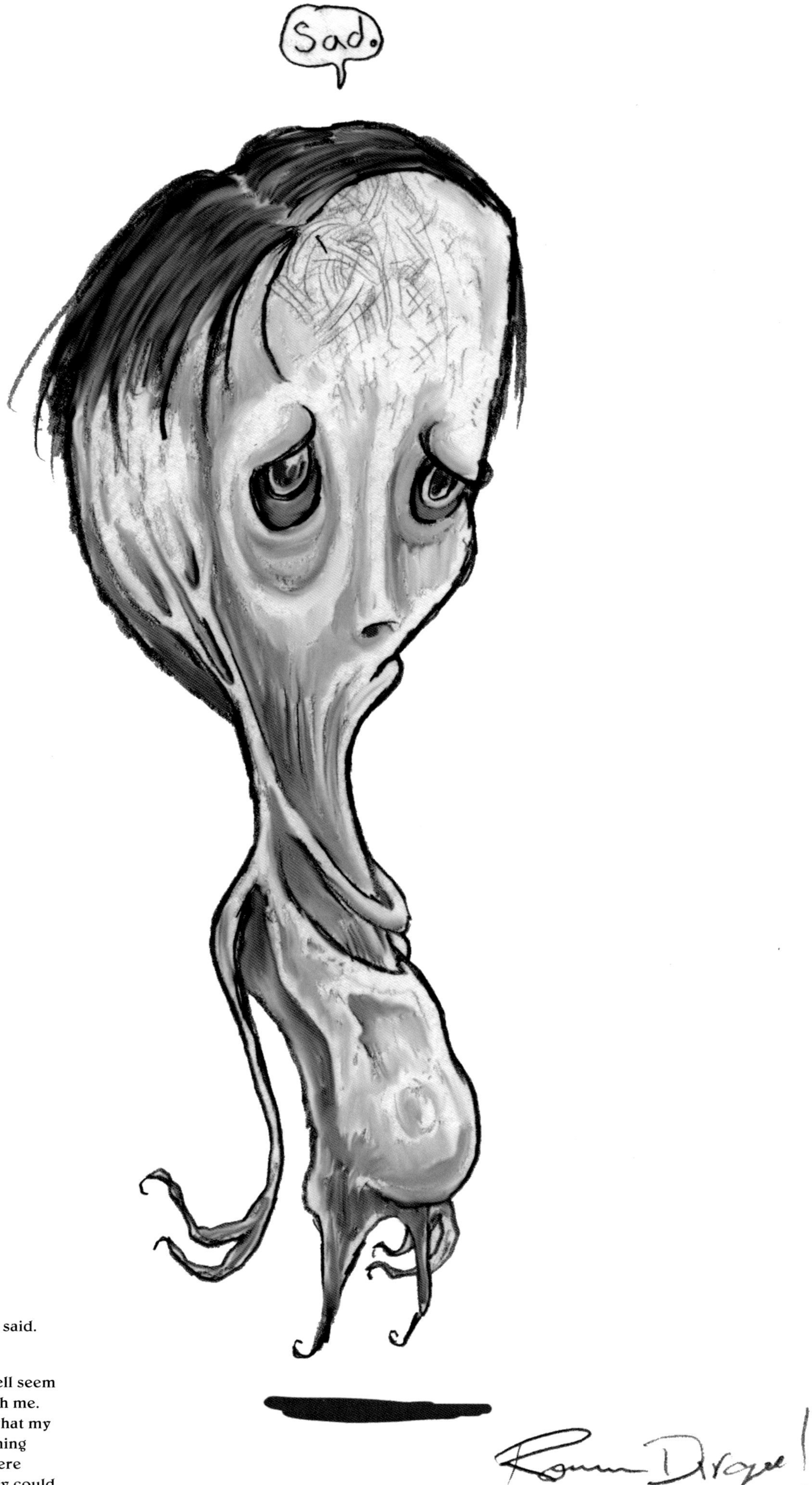

Right:
Floaty emo monster. 'Nuff said.

Opposite:
Demons escaping from Hell seem to be an ongoing thing with me. Maybe it's 'cause I know what my future holds and I'm planning ahead. These little guys were building a fake person they could ride in. Sort of a people car.

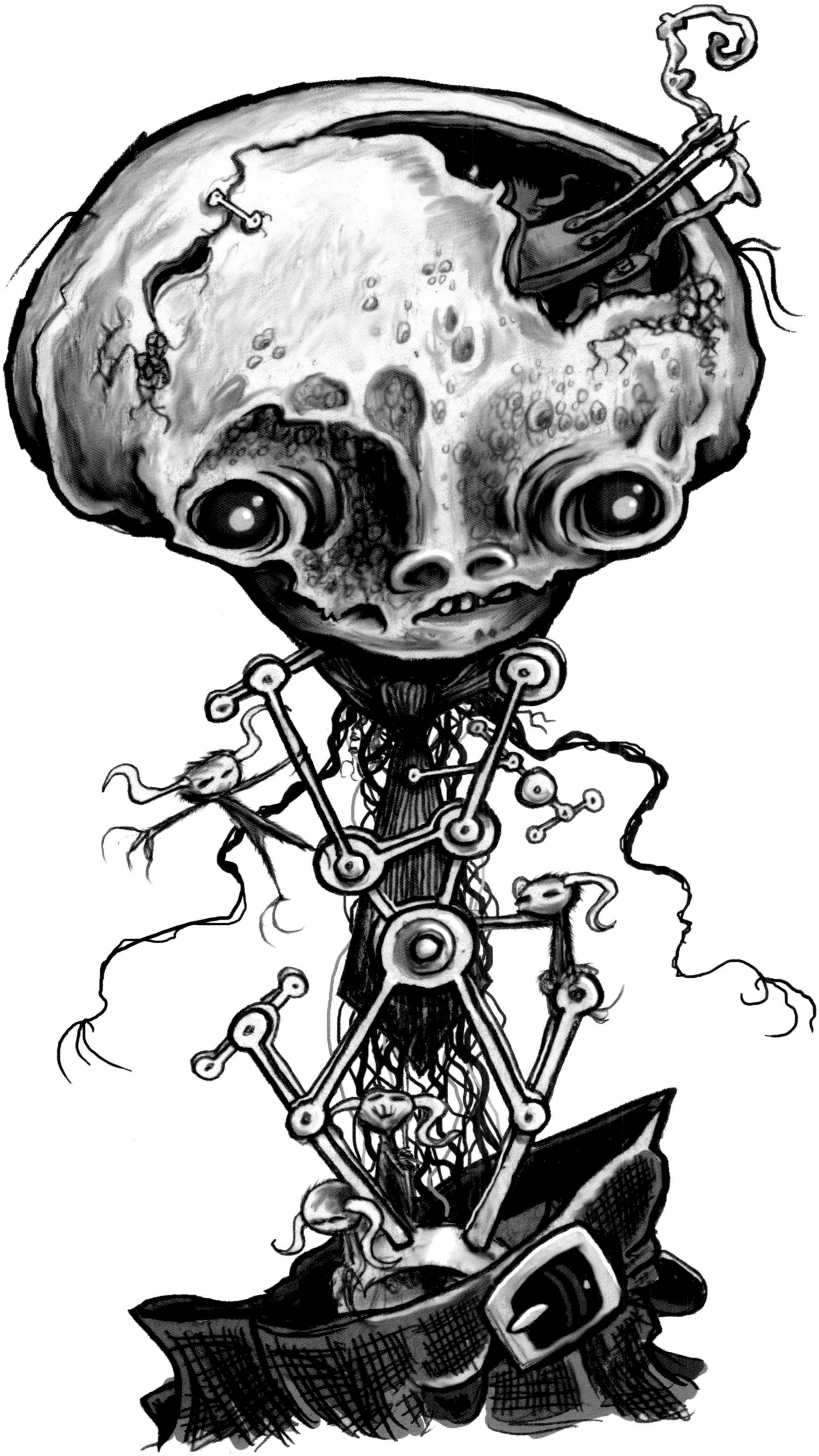

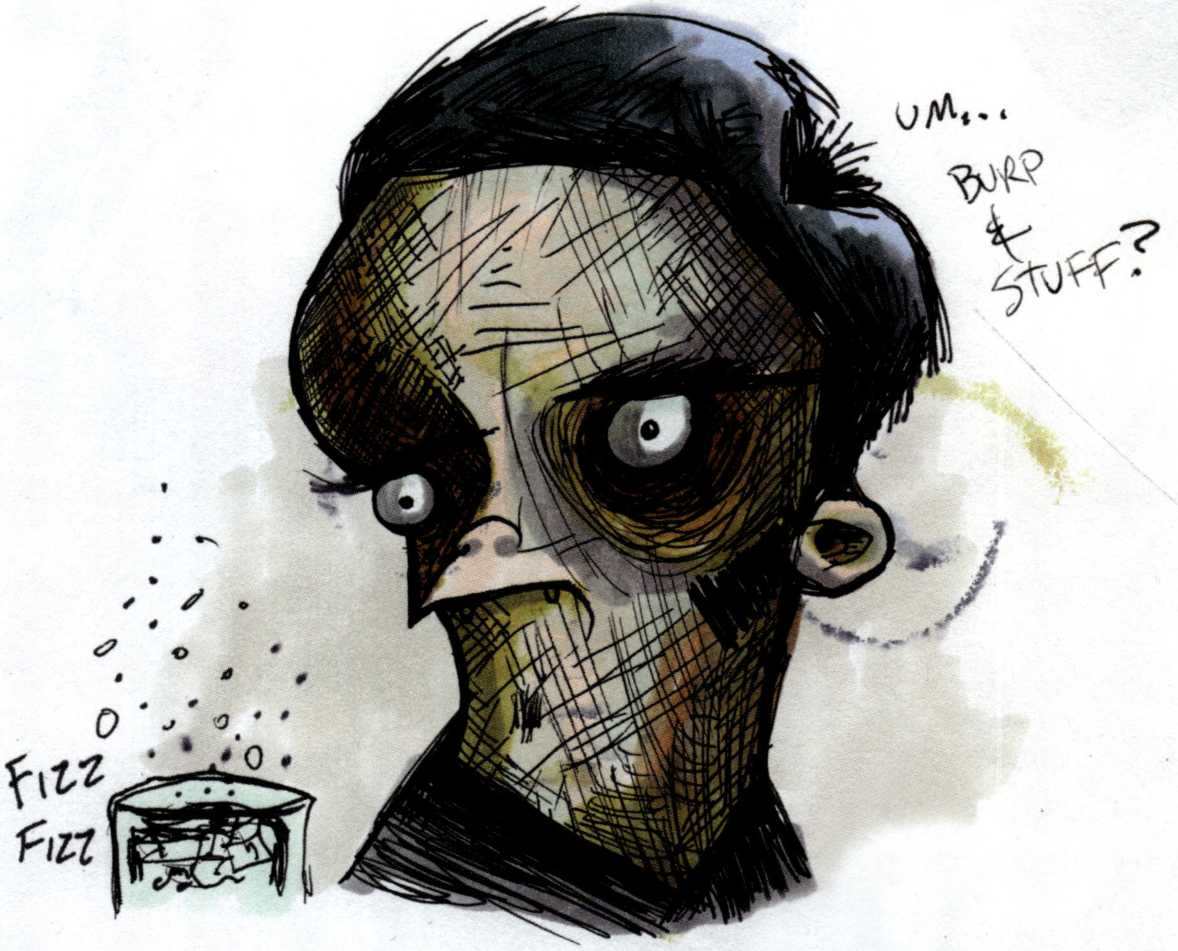
UM...
BURP
&
STUFF?
FIZZ
FIZZ

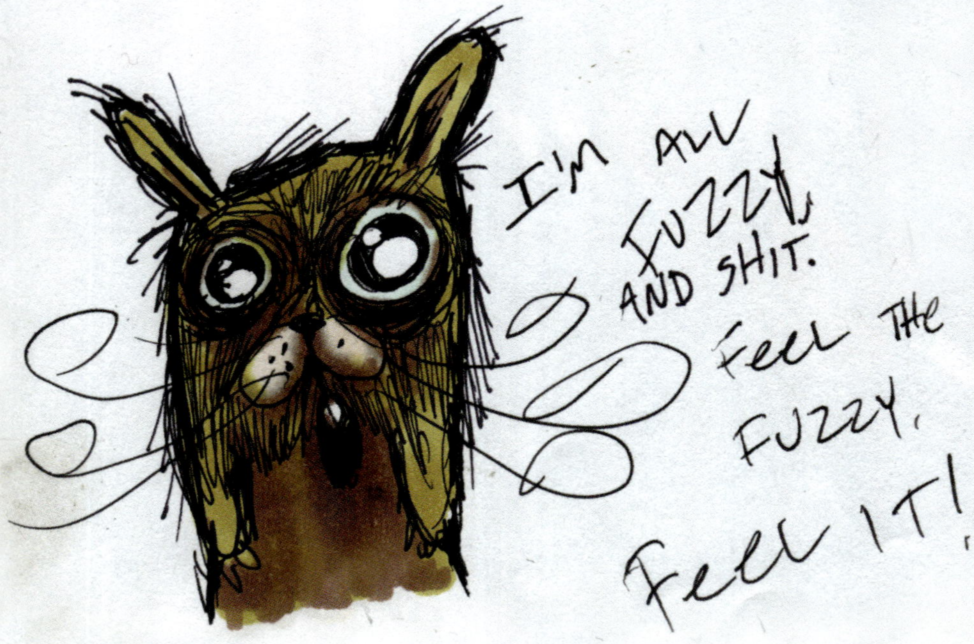
I'M ALL
FUZZY
AND SHIT.
Feel the
FUZZY,
Feel IT!

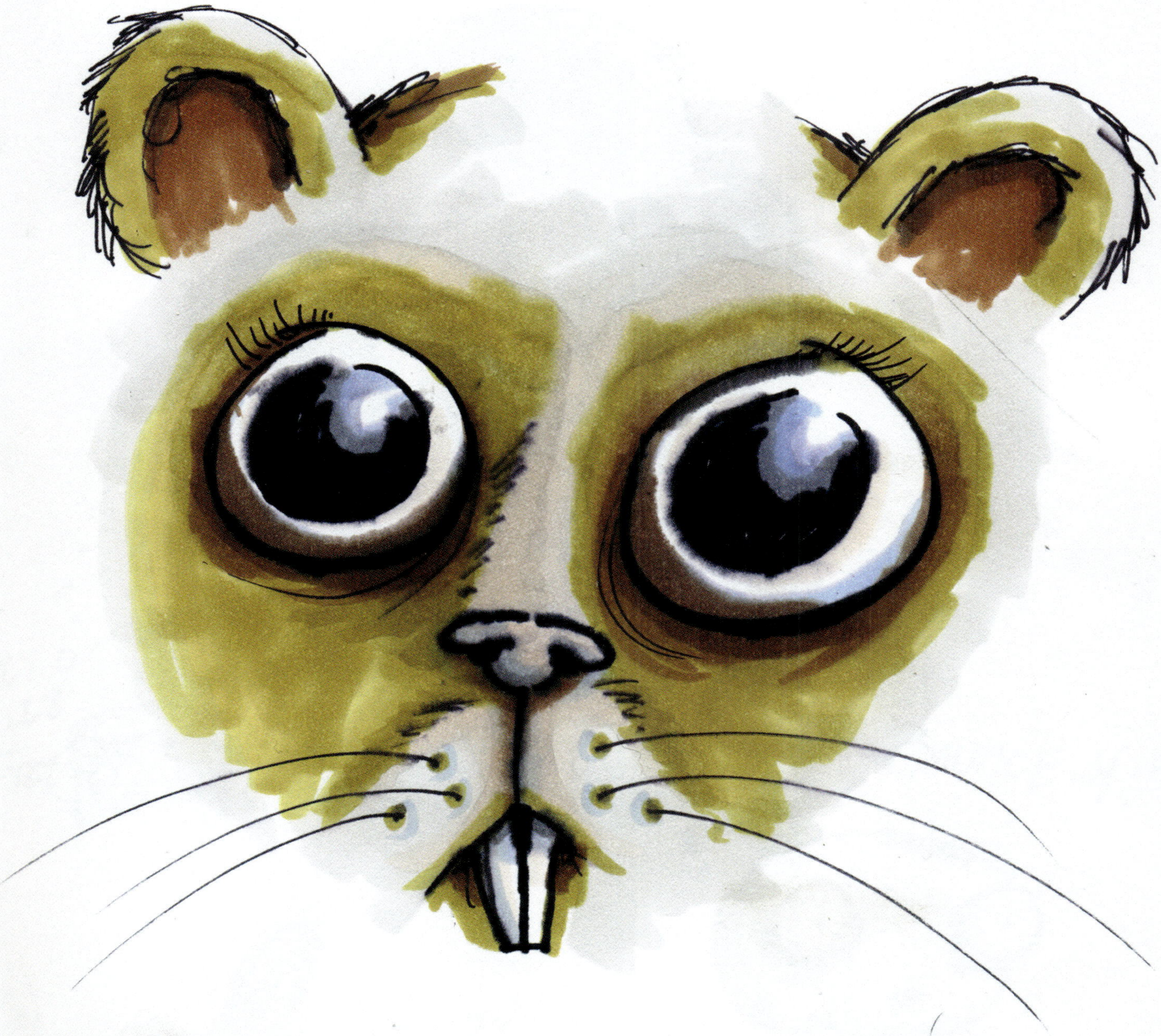

Opposite:
Nuthin'.

Above:
Still nuthin'.

Artwork

Most of these were done in the wee hours of the night. I was drinking heavily and have the bladder of a hummingbird, so "wee hours" has a whole new context behind it. Most of the time I don't really have a plan when I start a piece and just let it flow naturally, but there is always, absolutely a concept…usually. The piece opposite is called "Cased Away", and was a present for my Mom.

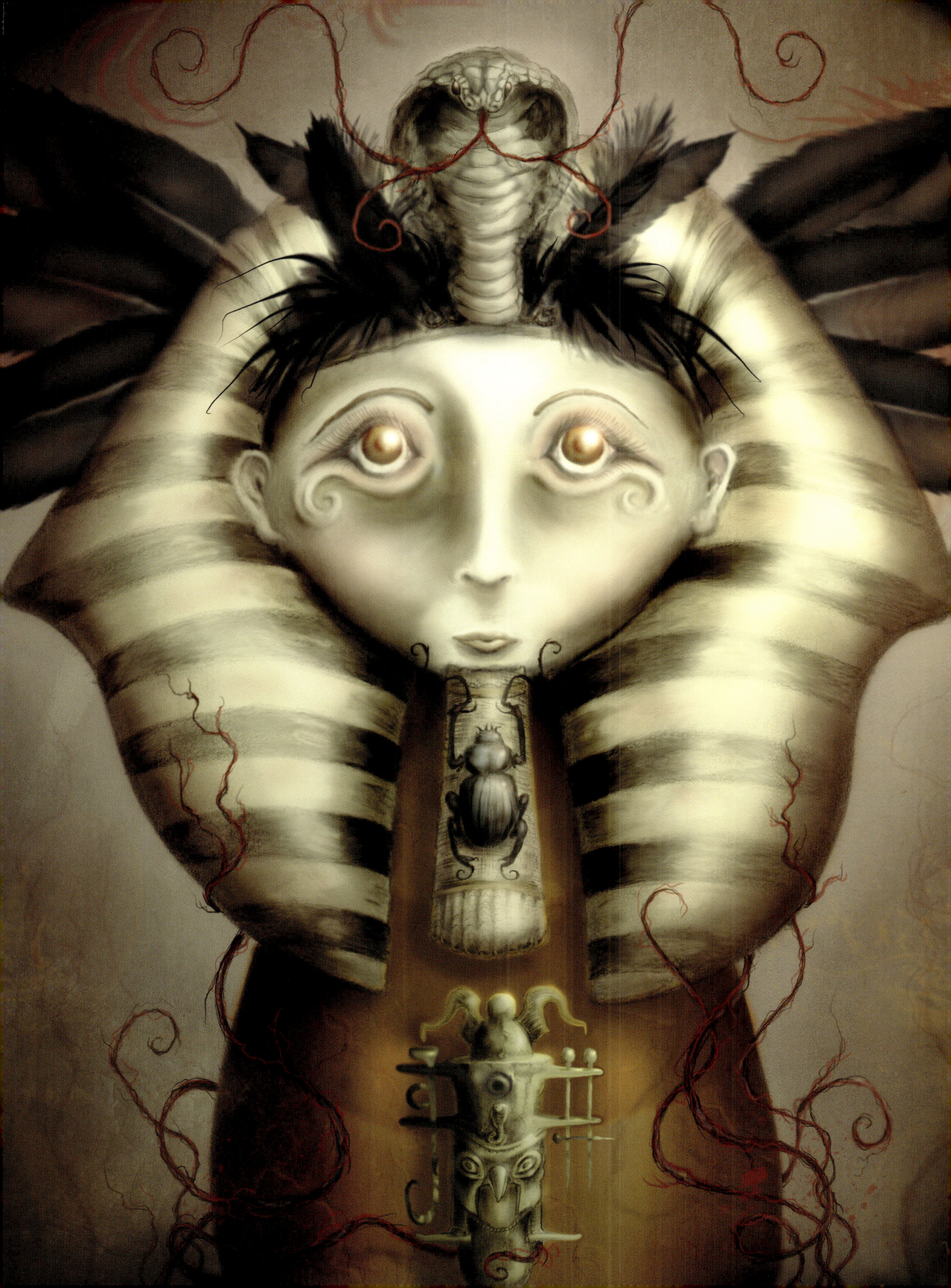

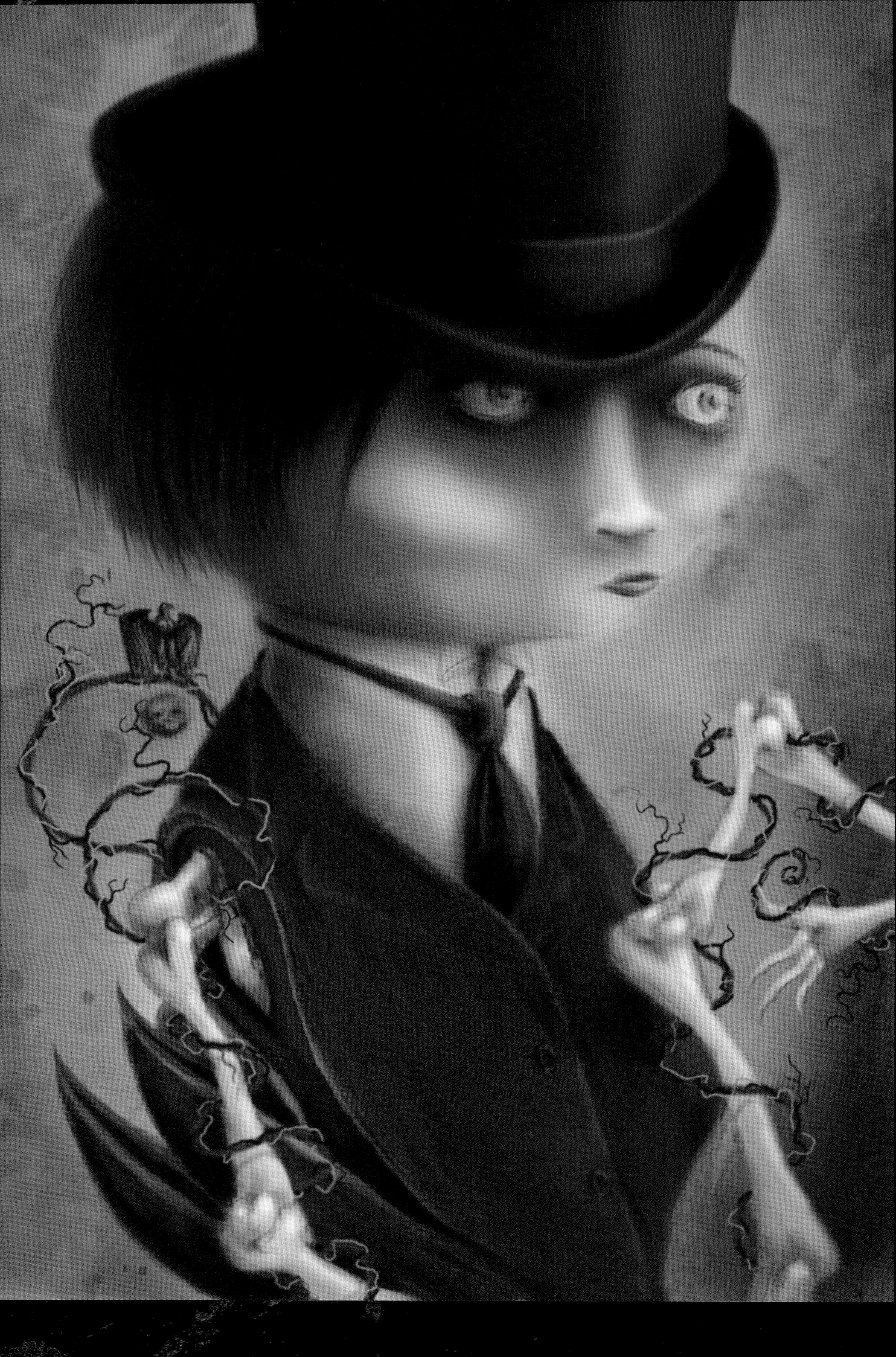

Above: "Bones McBoney

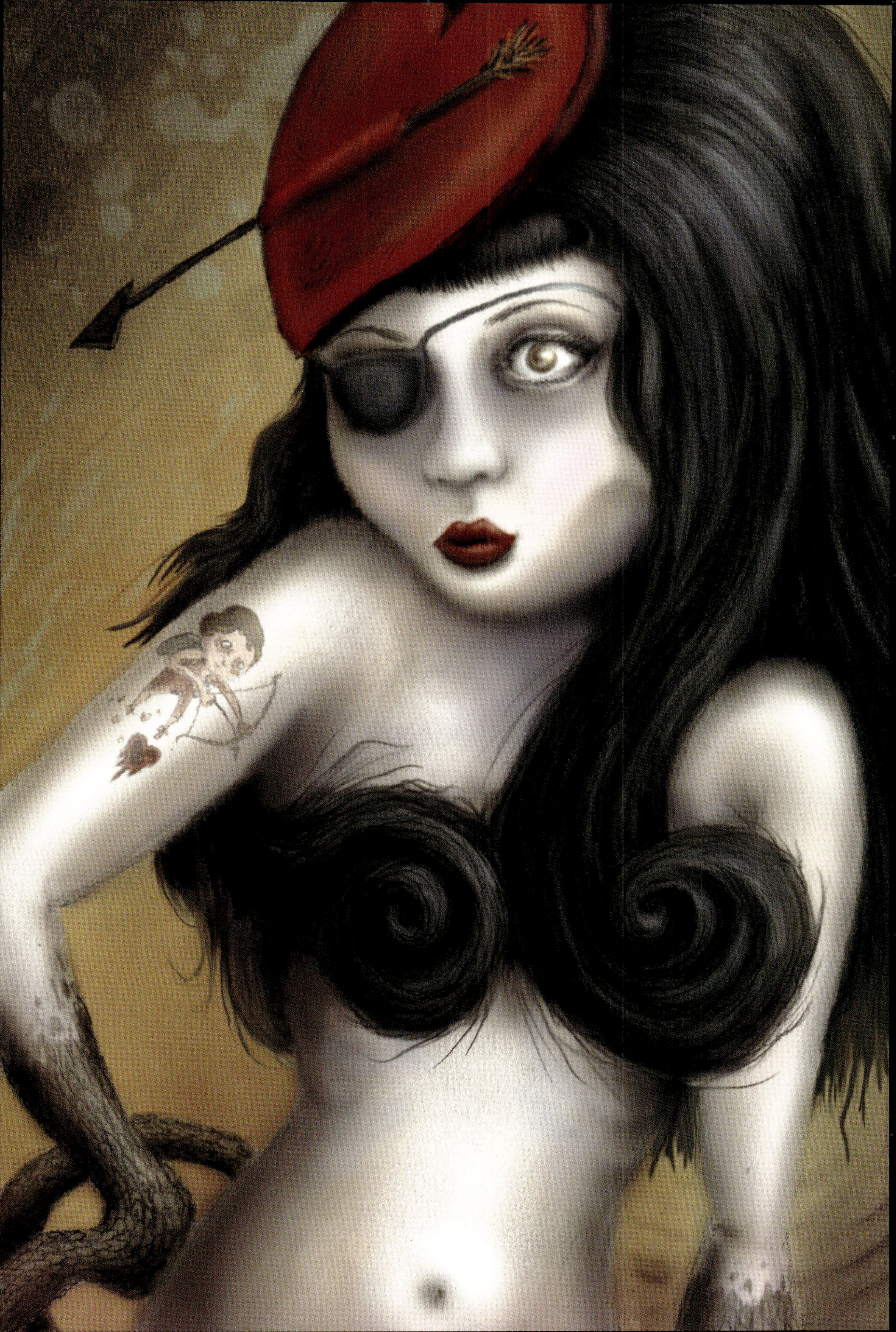

Above: "Arrowcide."

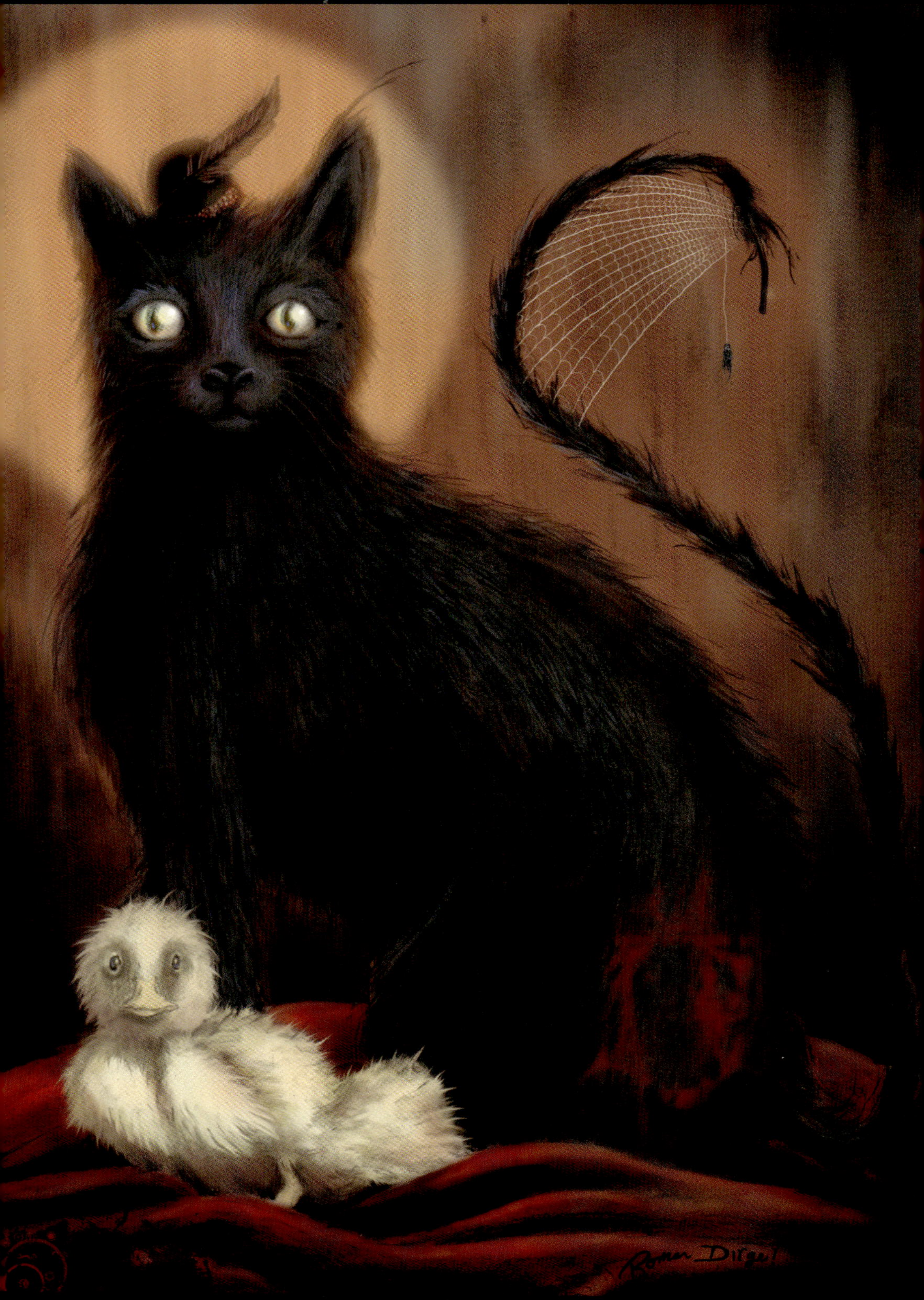

bove: "Fancy, Fancy Kitty."
ats make everything fancy.

pposite: "Dahlia."
fter the Black Dahlia case, a
otoriously unsolved murder
here the victim was cut in half. Ew.

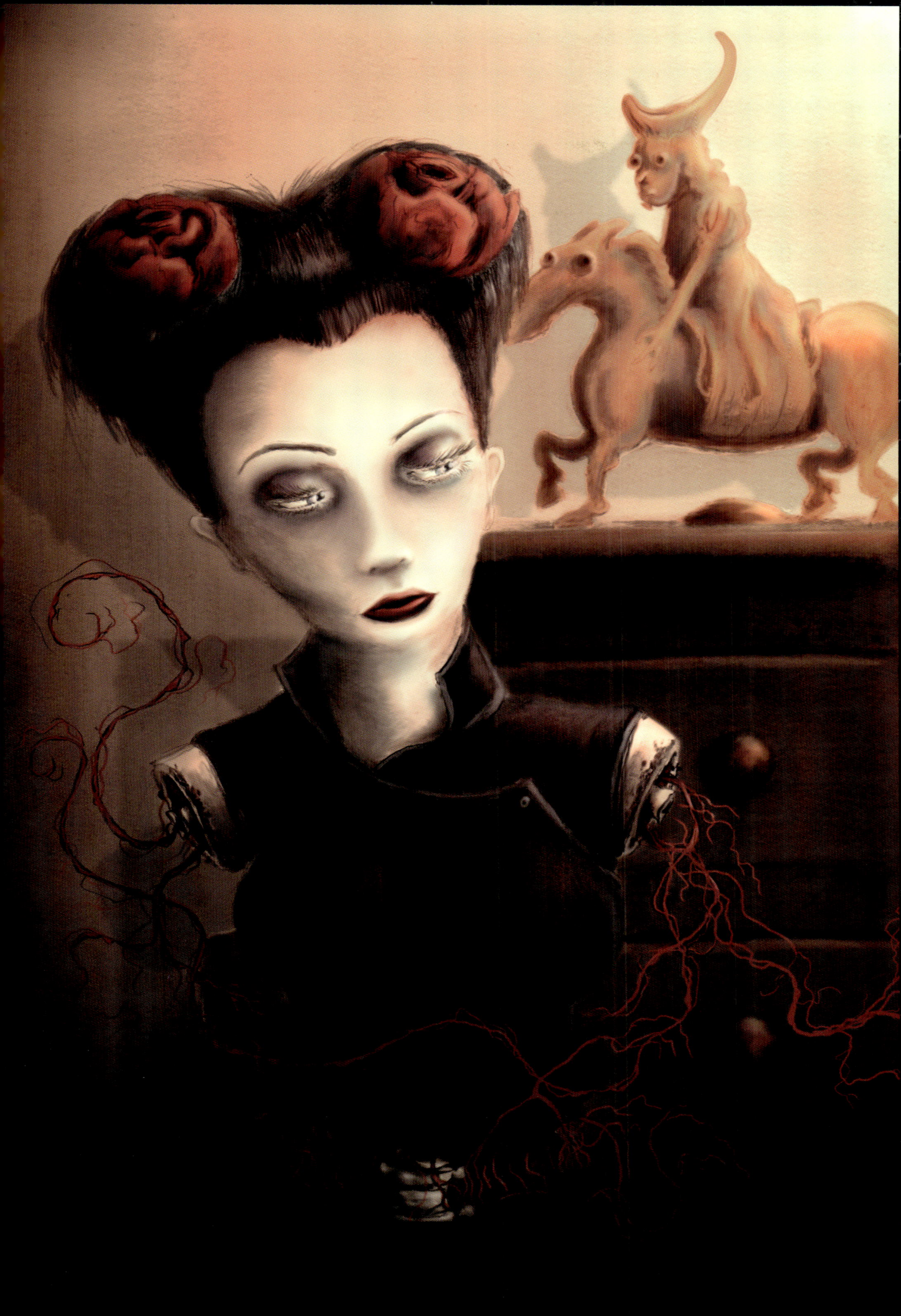

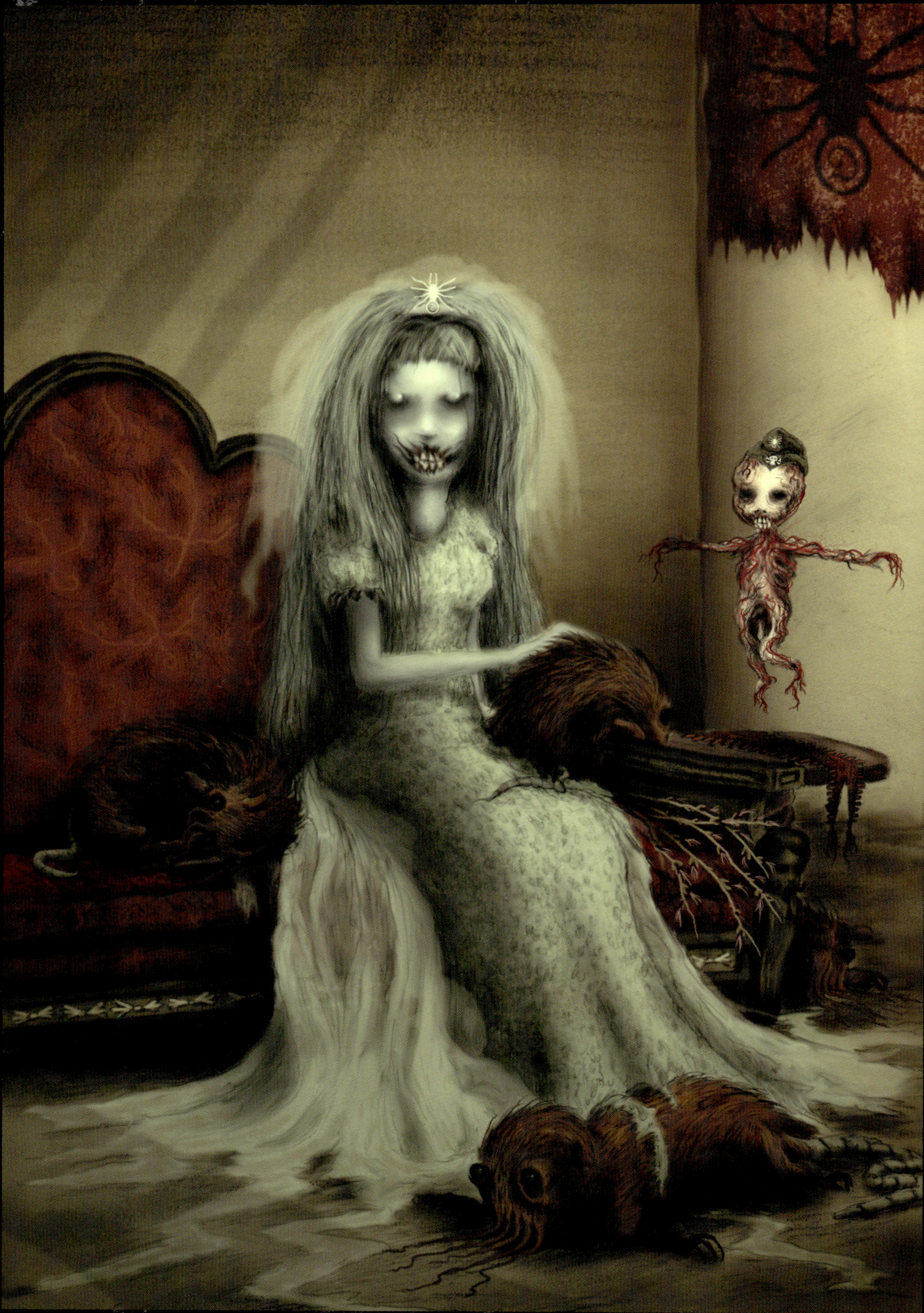

Above: "The Bride Wore Death."
I had a dream I married a zombie so this piece happened. Don't remember how the dream ended but it couldn't have been good.

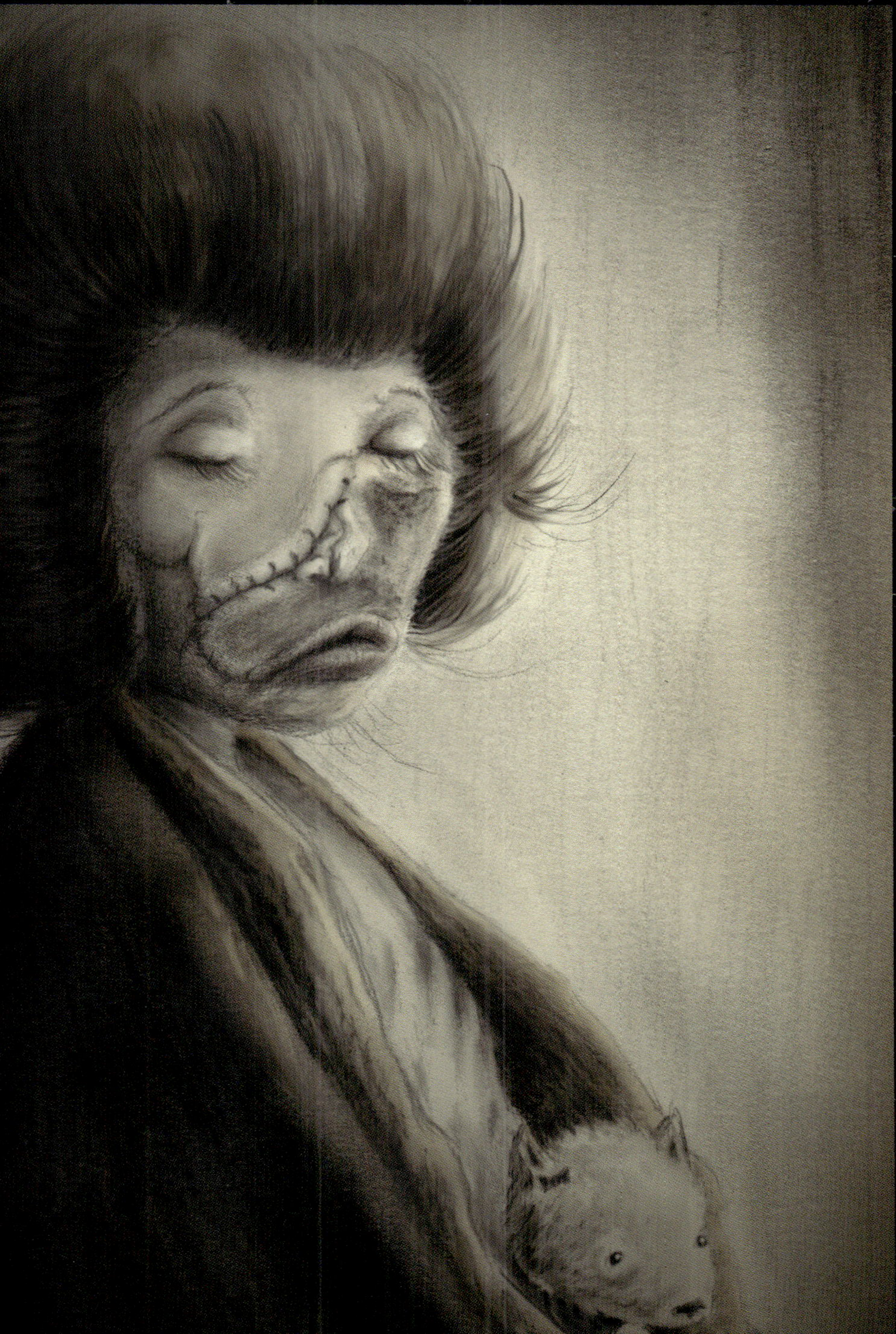

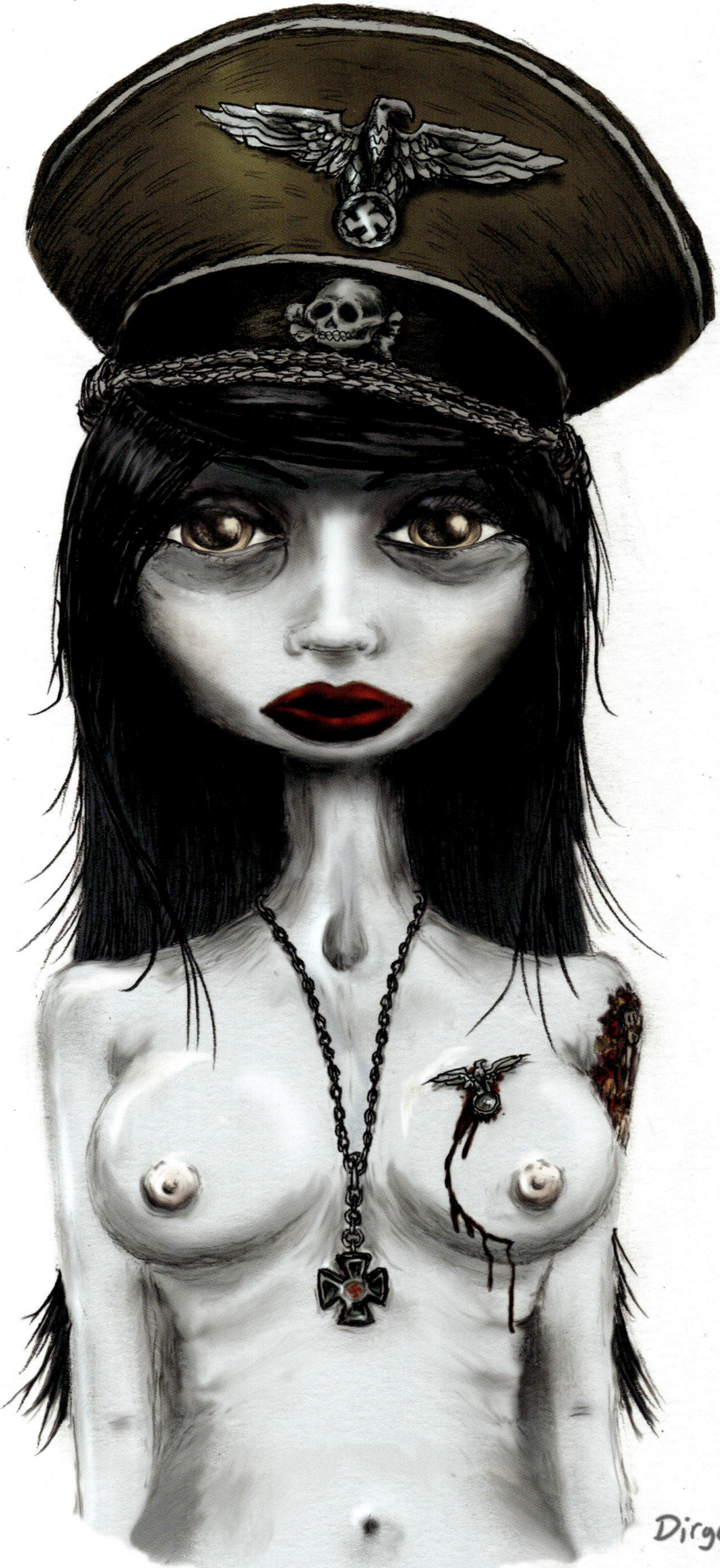
Dirge

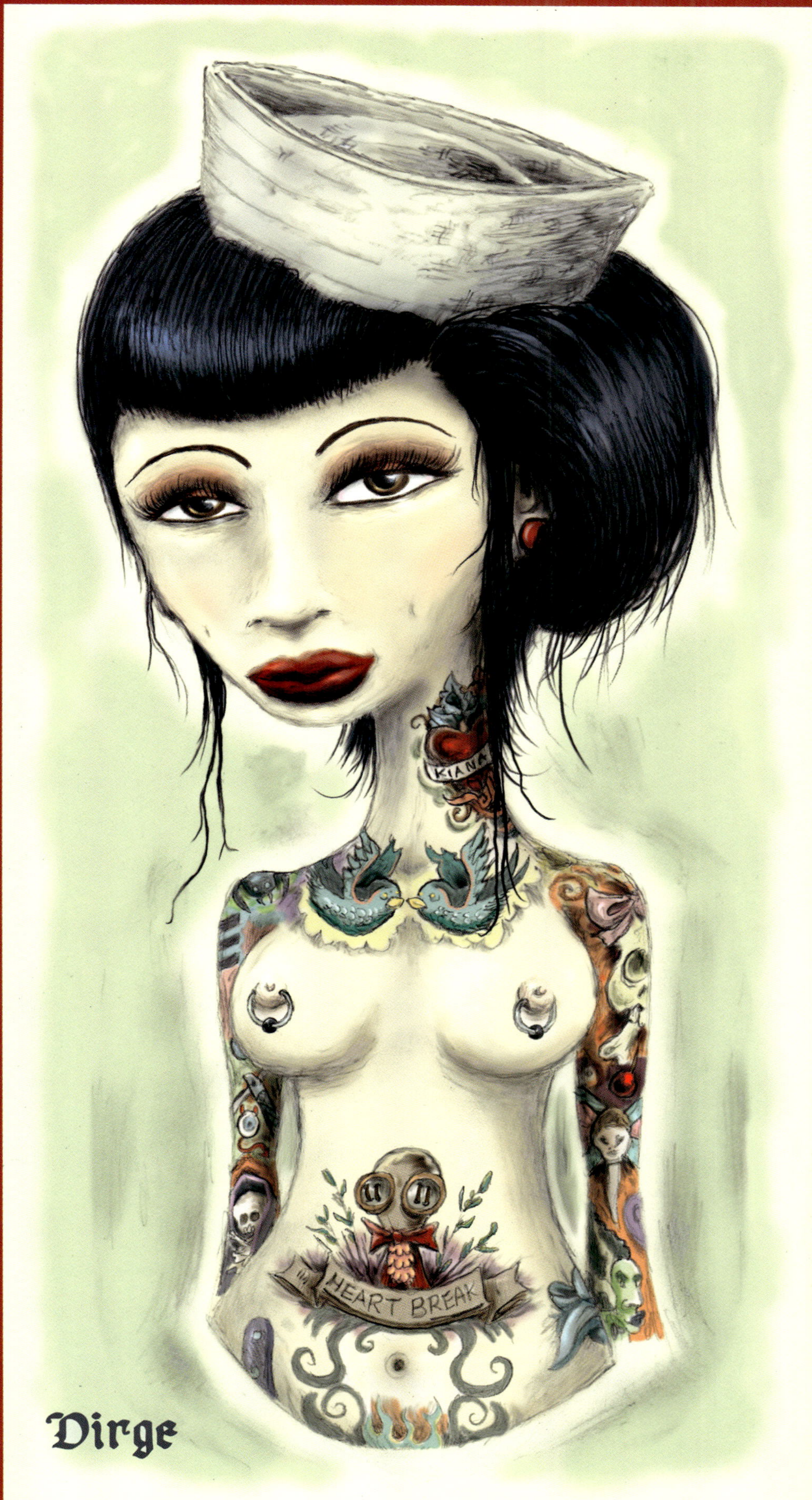

Opposite and left: Both of these lovely ladies are actually the same woman, who I was seeing at the time. I wanted to practice drawing a Nazi hat for the Lenore Nazi zombie issue of my comic and she posed for me.

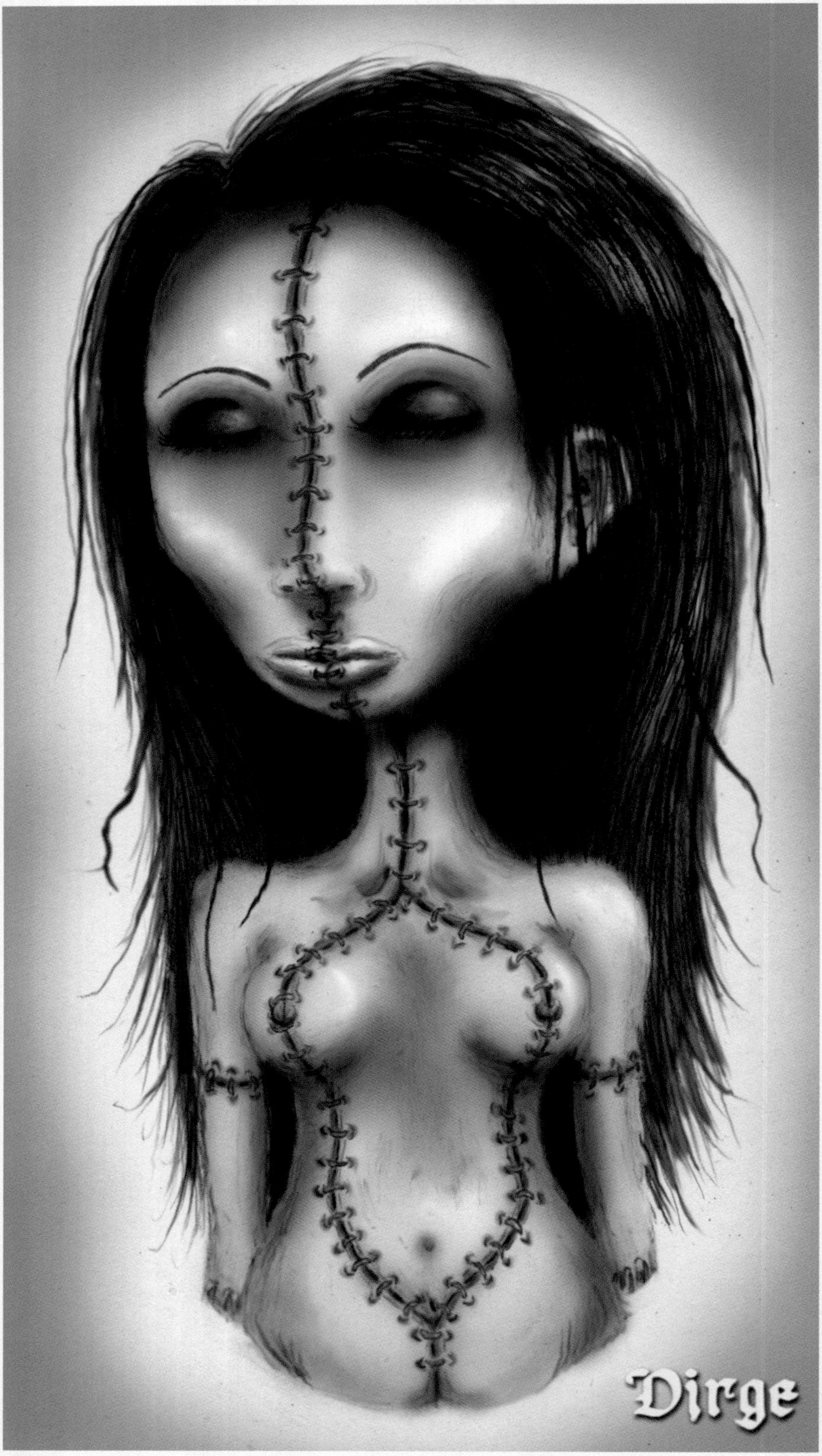
Dirge

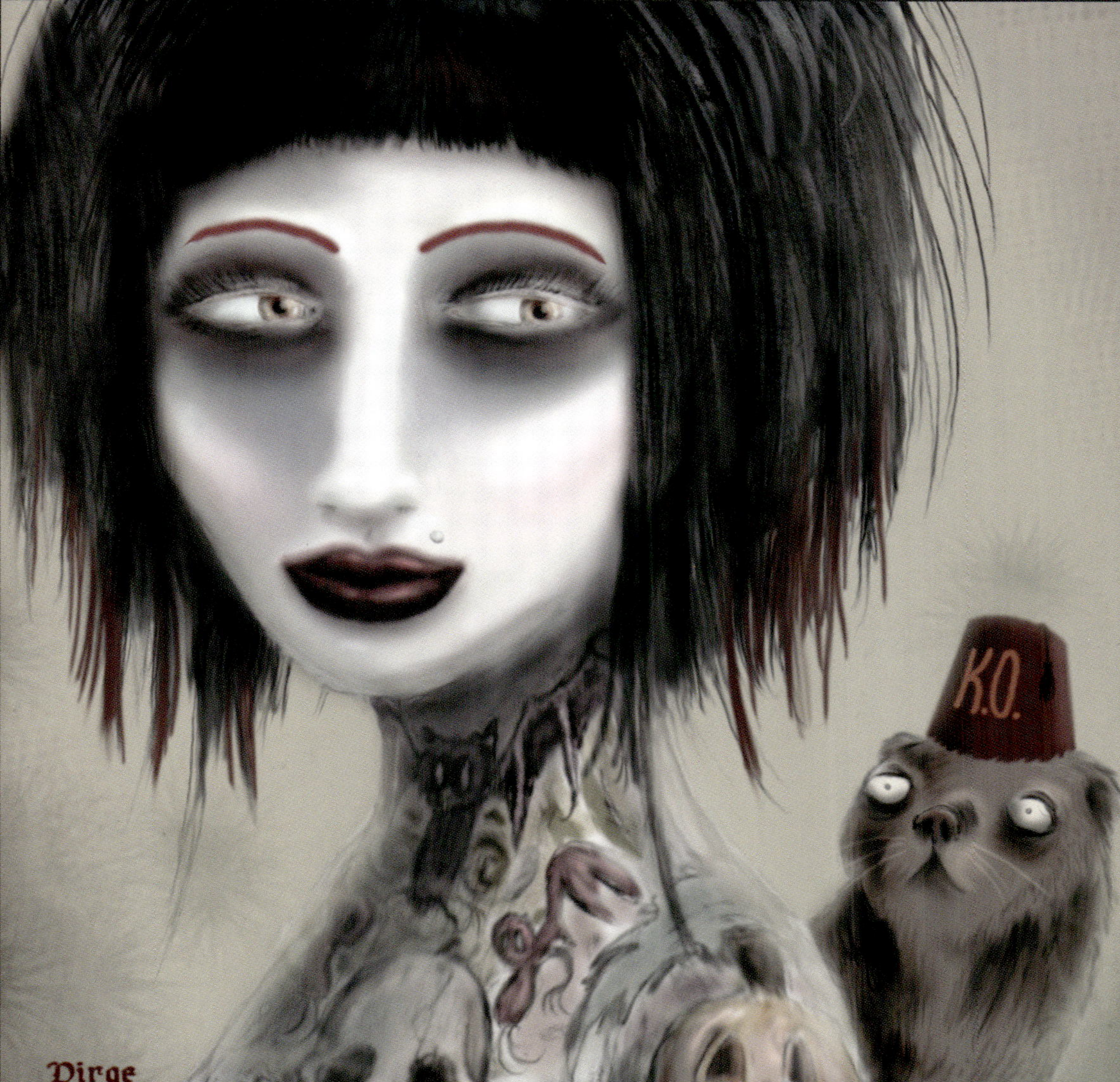

Opposite:

Above, and next spread: "Th

My favorite bar in Hollywood was th
Tiny's K.O. I did a series of art pieces

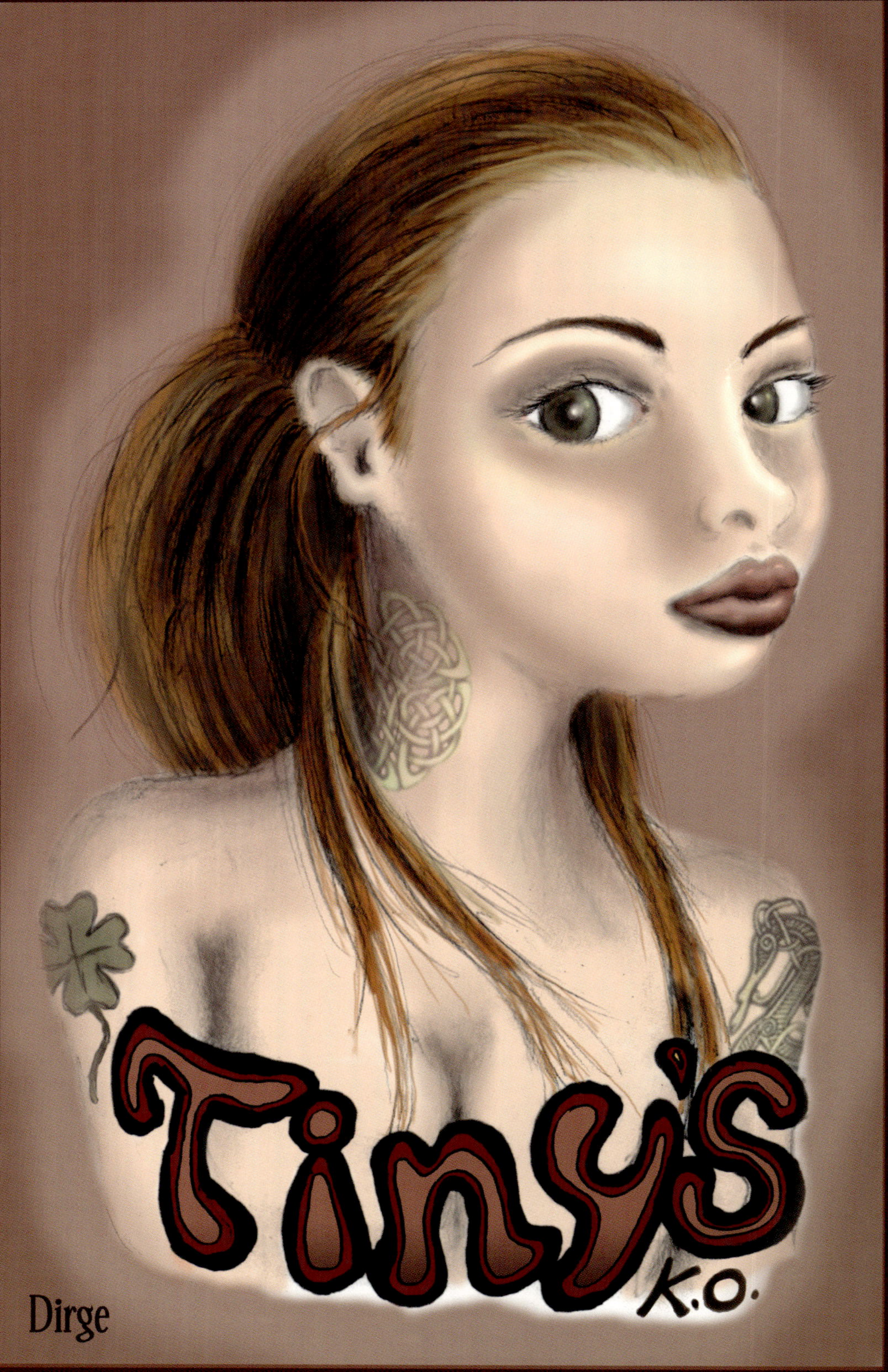
Tiny's
K.O.
Dirge

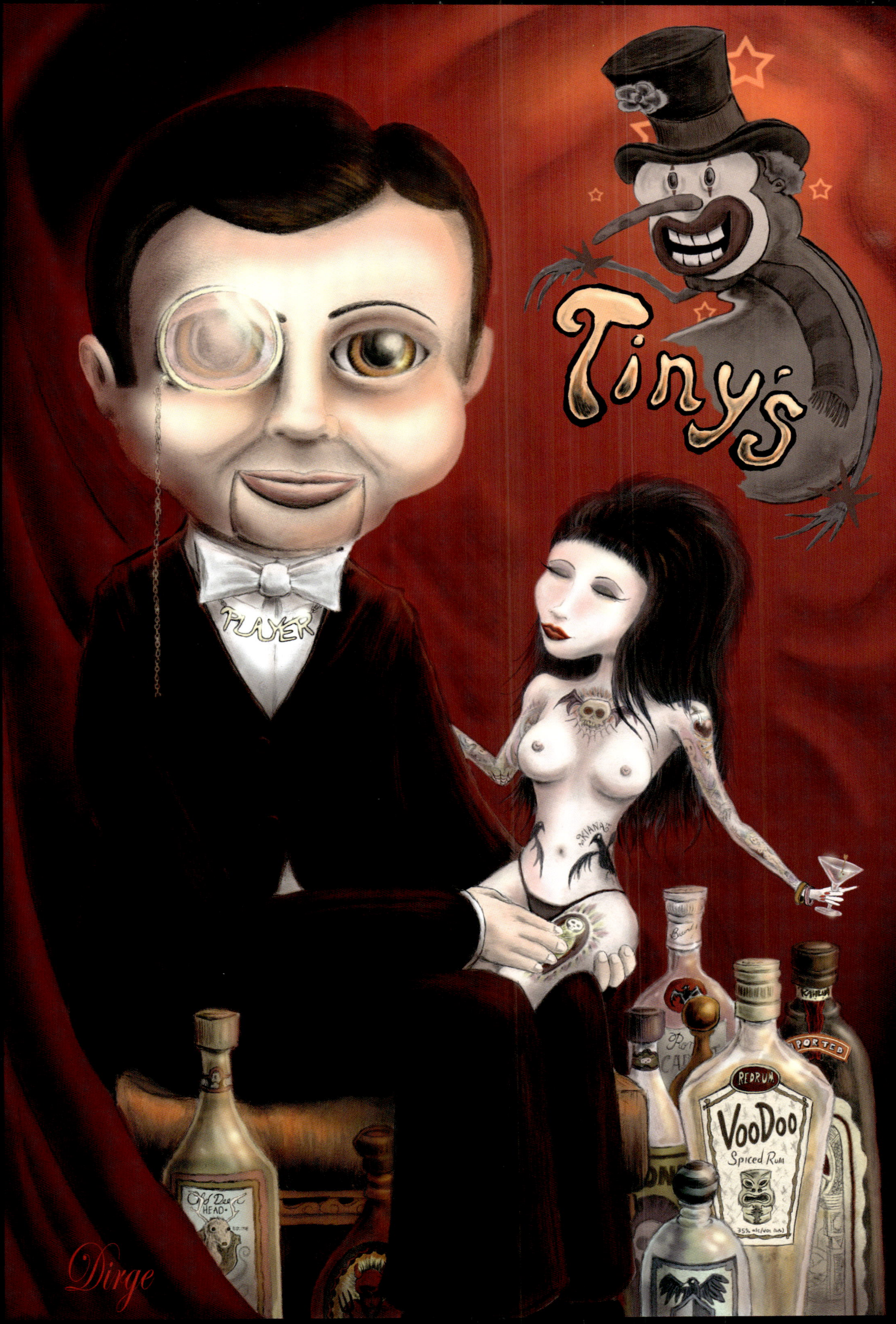
Tiny's
PLAYER
RED RUM
VooDoo
Spiced Rum
Dirge

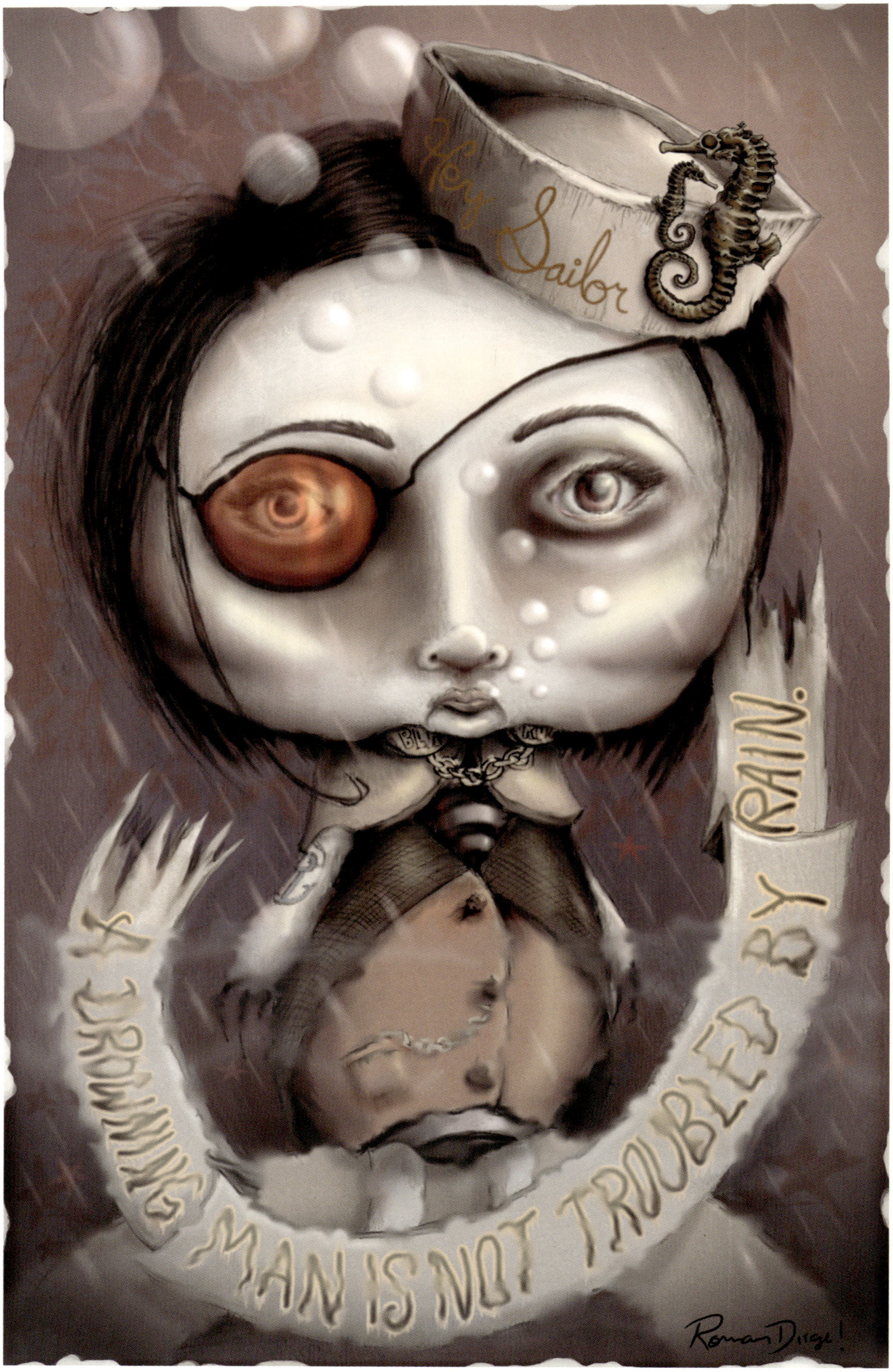

Above: "Troubled."
I was having a bad day so I did this one to put things in perspective for myself.

Opposite: "IVYPUS."
Completed for an ex that had an octopus fixation. What is up with these women I date?

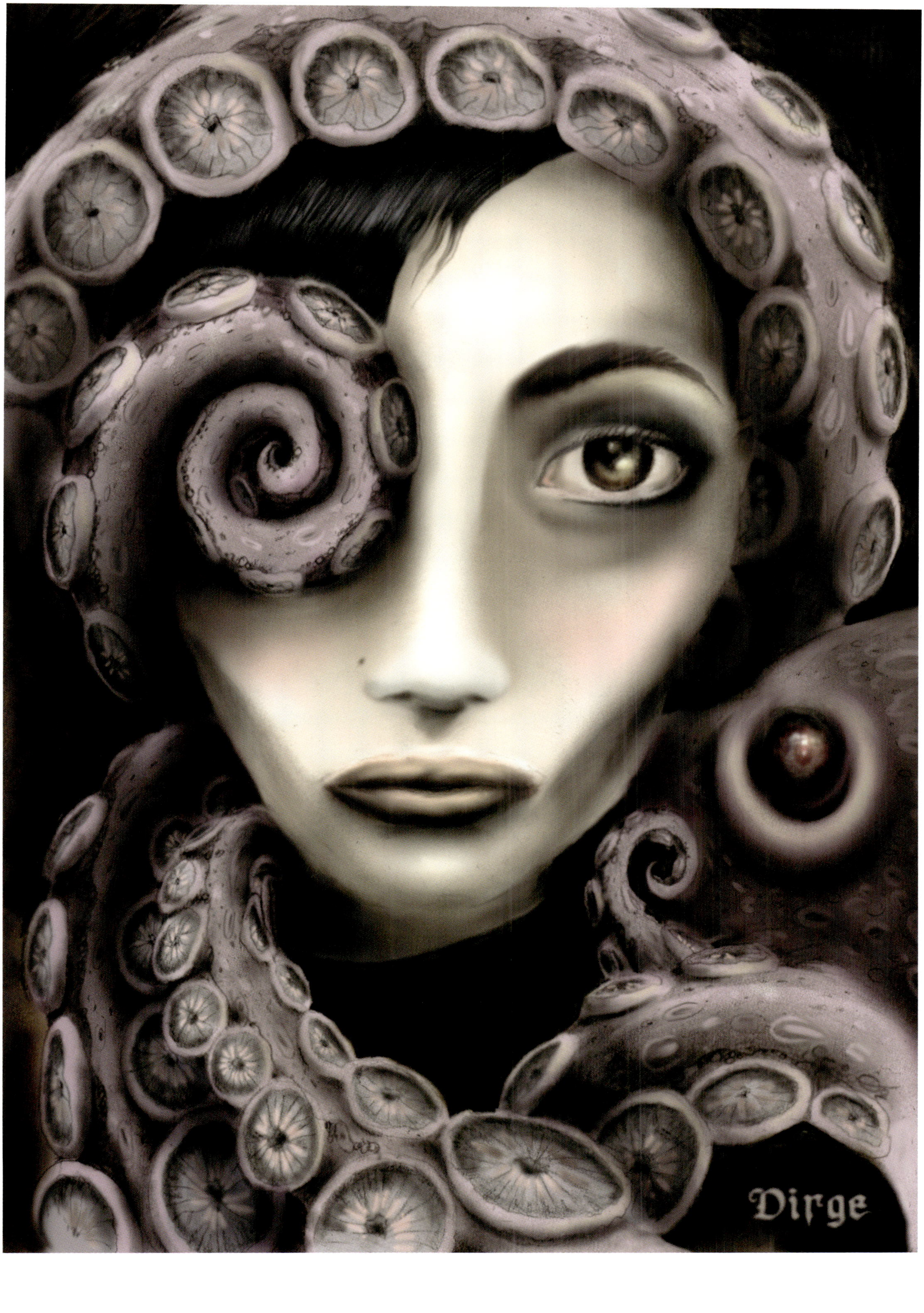
Dirge

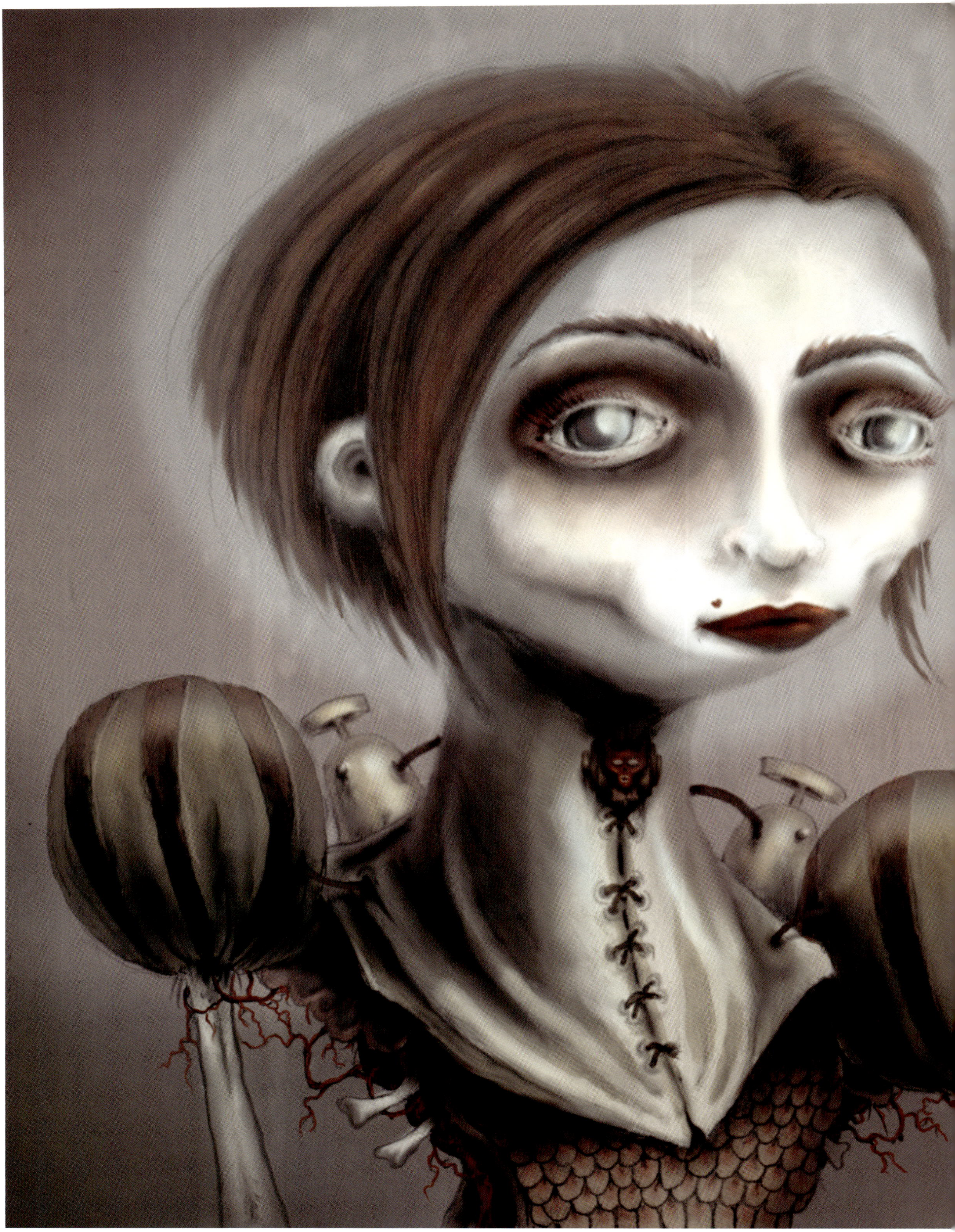

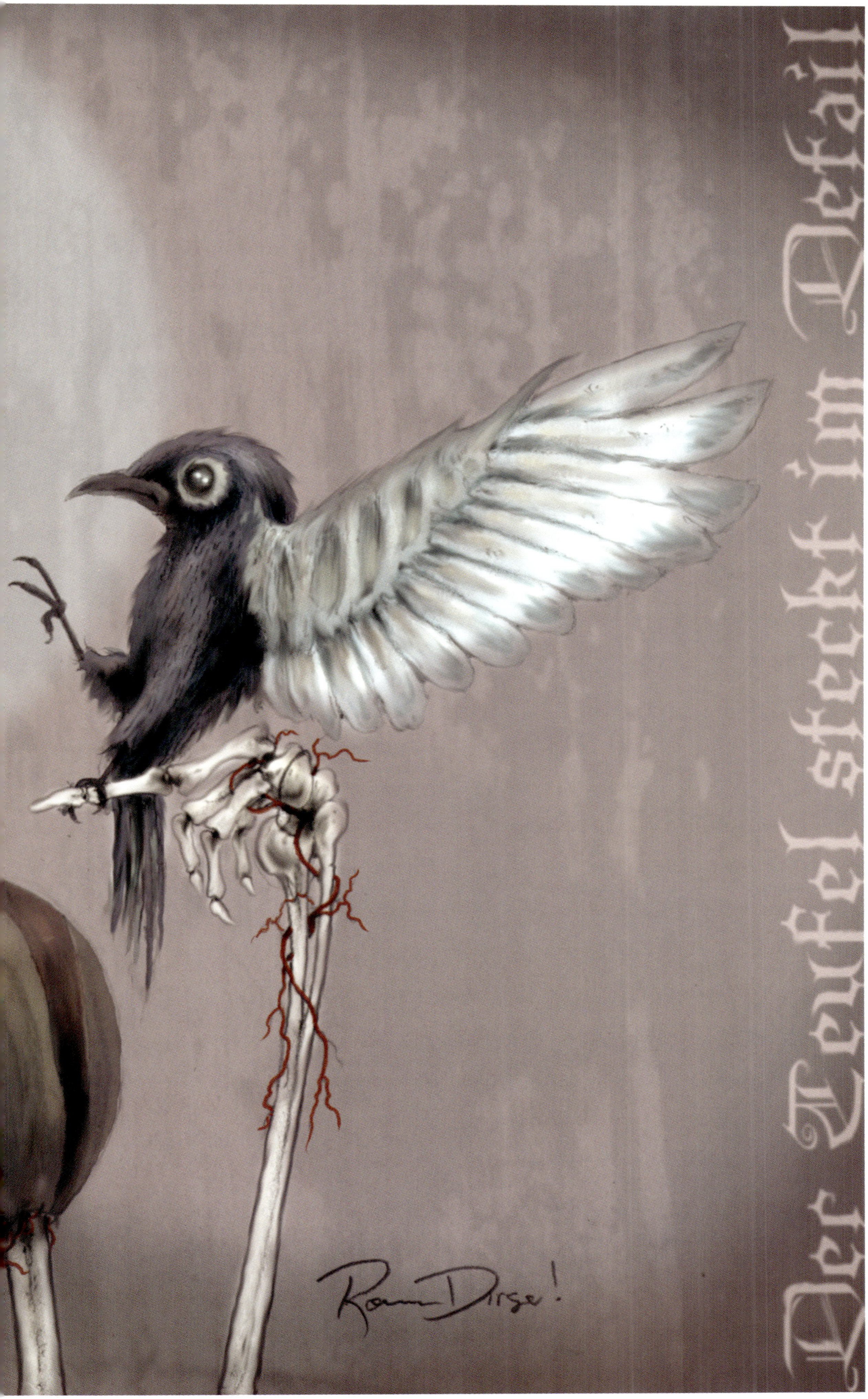

Left:
"Der Teufel Steckt Im Detail."
The Devil is in the detail.
He is actually if you look.

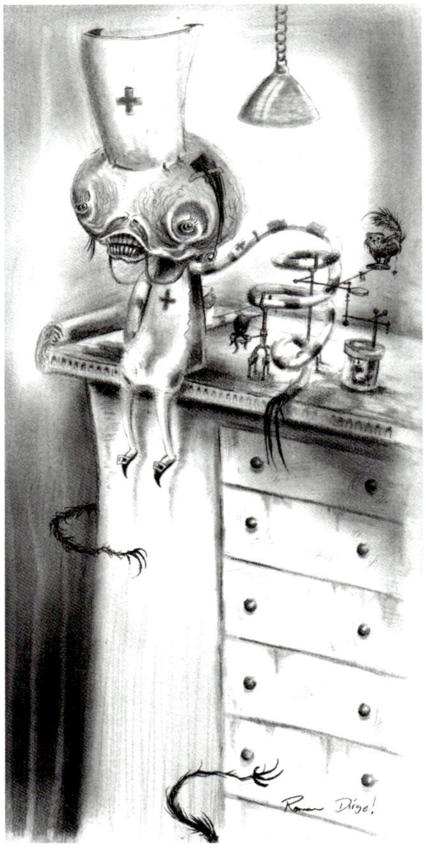

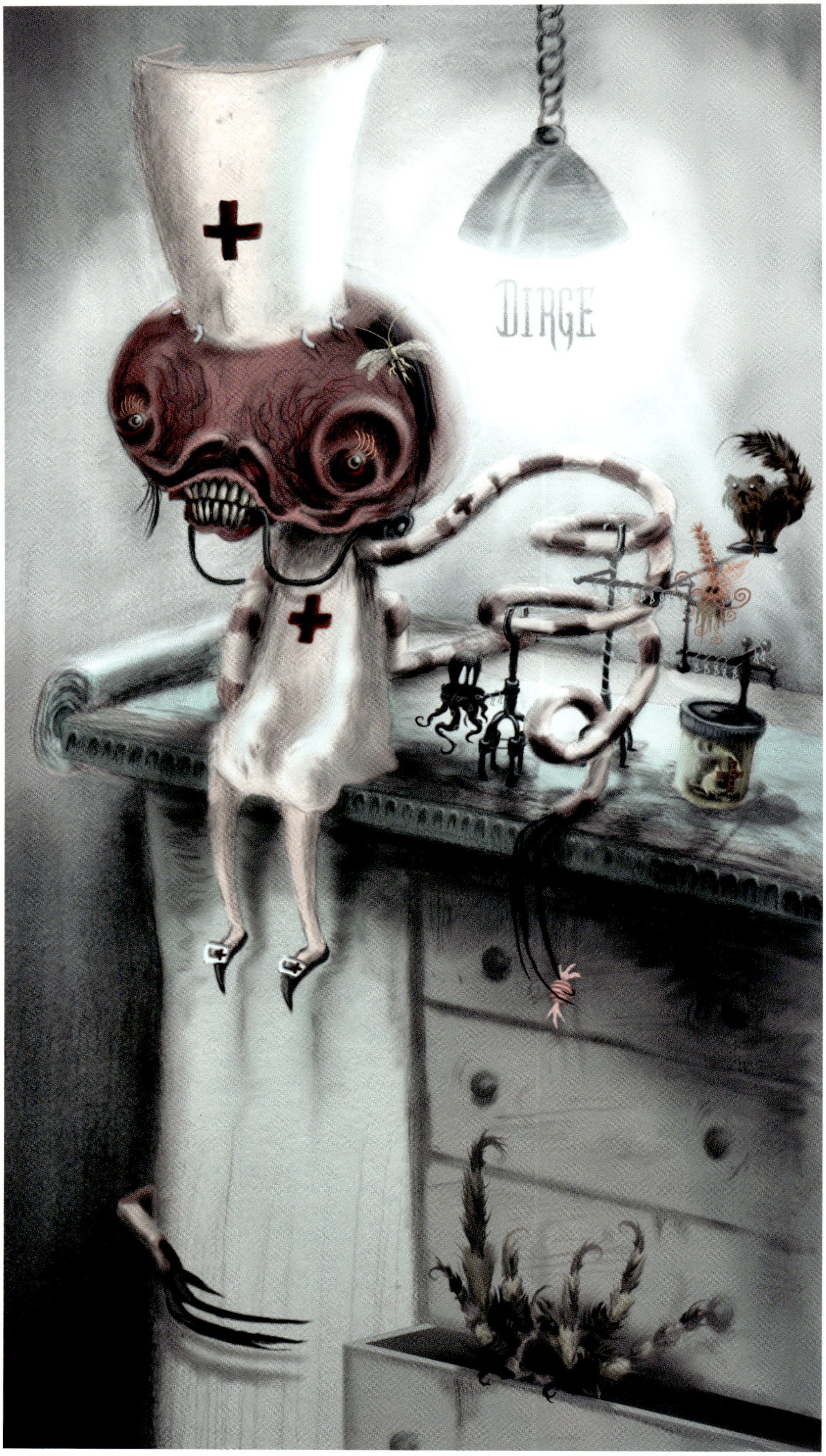

Above and right: "Nurse Monster What Gives Candy To A Spider Thing In A Drawer."
These are good examples of what the drawing looks like before the coloring happens.

Opposite: "Mary Toft And The Rabbit Babies."
This was a piece I did honoring the real life Mary Toft, an English woman who claimed to be giving birth to dead rabbits. She tried so hard to convince the populace it was true, doctors found rabbit chunks in her no-no bits. She was later imprisoned for fraud.

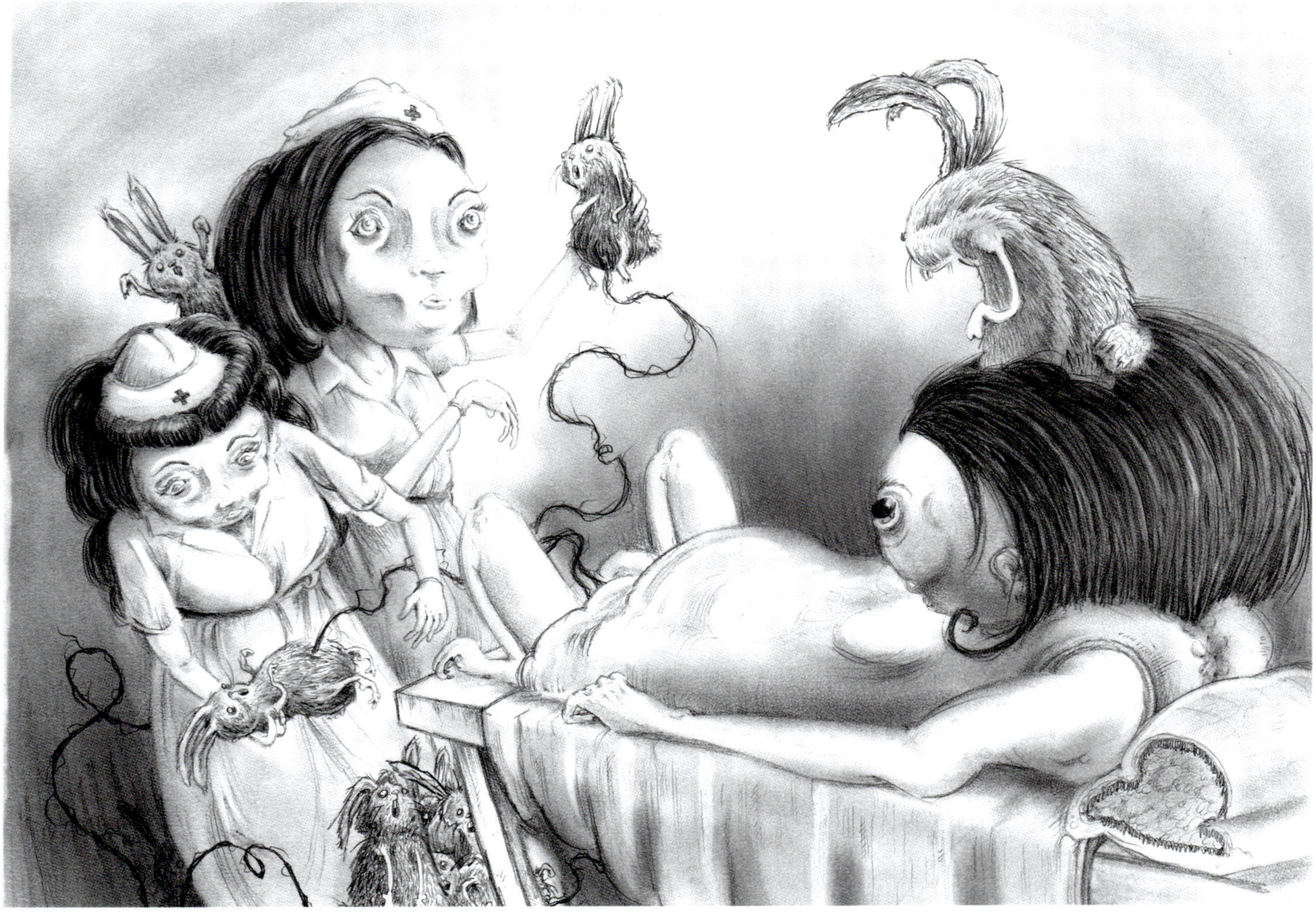

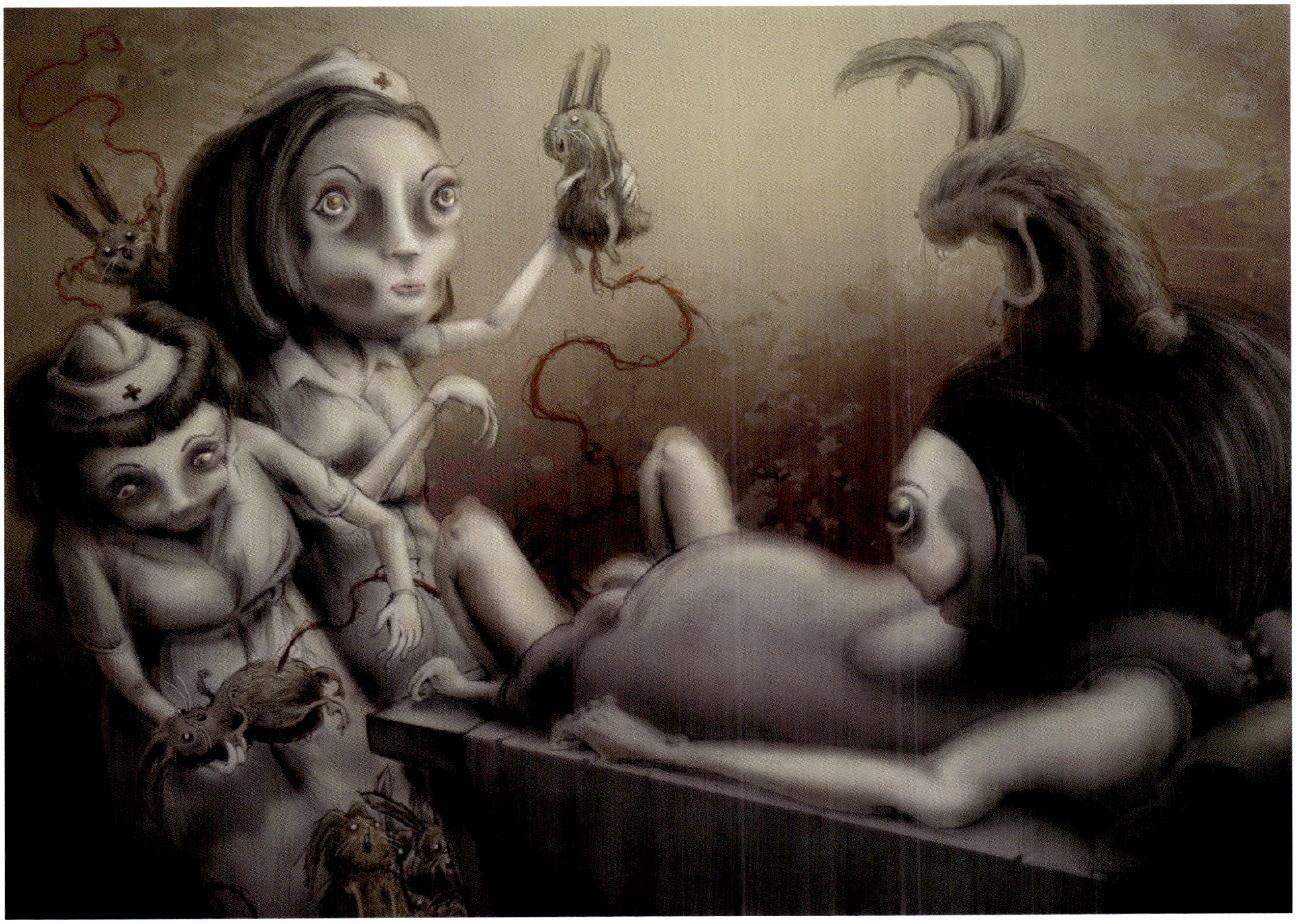

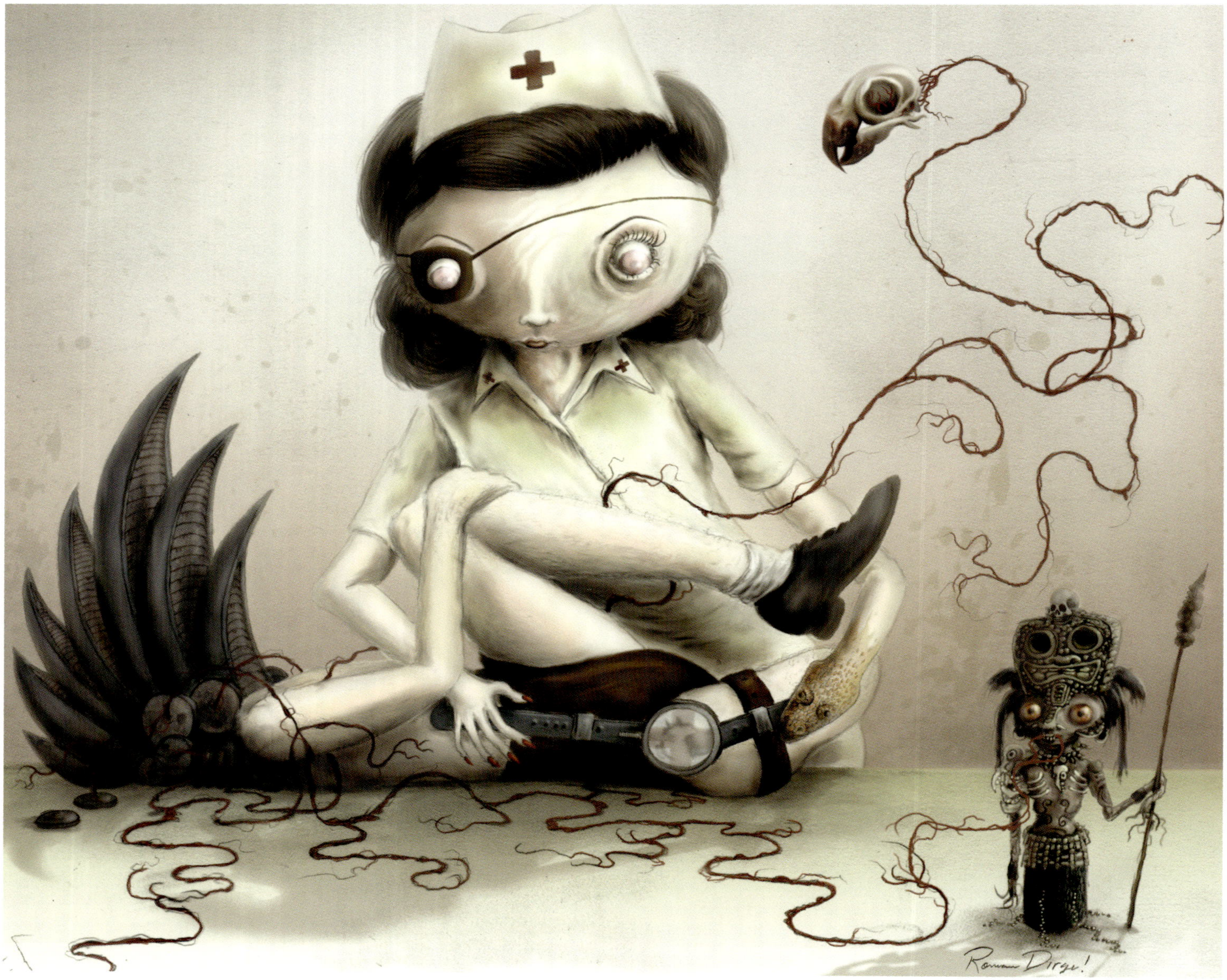

Above: "Amputation."
Inspired by a photo I saw in an old book entitled *An Atlas of Amputations*.

Opposite: "Maya."
Based on the facial structure of my friend Maya. Then, for reasons unknown, I just knew she needed to be holding a rooster wearing a mask while her hand unraveled.

Next spread: "Mermaids."

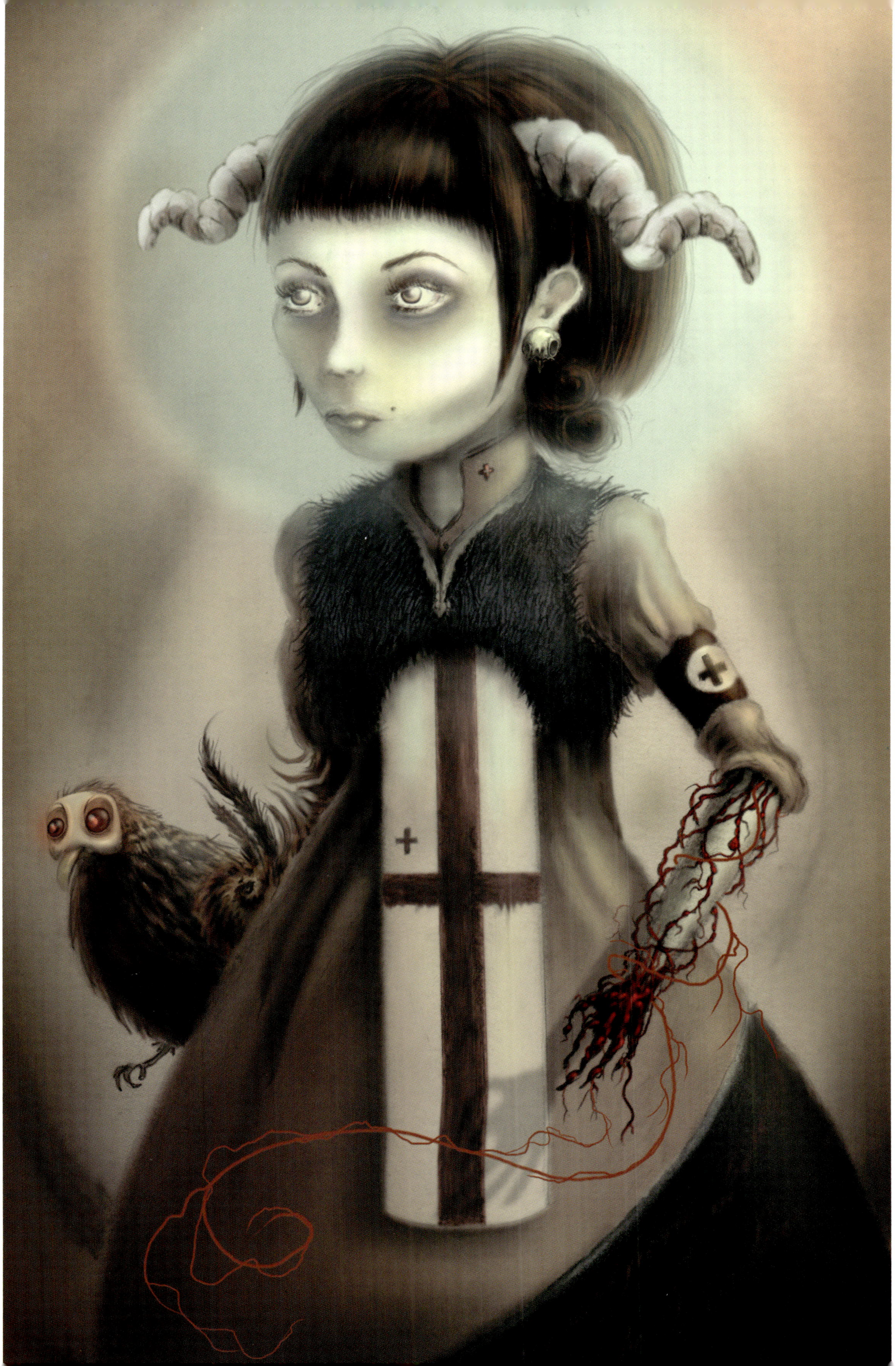

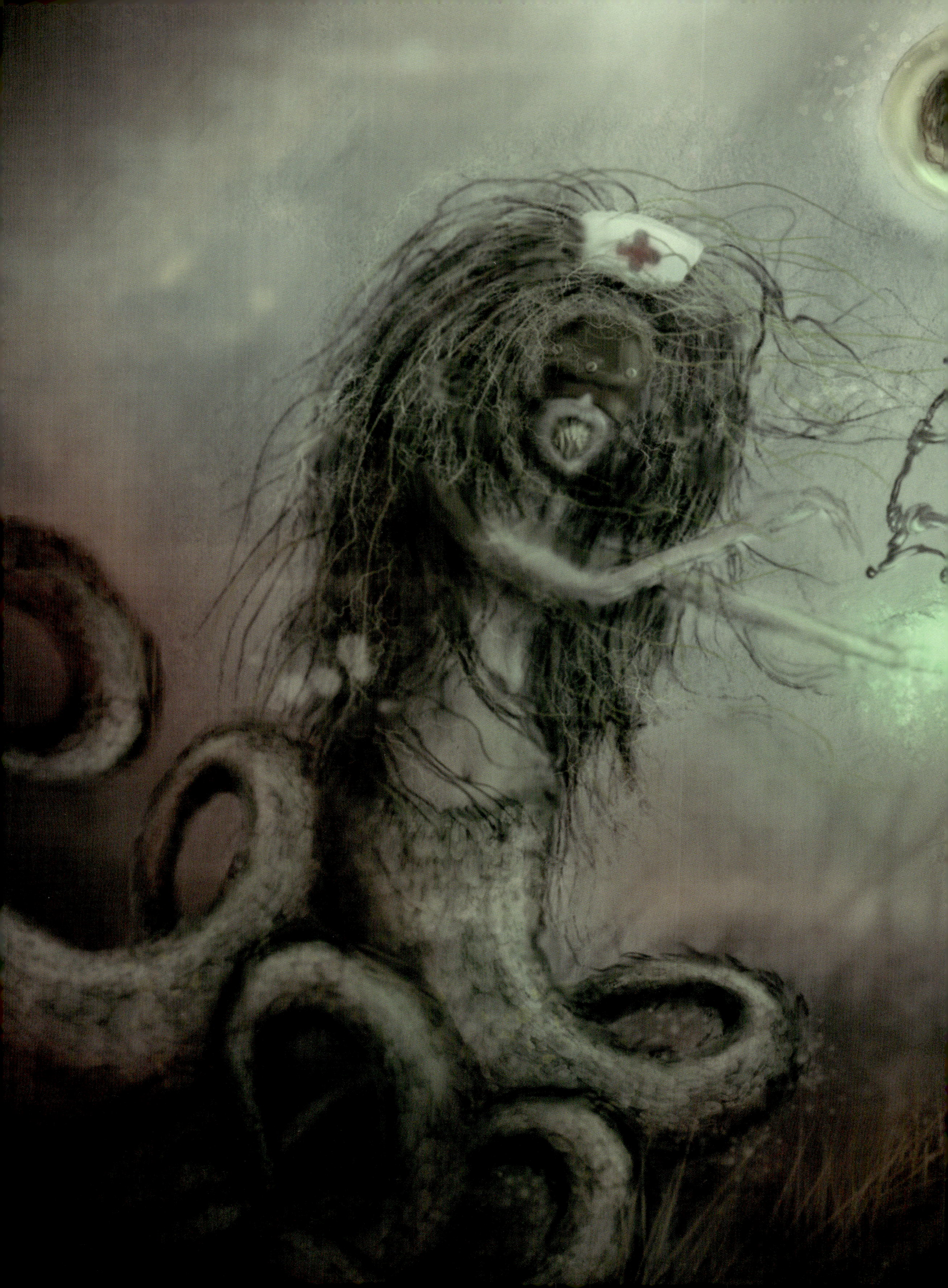

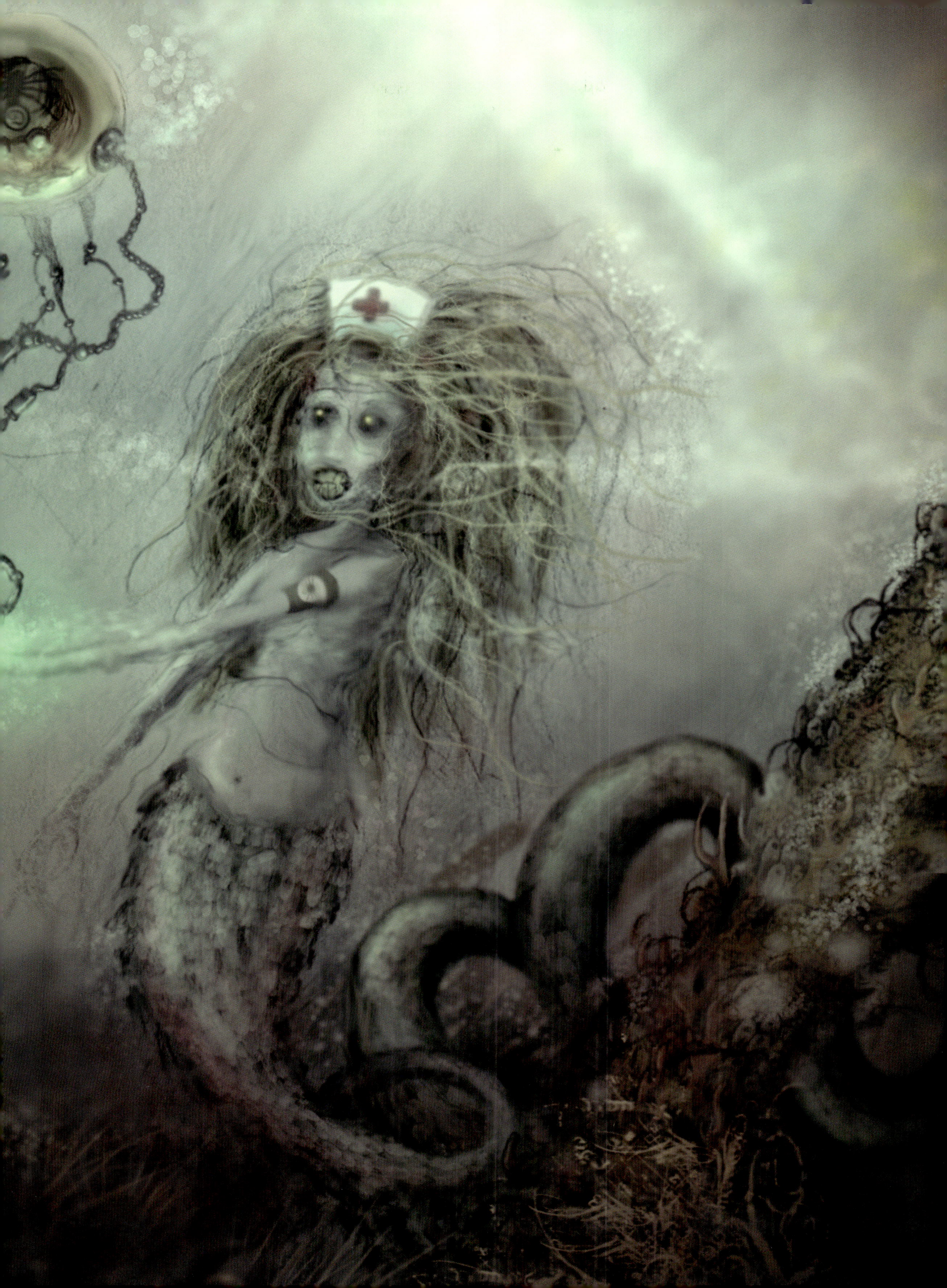

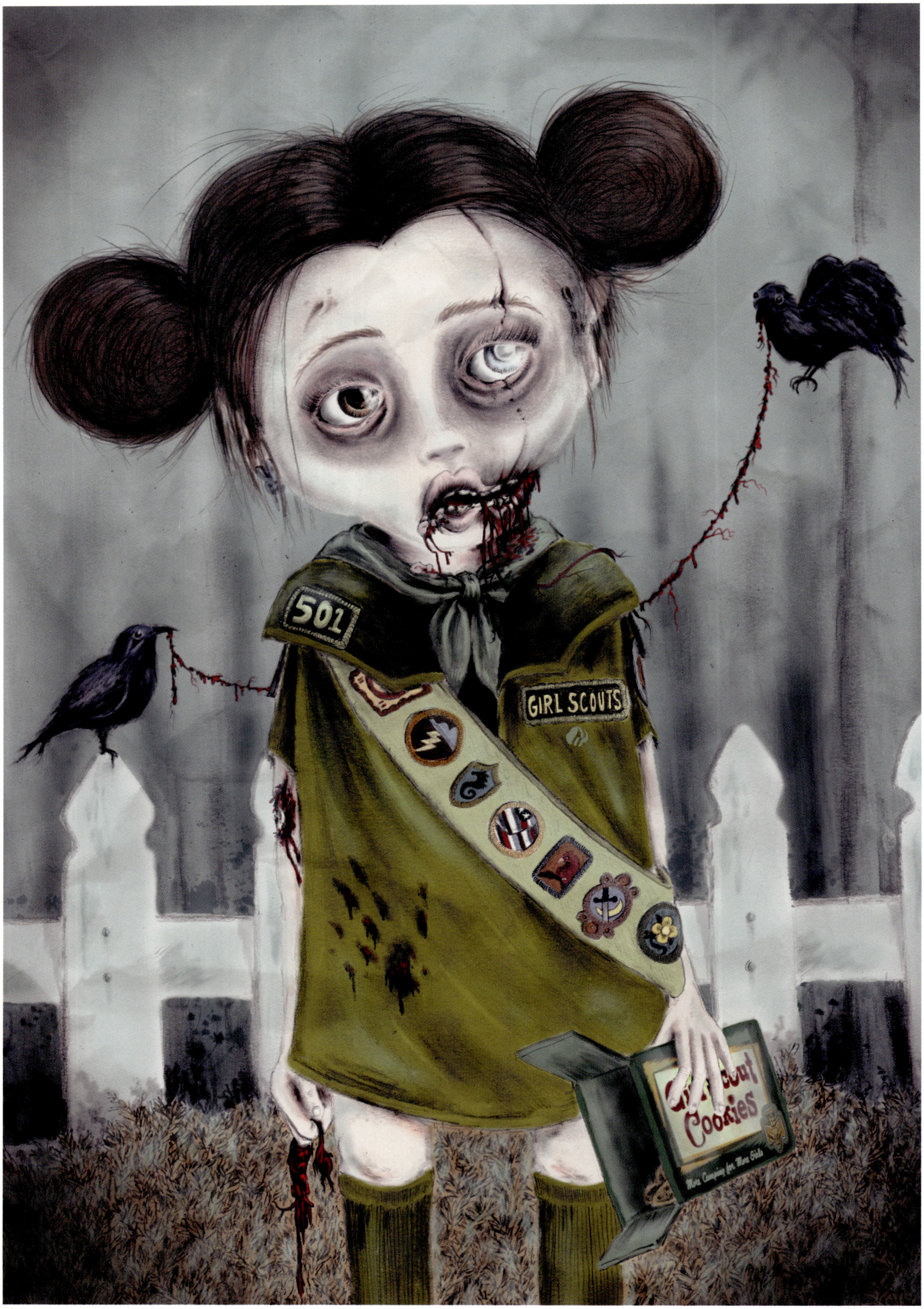
501
GIRL SCOUTS
Cookies
More Camping for More Girls

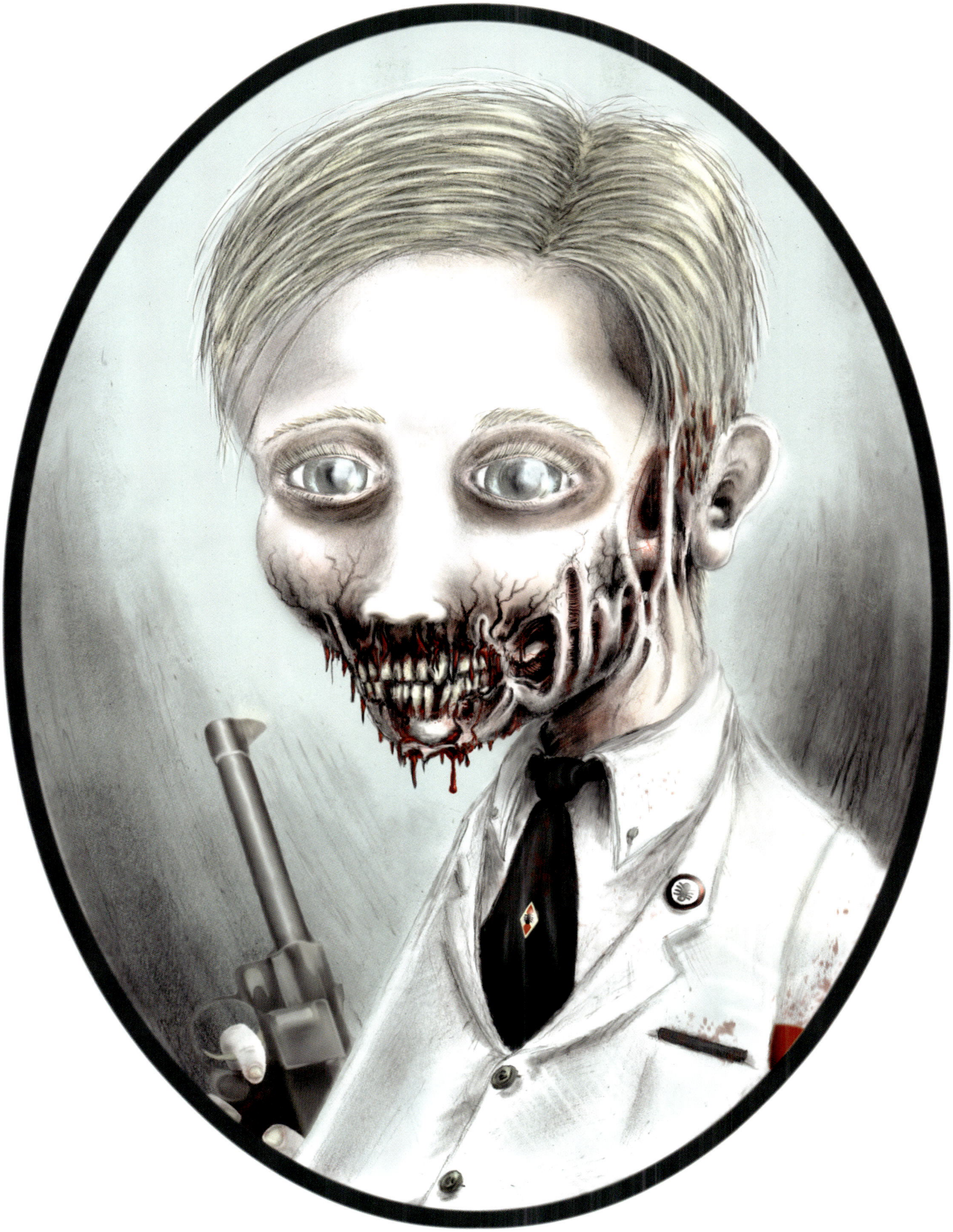

Opposite: "Cookies."
I'll take any excuse to draw zombies.

Above: "The Final Day."

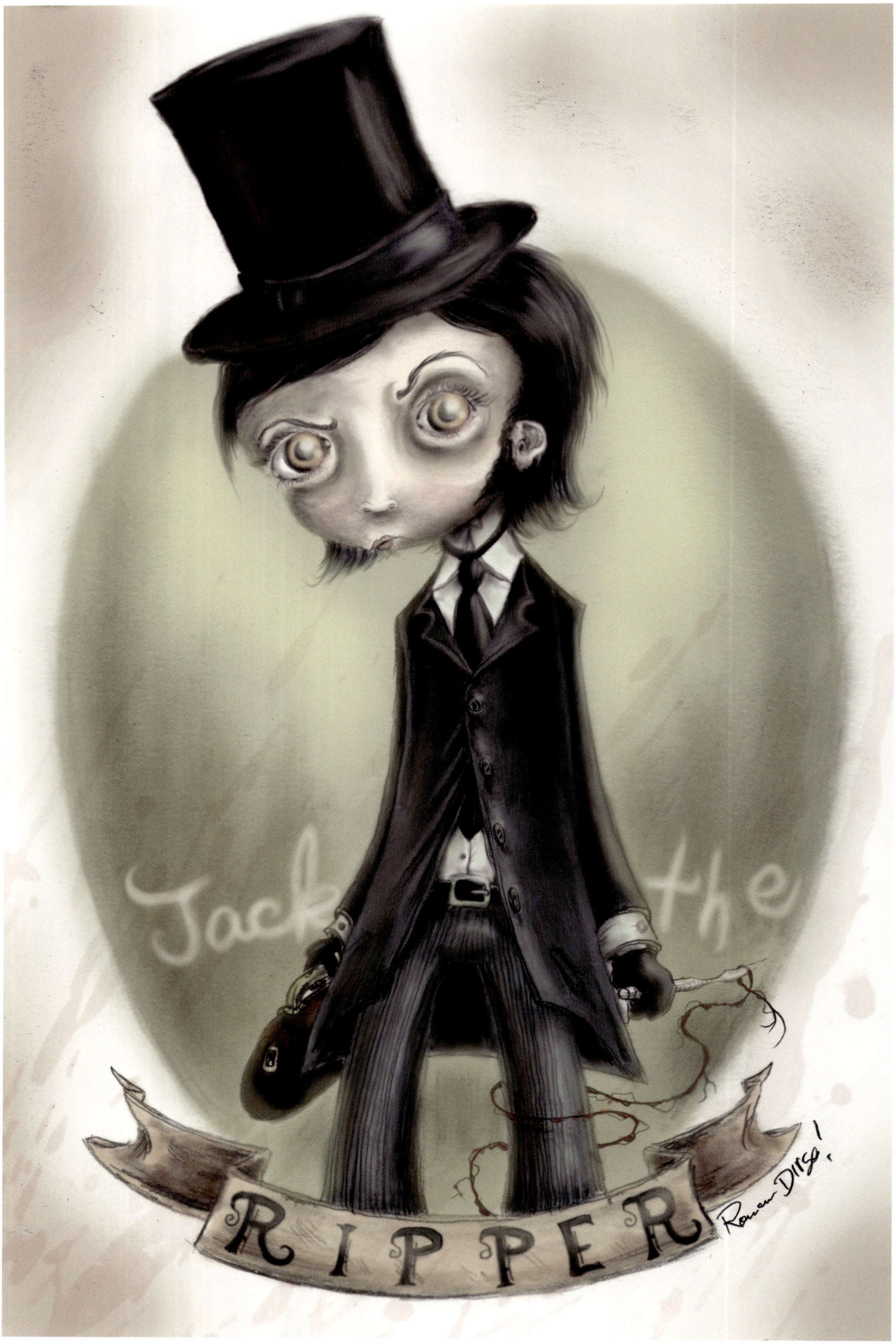

Above: "Jack."

Opposite: "Tea Time."

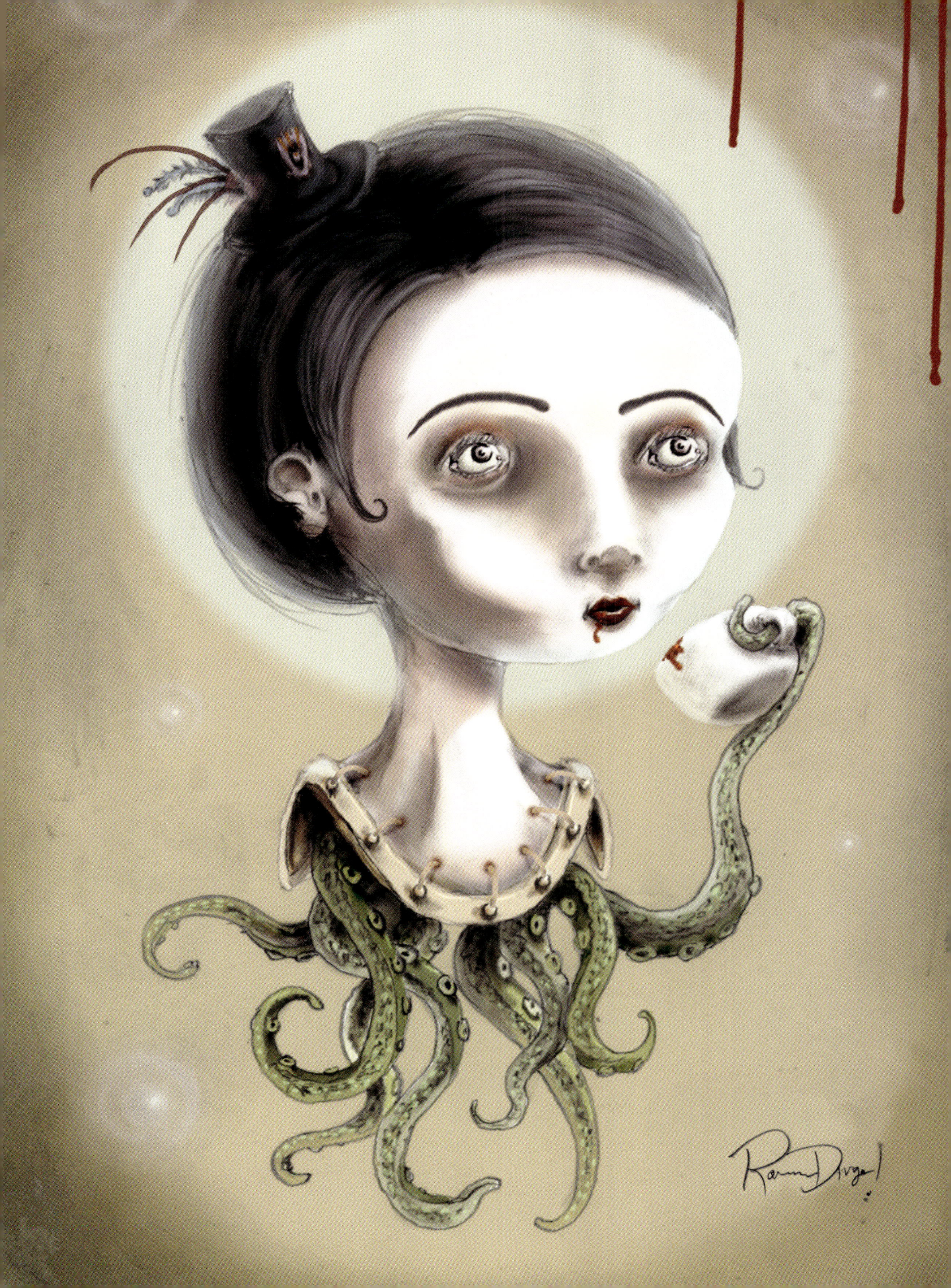

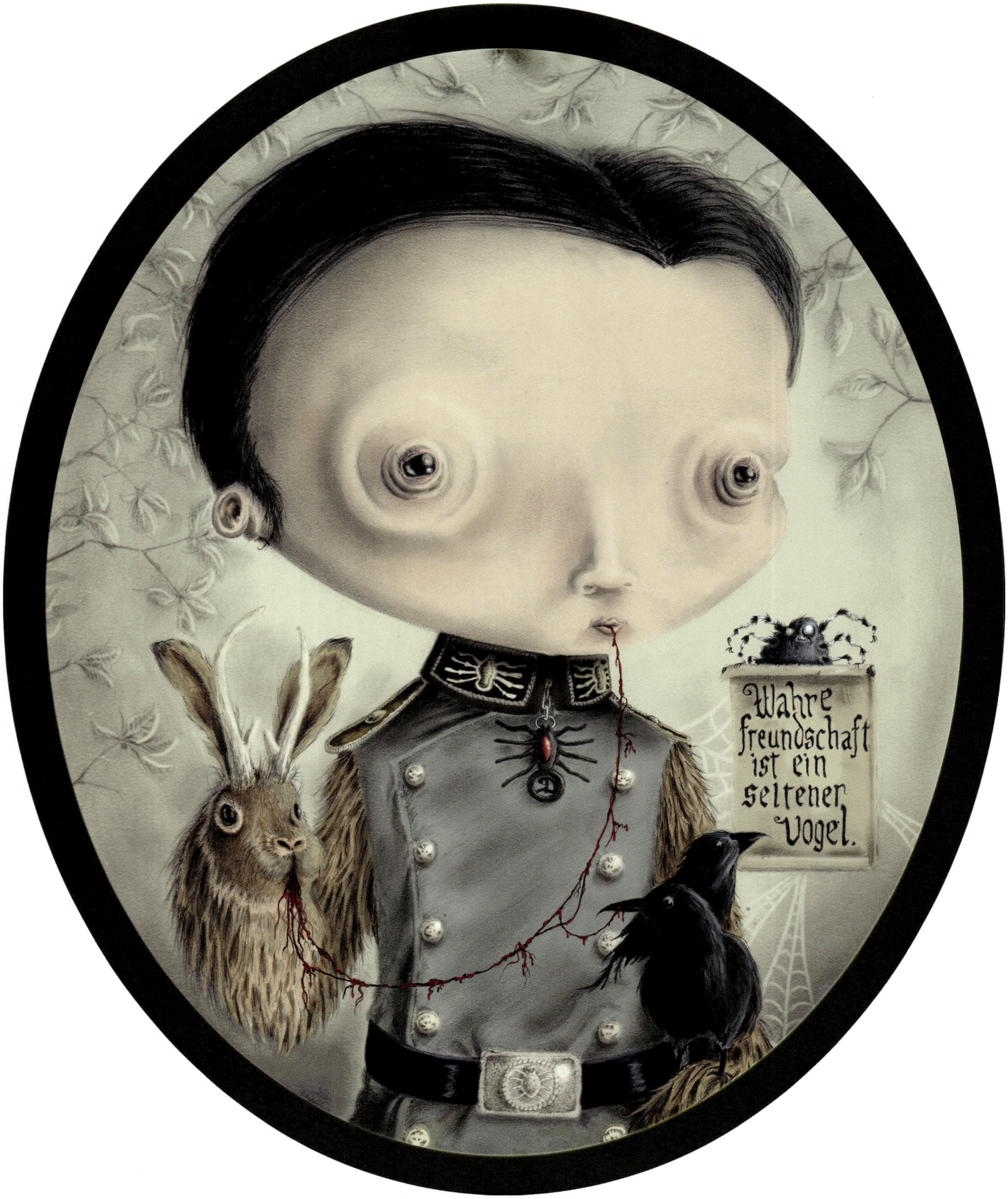

Above: "Wahre Freundschaft Ist Ein Seltener Vogel."
True friendship is a rare bird.

Opposite: "The Hanged Man-Thing."

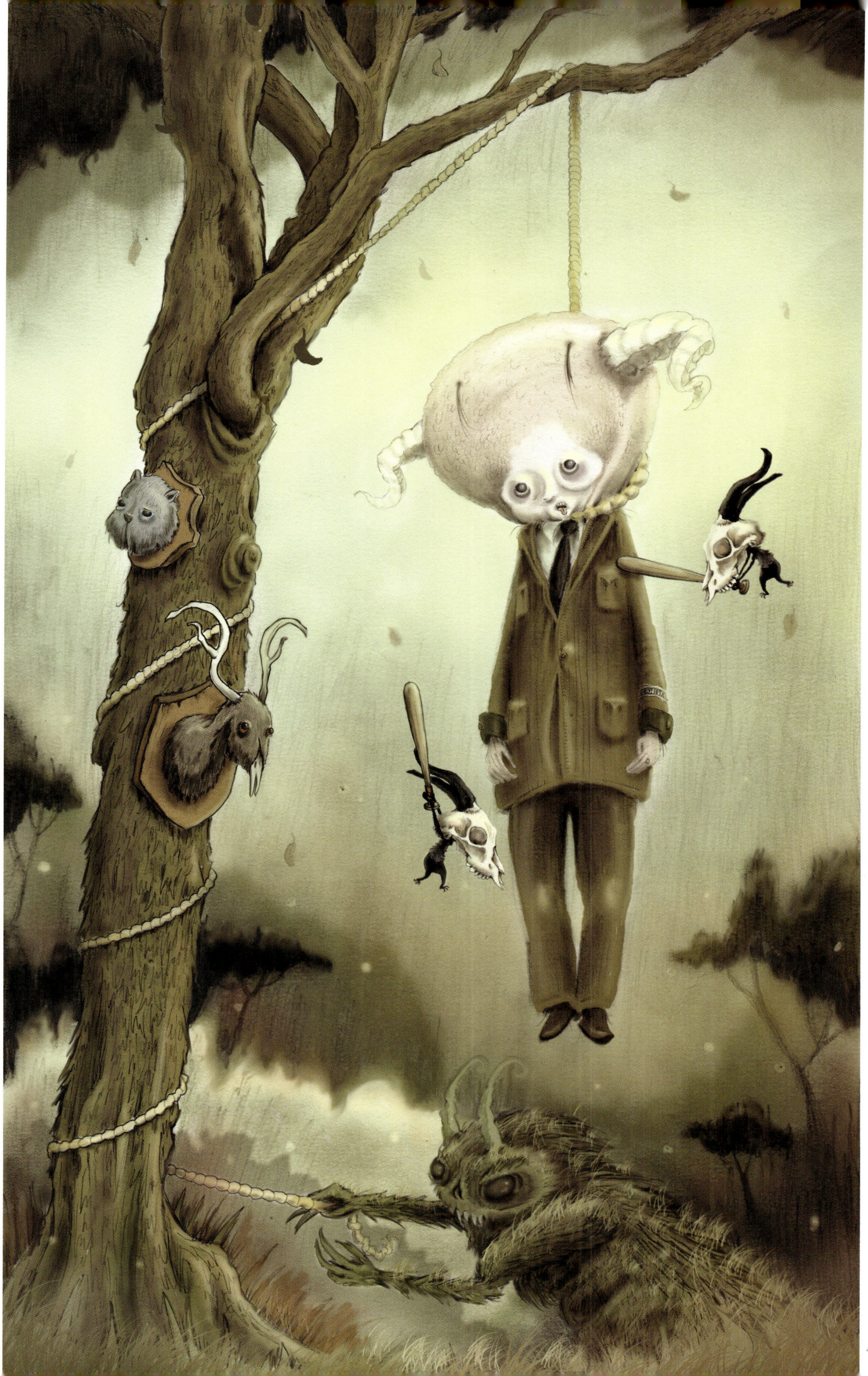

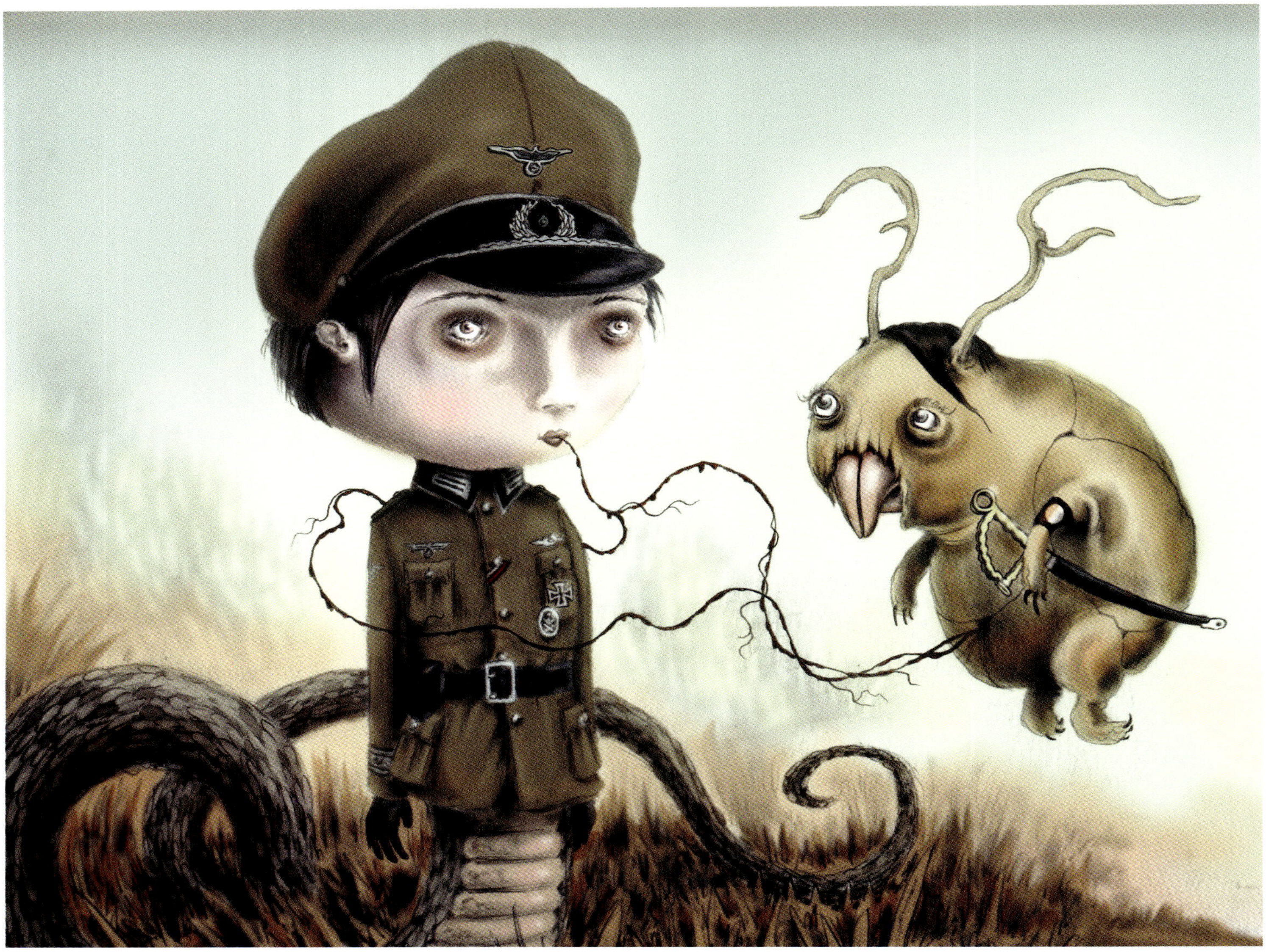

Above: "Snake In The Grass."

Opposite: "Einmal Ist Keinmal."
Once is Never.

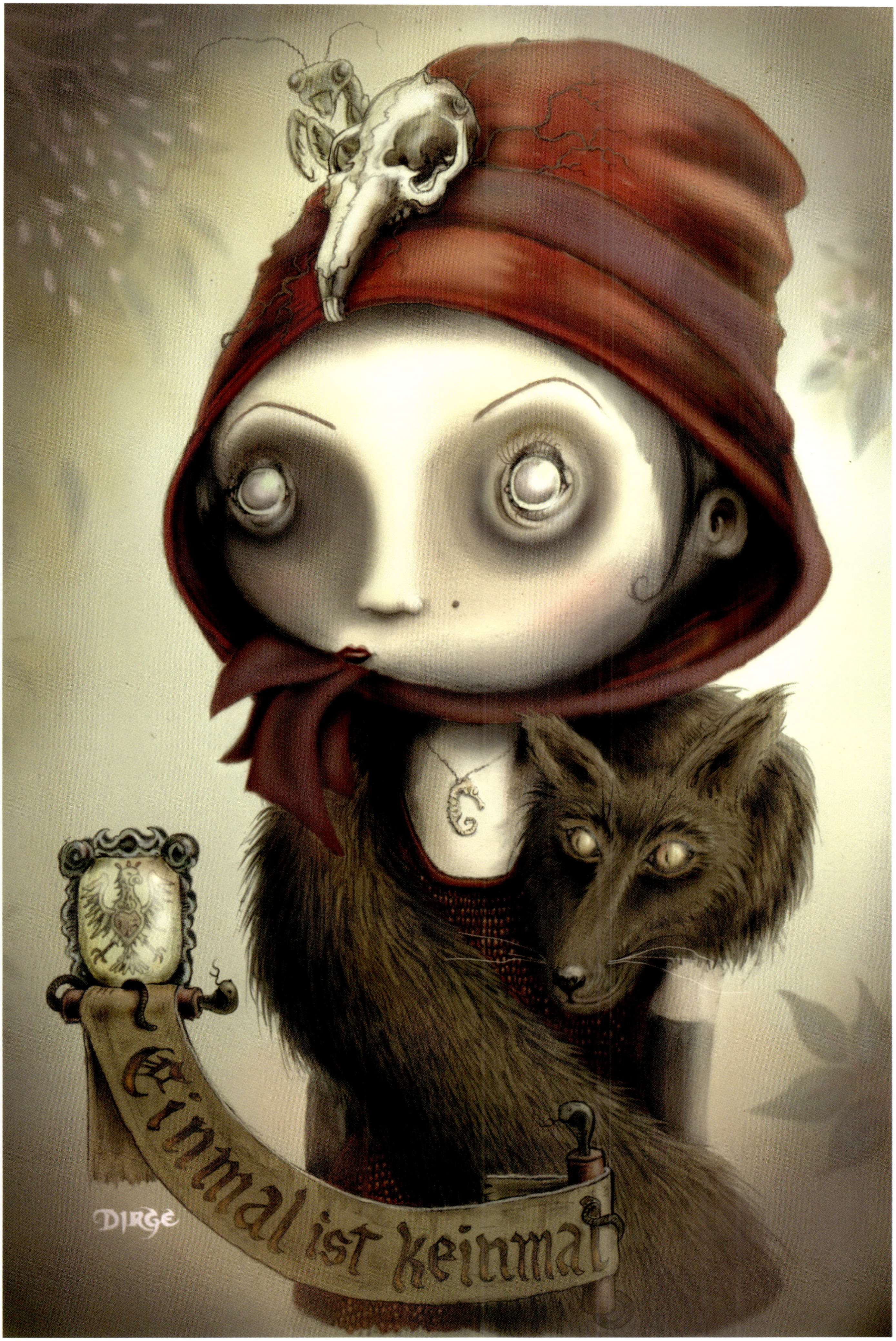
Einmal ist keinmal
DIRGE

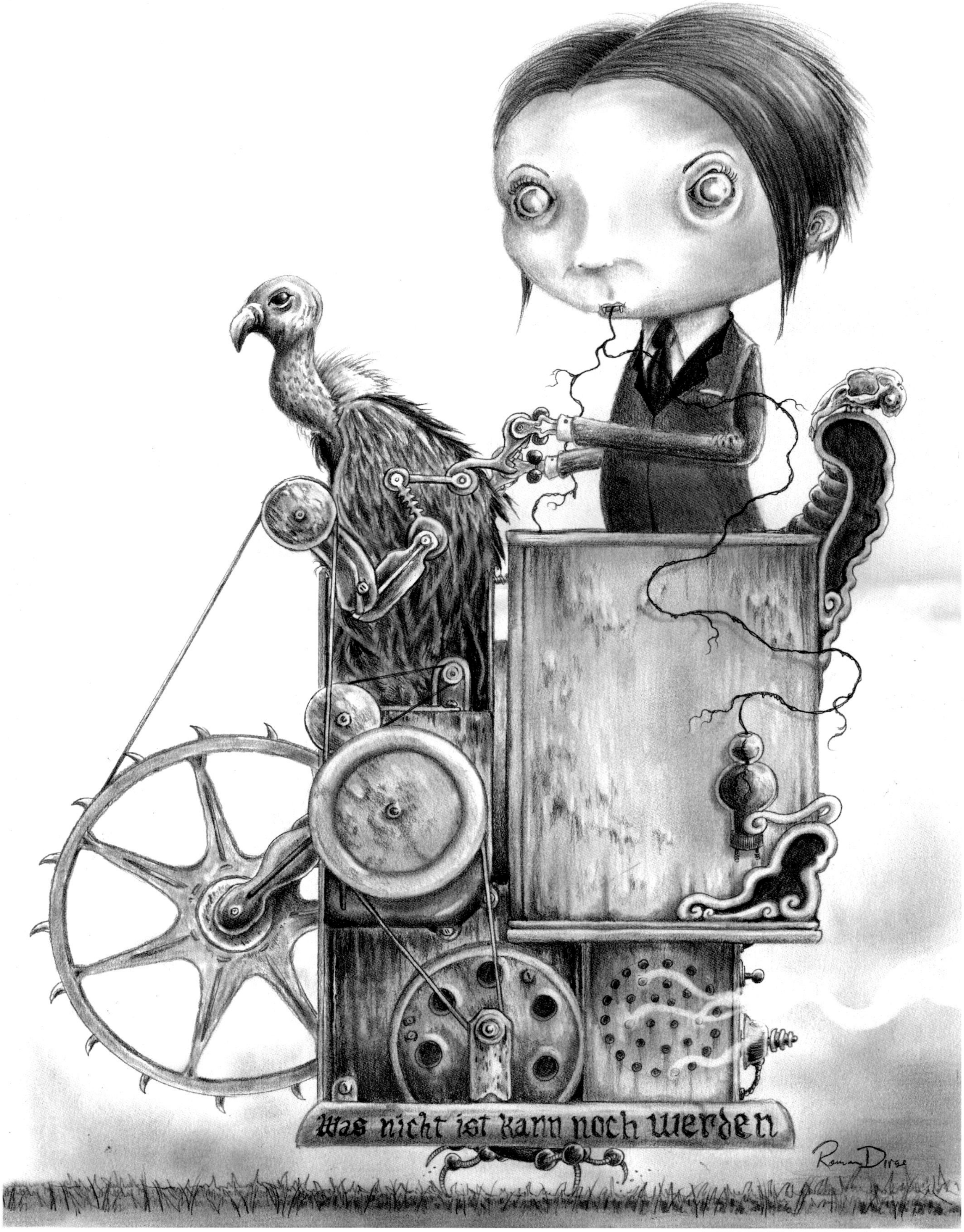

Above and opposite: "Vampire Vulture Walker."
I found an old projector on the street, drew it...
and it went from there.

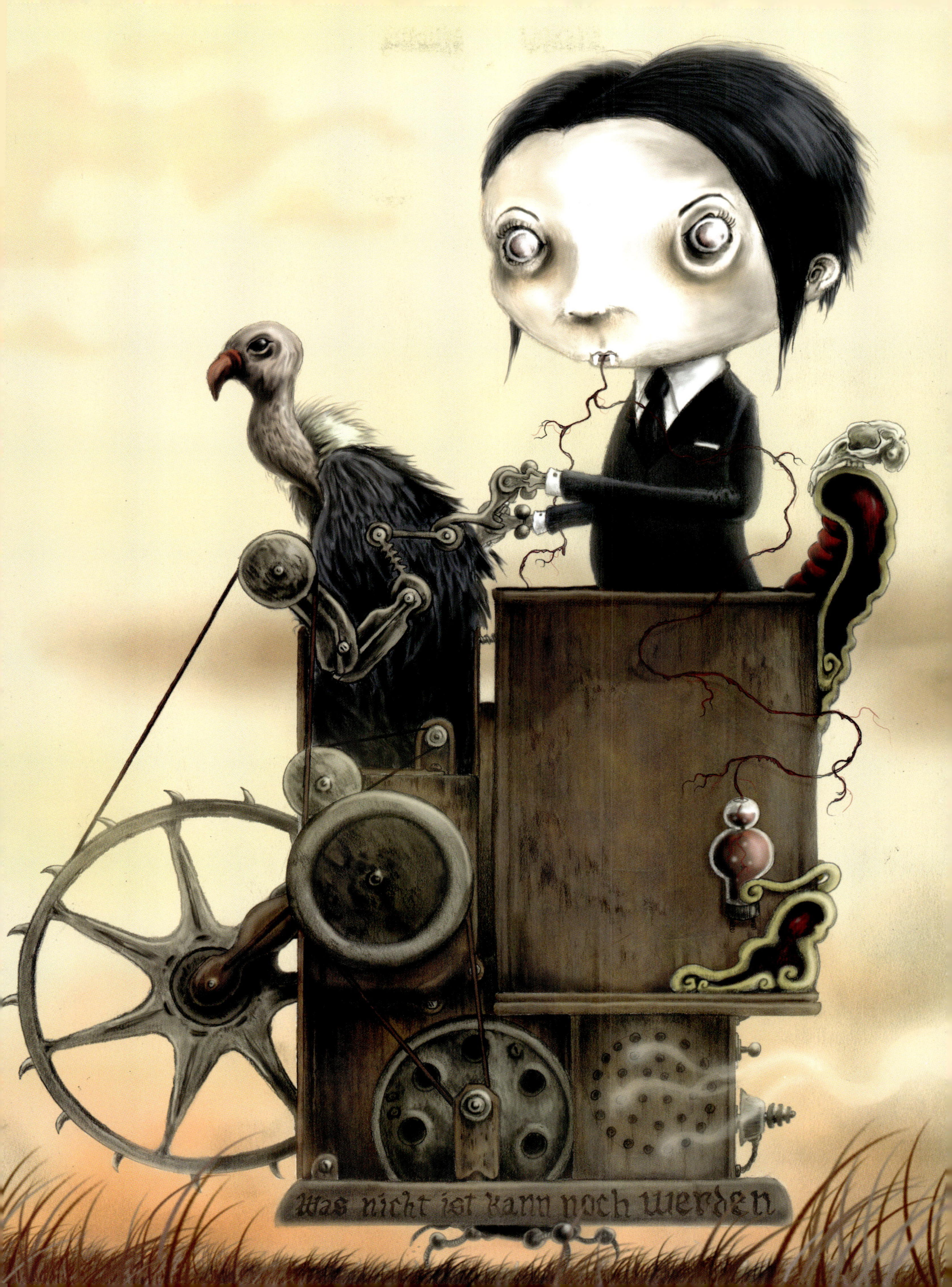
Was nicht ist kann noch werden

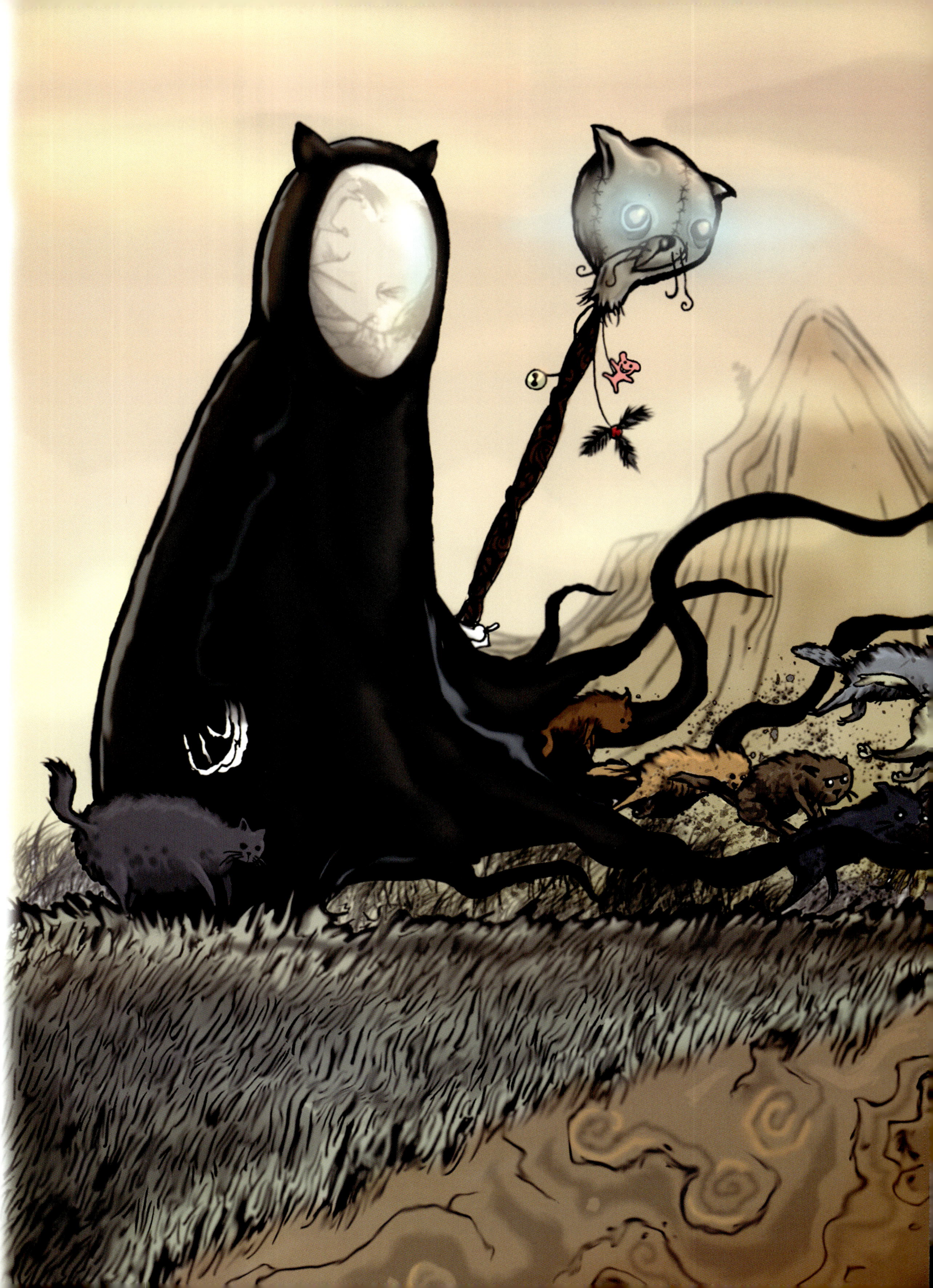

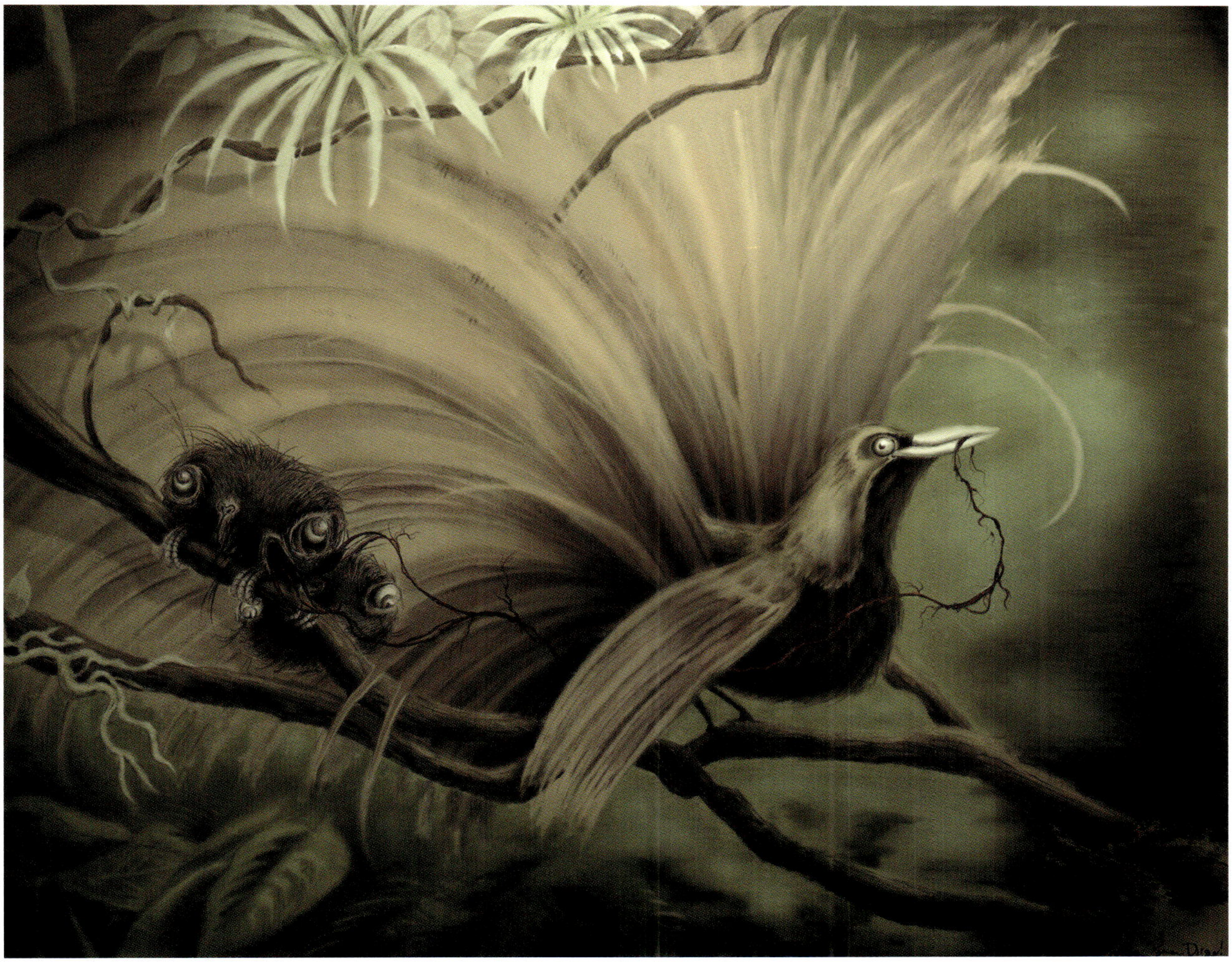

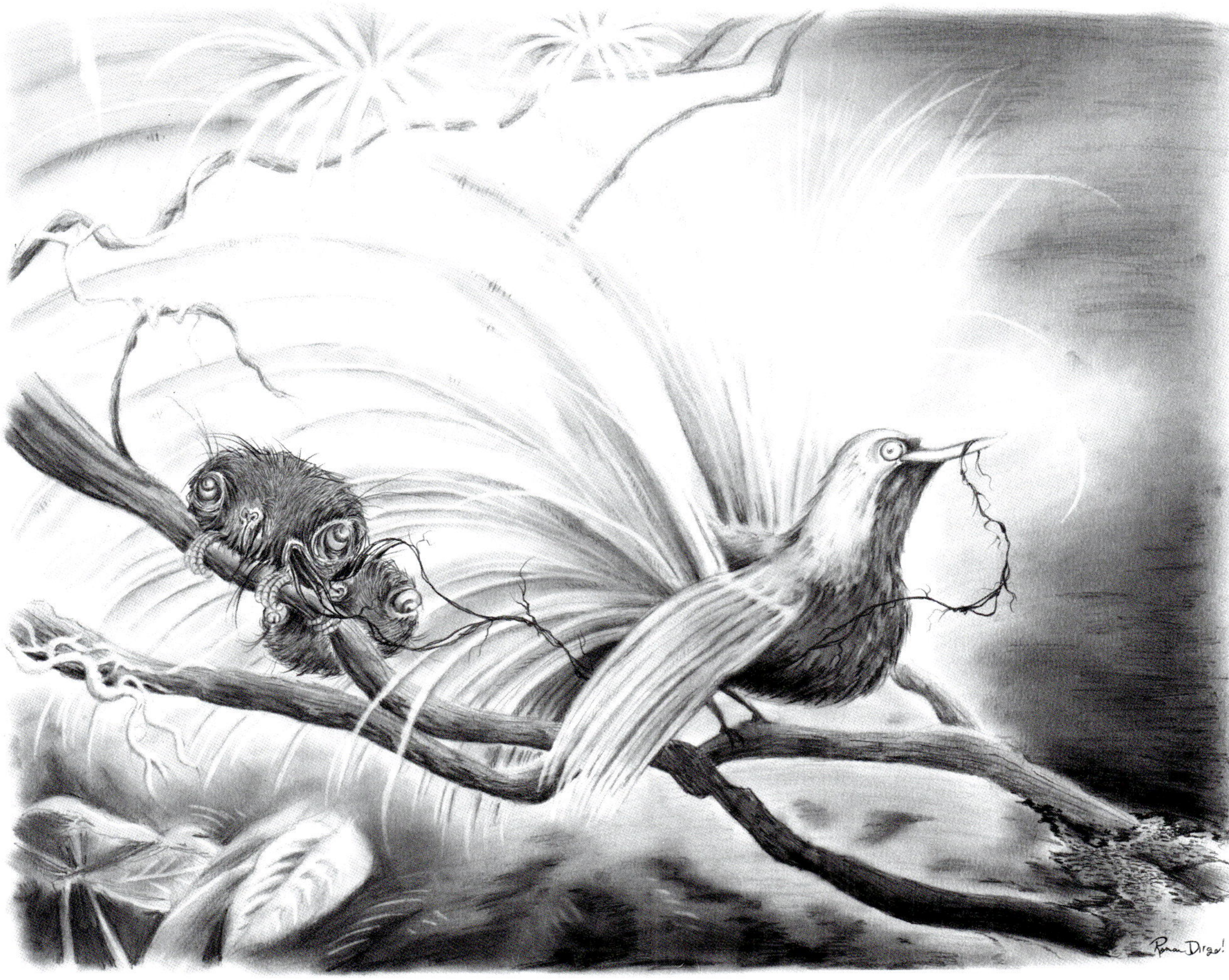

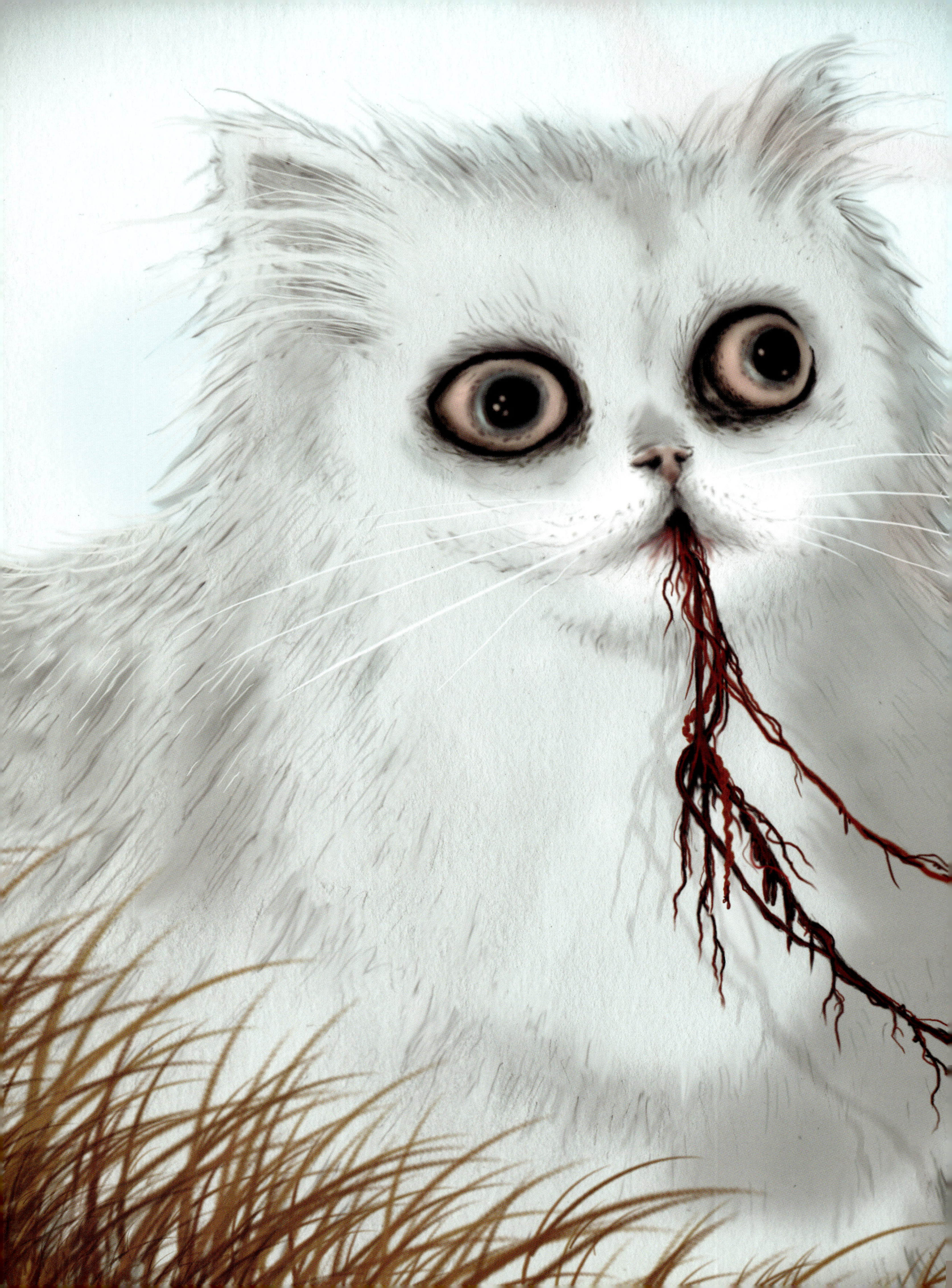

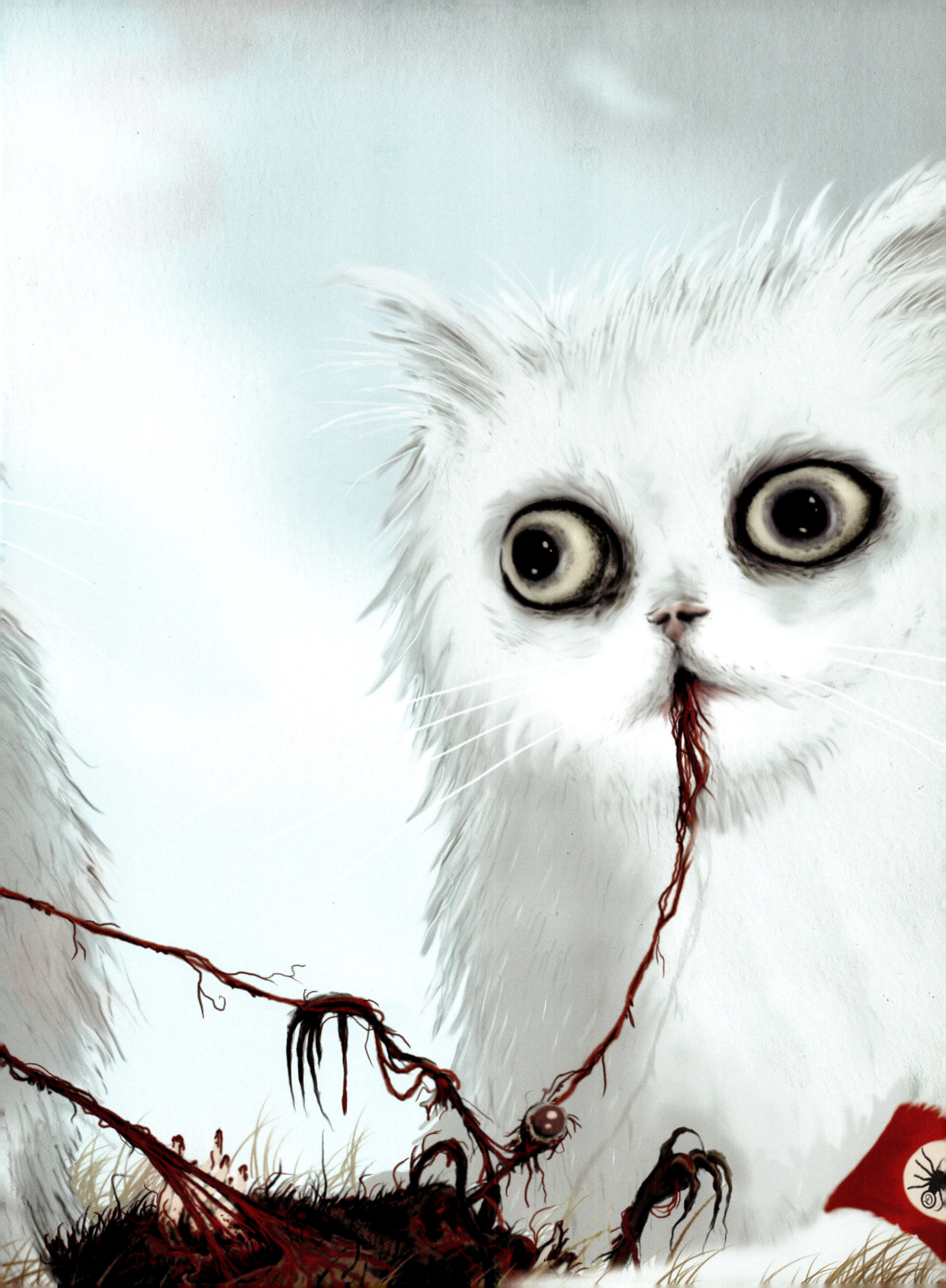

Scarytales

I looooove fairy tales. The originals are so dark and demented. No wonder people didn't live as long back when they were told at bedtime. It's easy to be inspired by these classic gems. Here are my humble takes on some classics. Opposite is the "Queen Of Horns." I've always wanted to do my own take on Alice in Wonderland, but it seems like everyone and their dog's dog have driven that into the ground at this point. Mine would have involved this queen.

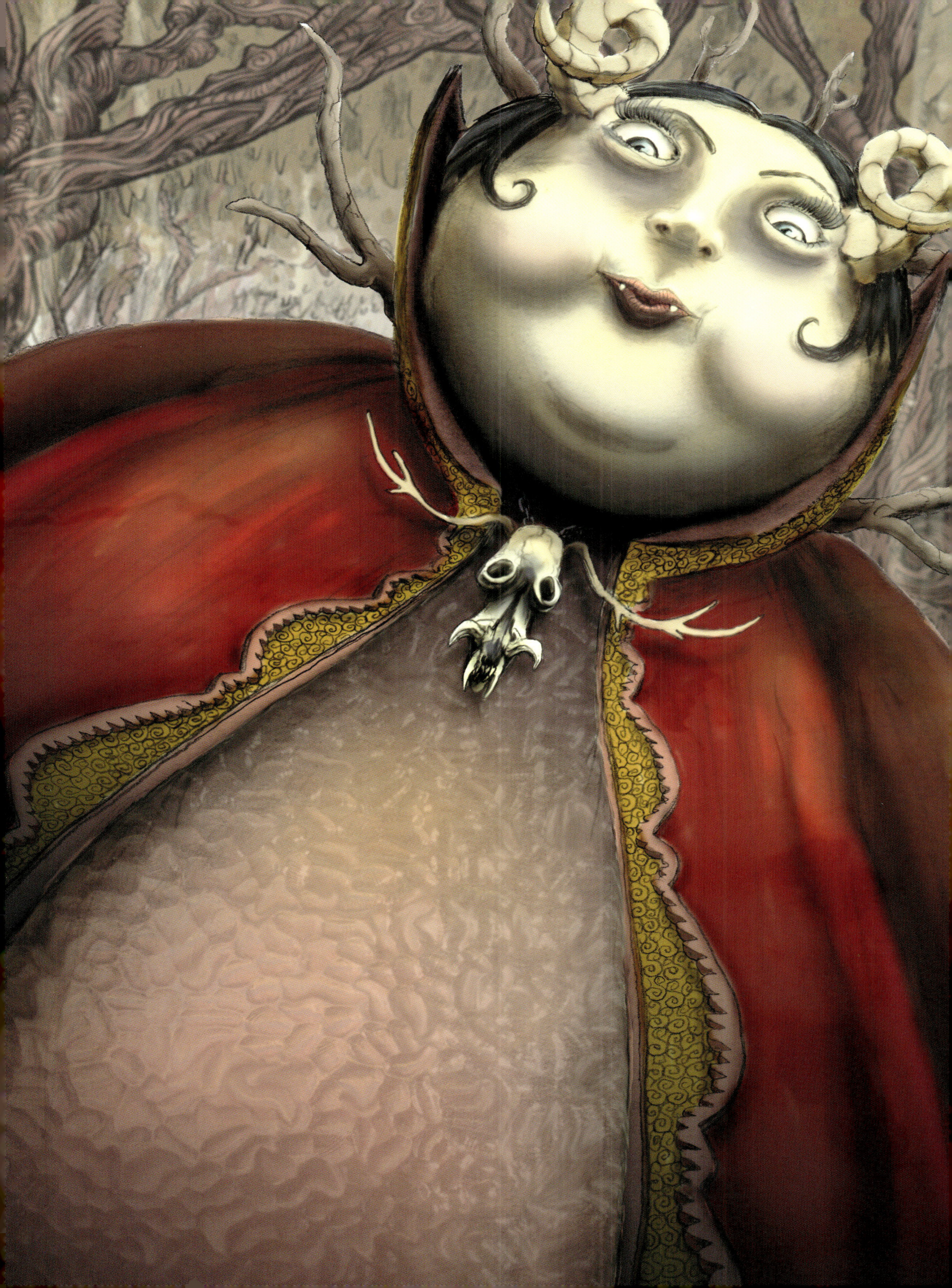

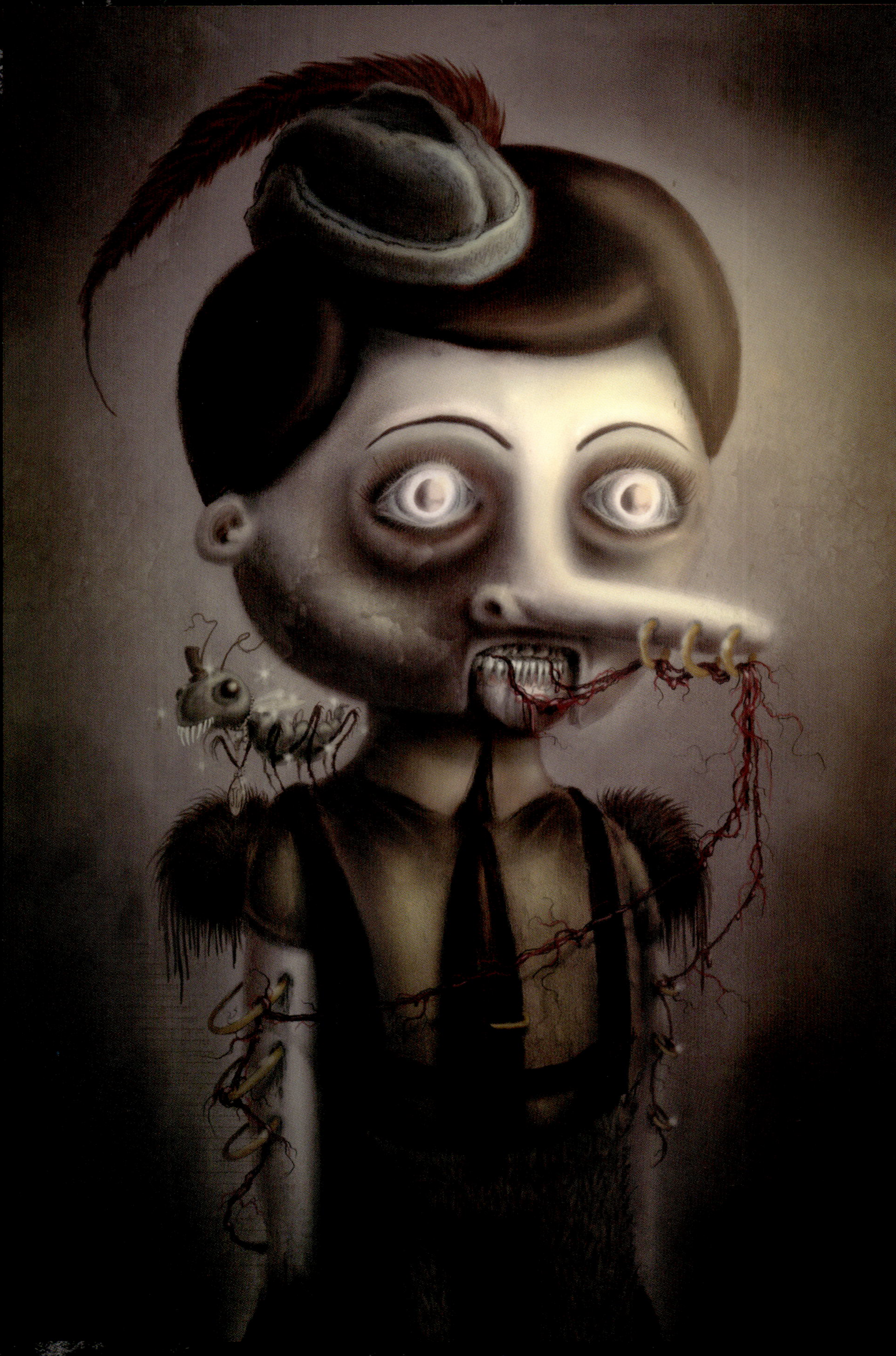

Above: "PinocchiUhOh."
Check out that pimp cricket's fly bling.

Opposite: "Wes Brot Ich Ess Des Lied Ich Sing."
(Whose bread I eat, his song I sing.) There were seven dwarves when this scene started.

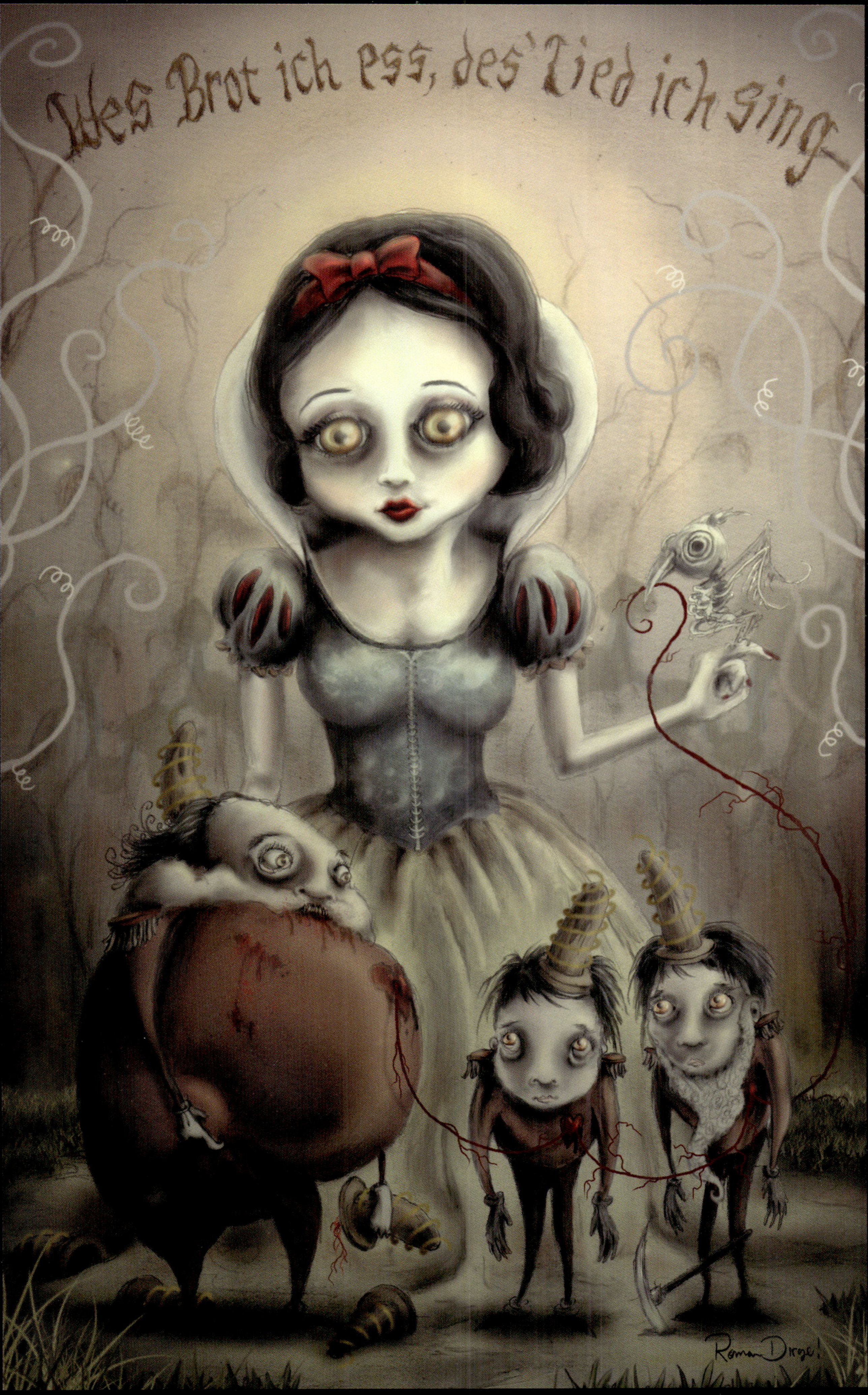
Wes Brot ich ess, des Lied ich sing
Roman Dirge

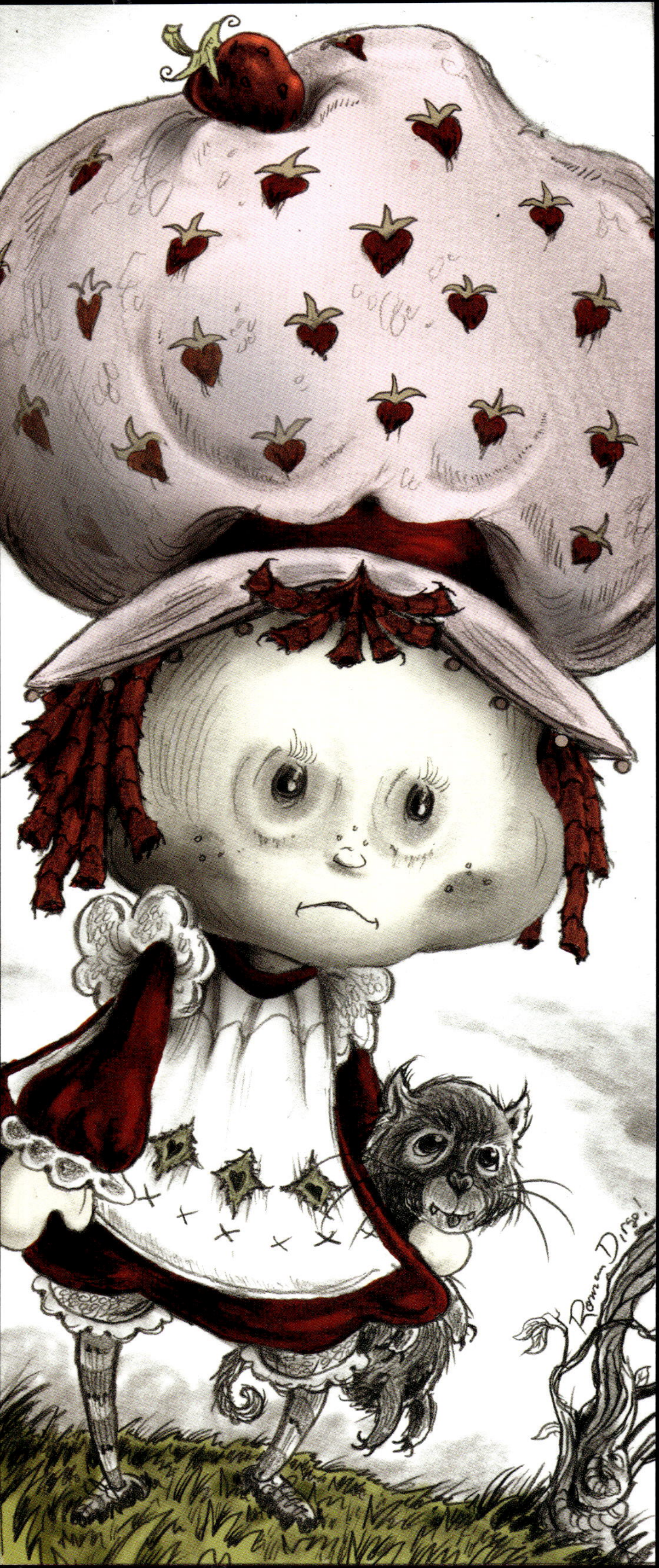

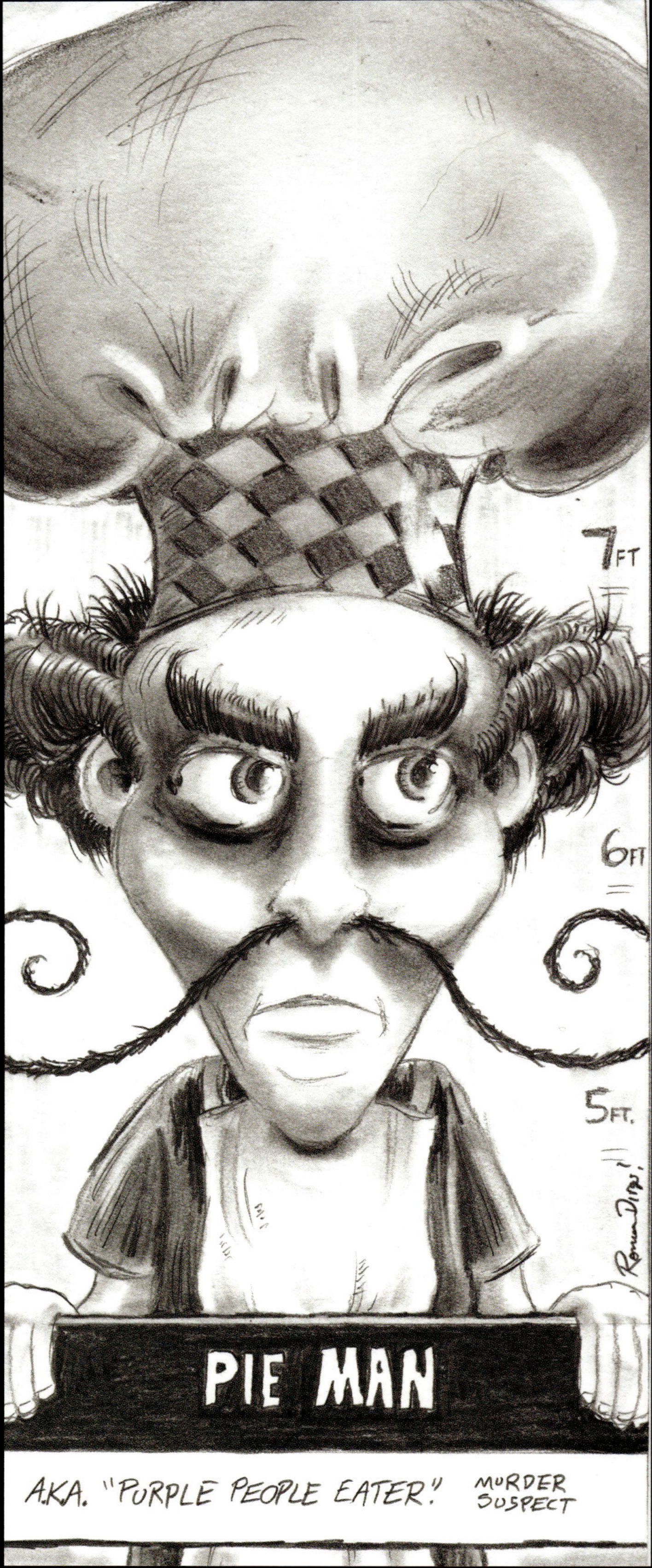

Above:
Not a fairytale but always liked it. The original of this was three parts that had a middle piece of a strawberry pie, but it has been lost to time… or cats. Or time-cats! They're the worst.

Opposite: "Changing Of The Cards."

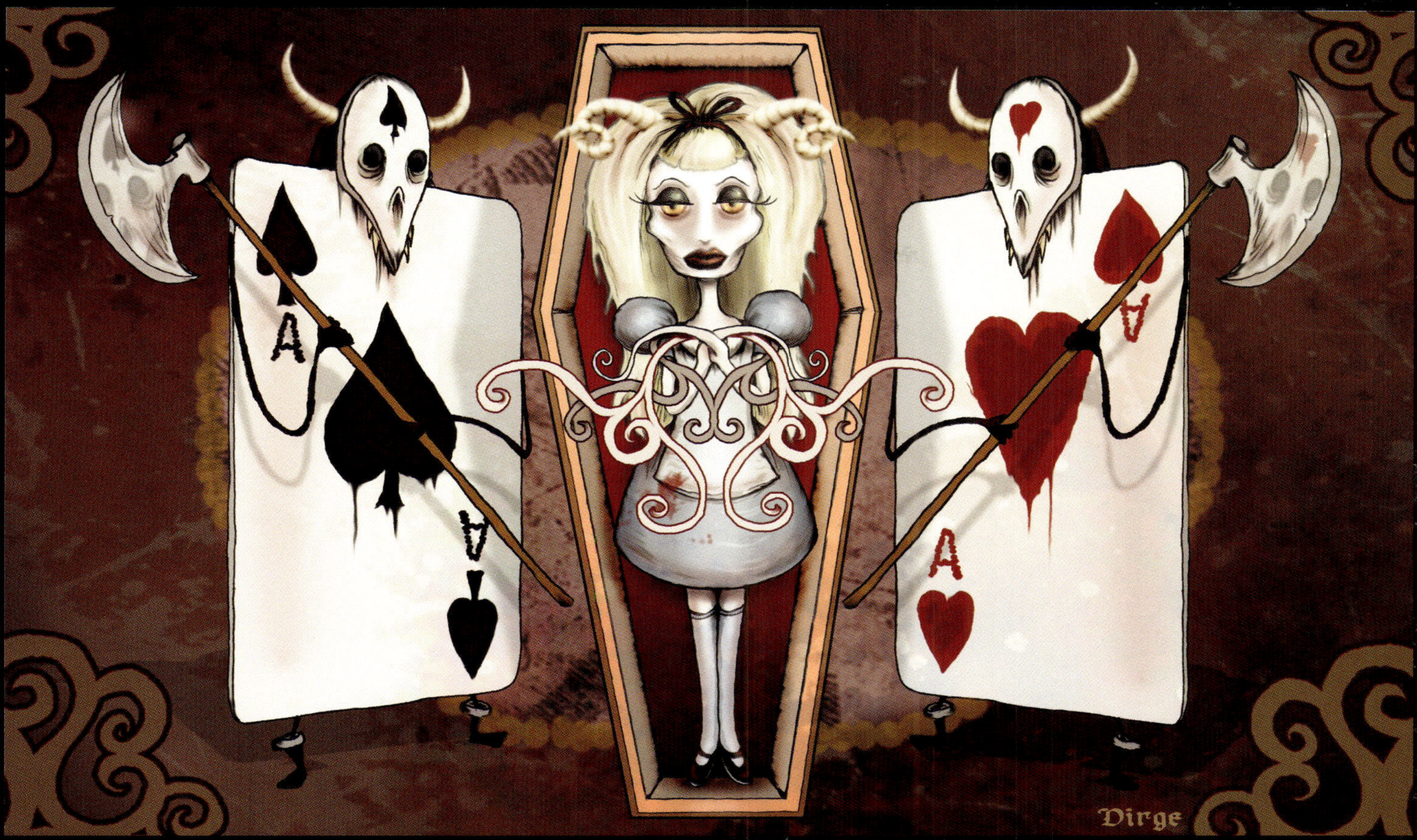
Dirge

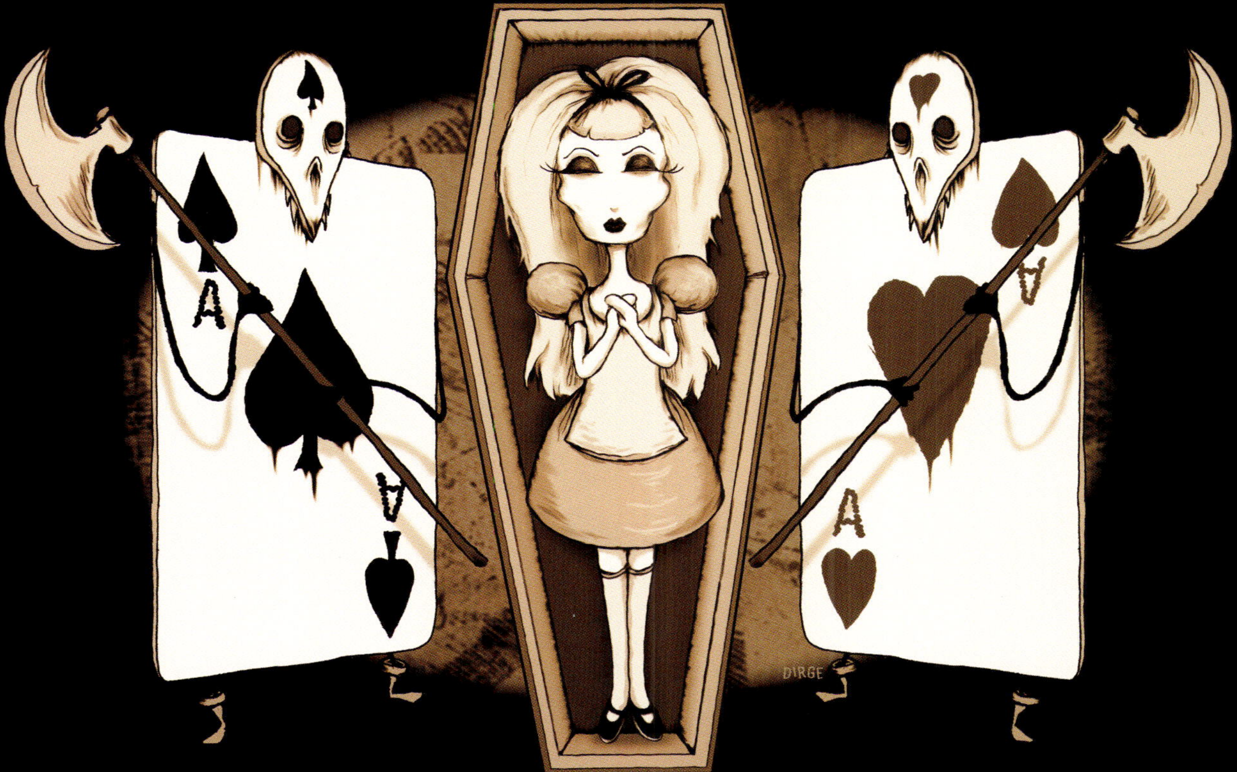
DIRGE

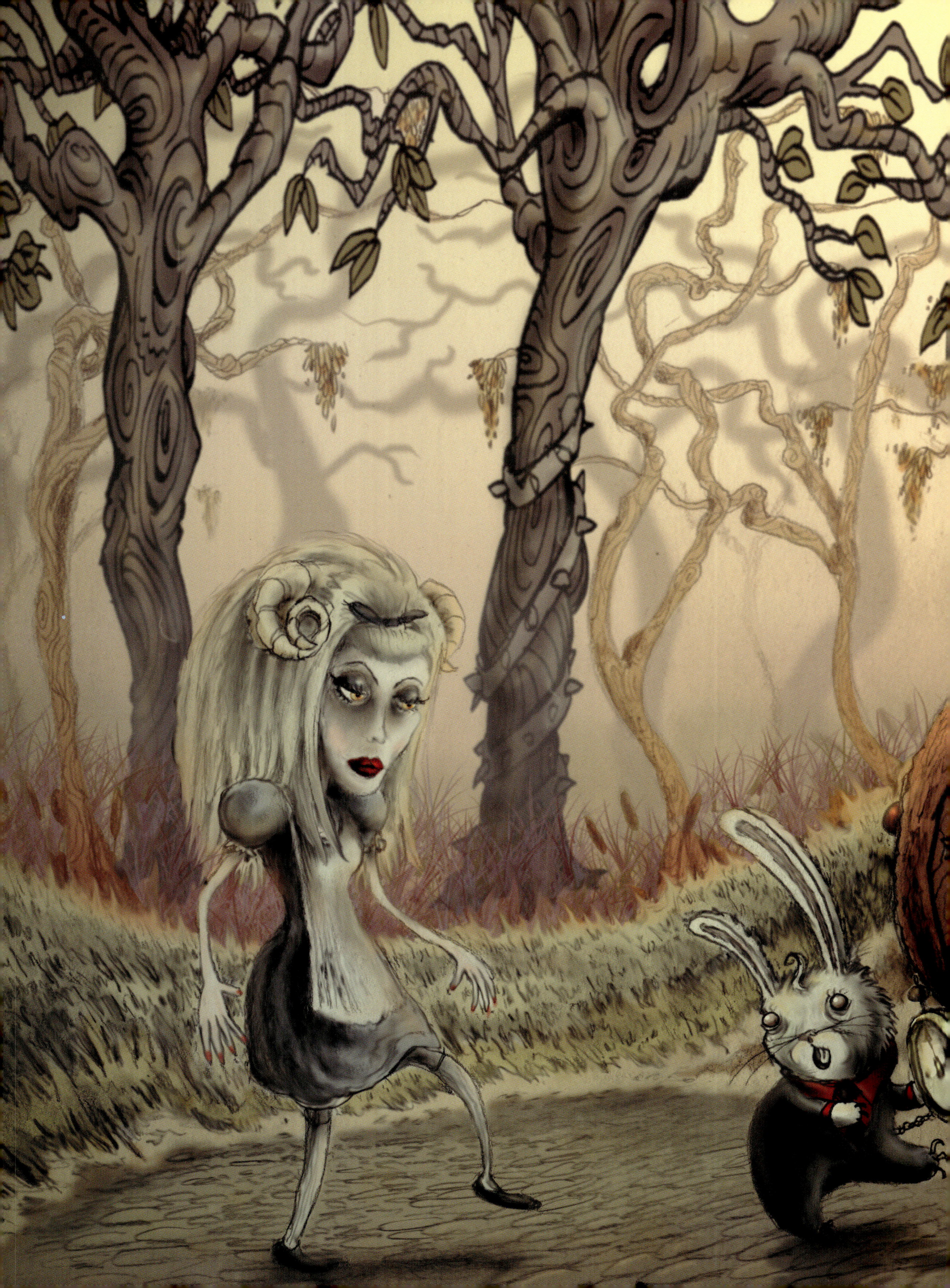

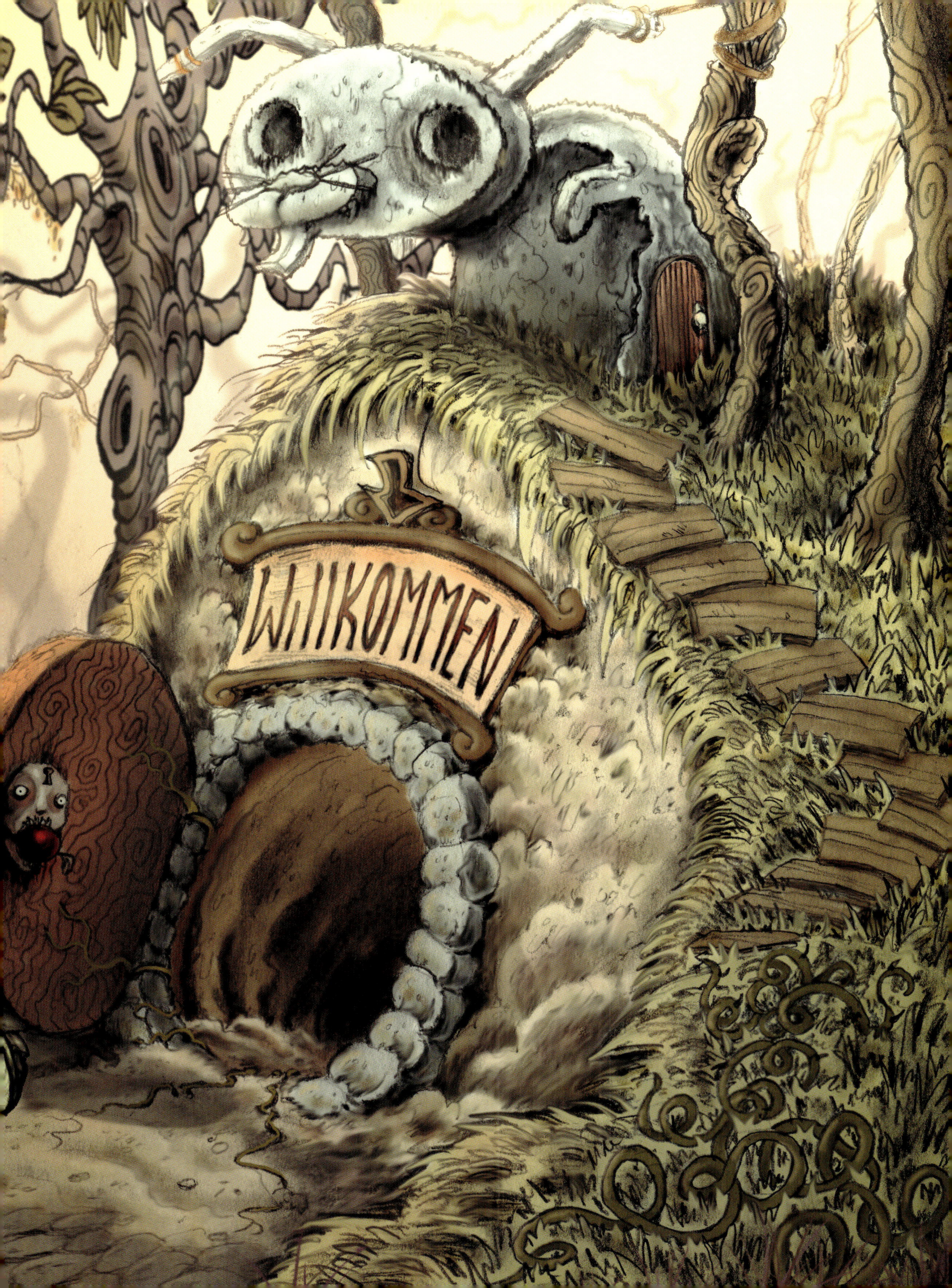
WILLKOMMEN

Monster!

Monsters are by far my favorite things to play with. Drawing-wise, not… you know, playing Scrabble with a yeti or something. Some of these visited me more than once in my head while I dreamt, so I output them to exorcise them, so to speak. Sometimes it worked, most often it didn't.

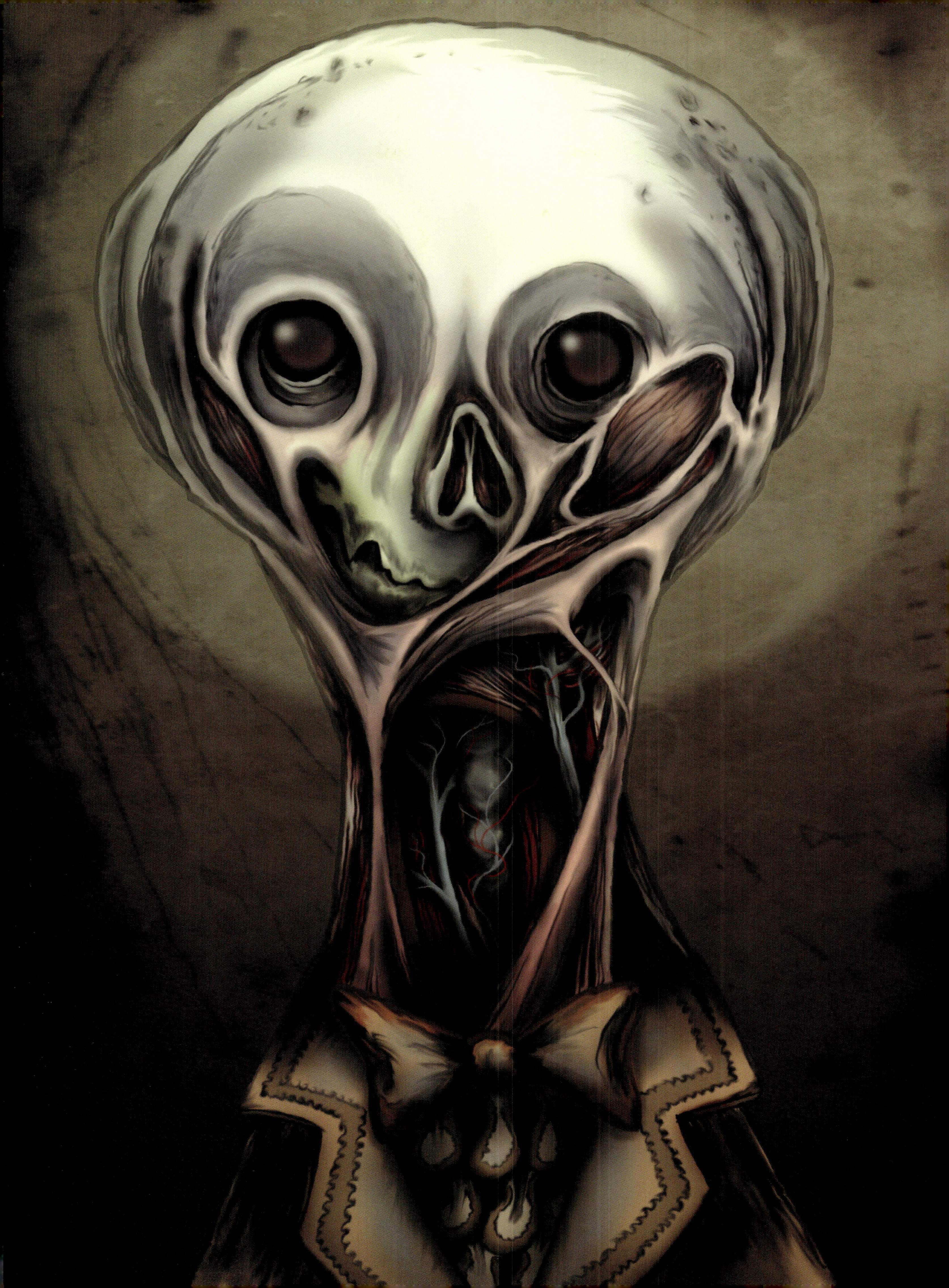

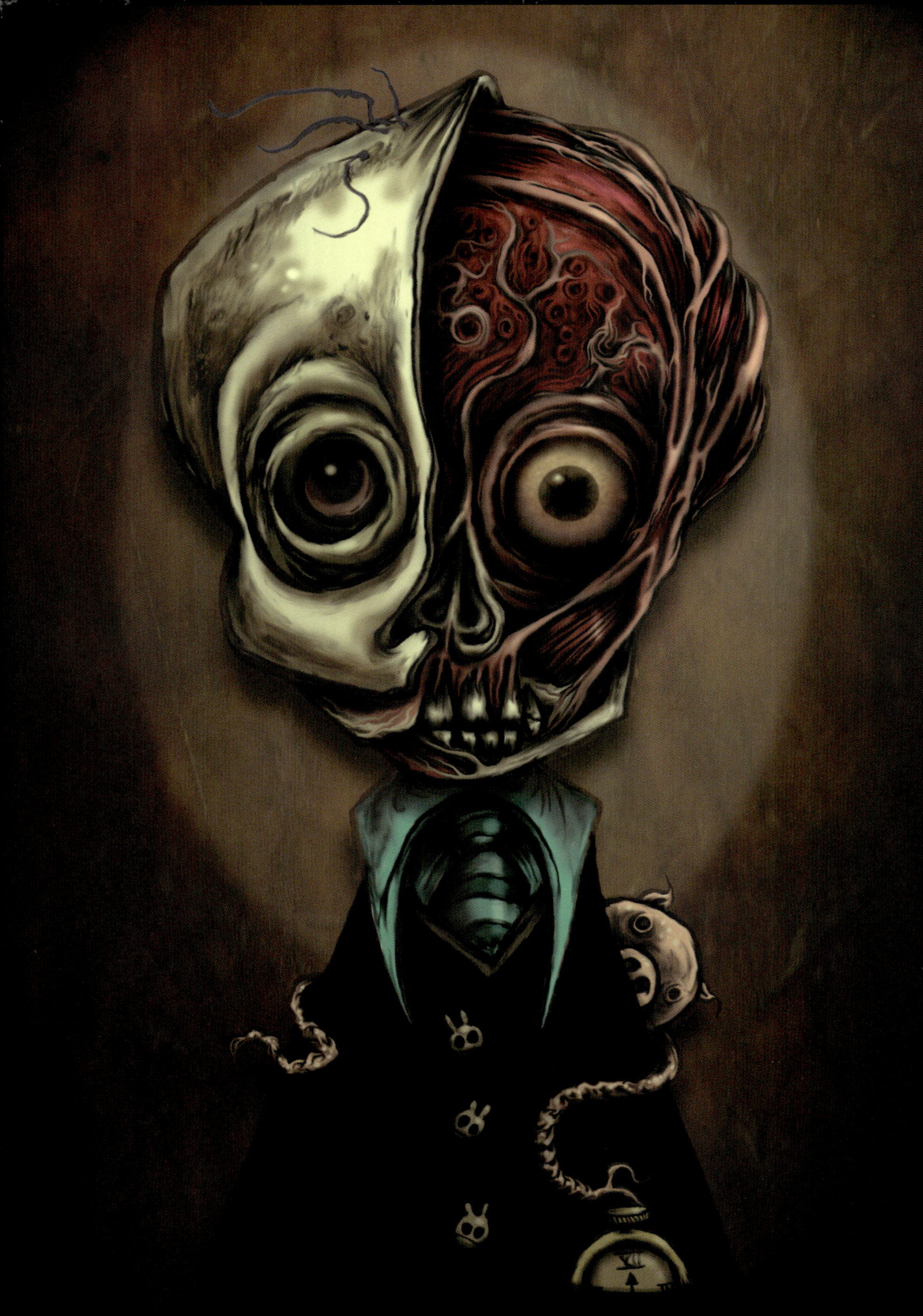

Previous page: "Mr. Bulb."

Above: "Mr. Piggy."

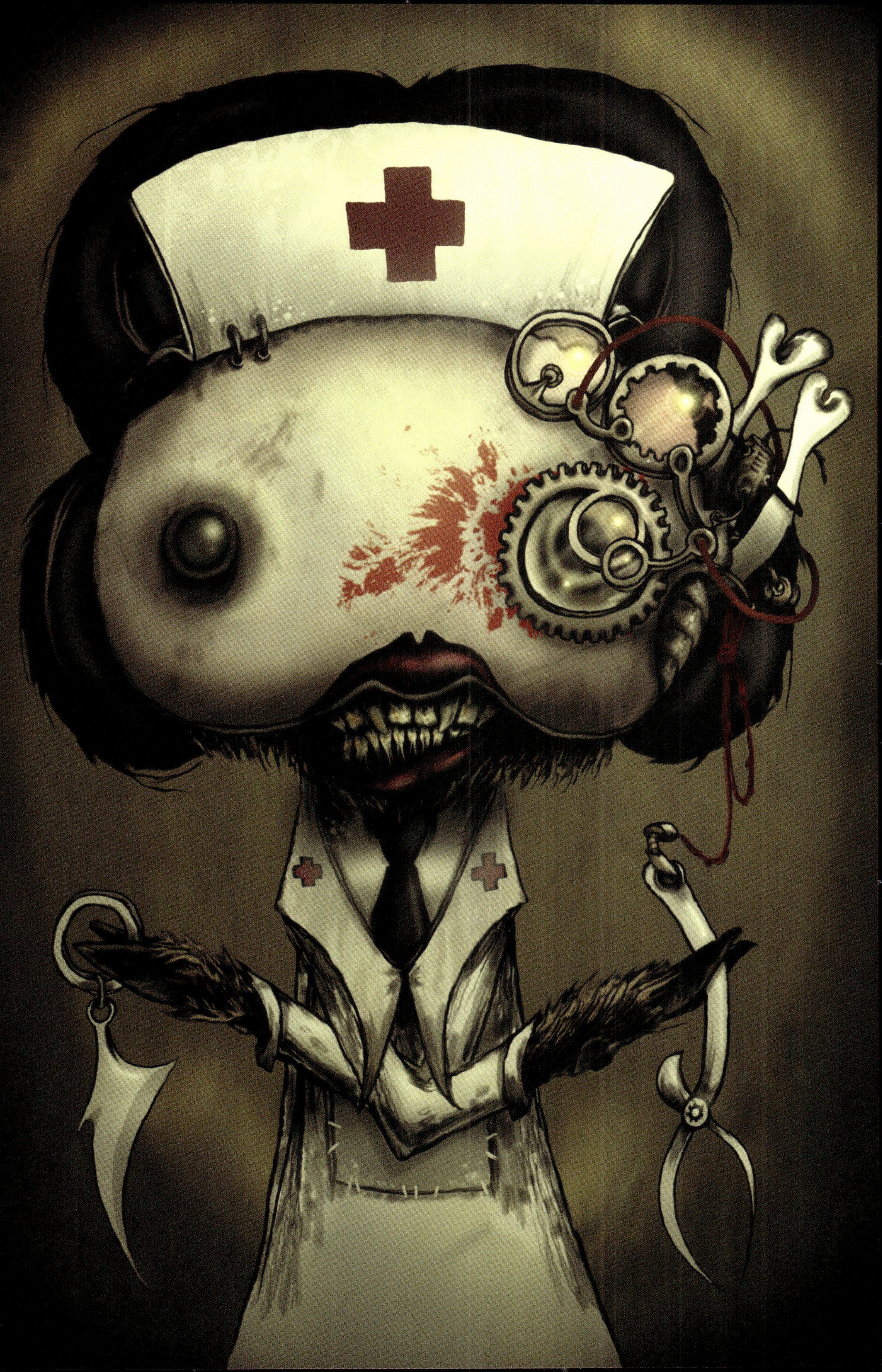

Above: "Nurse Hatchet."

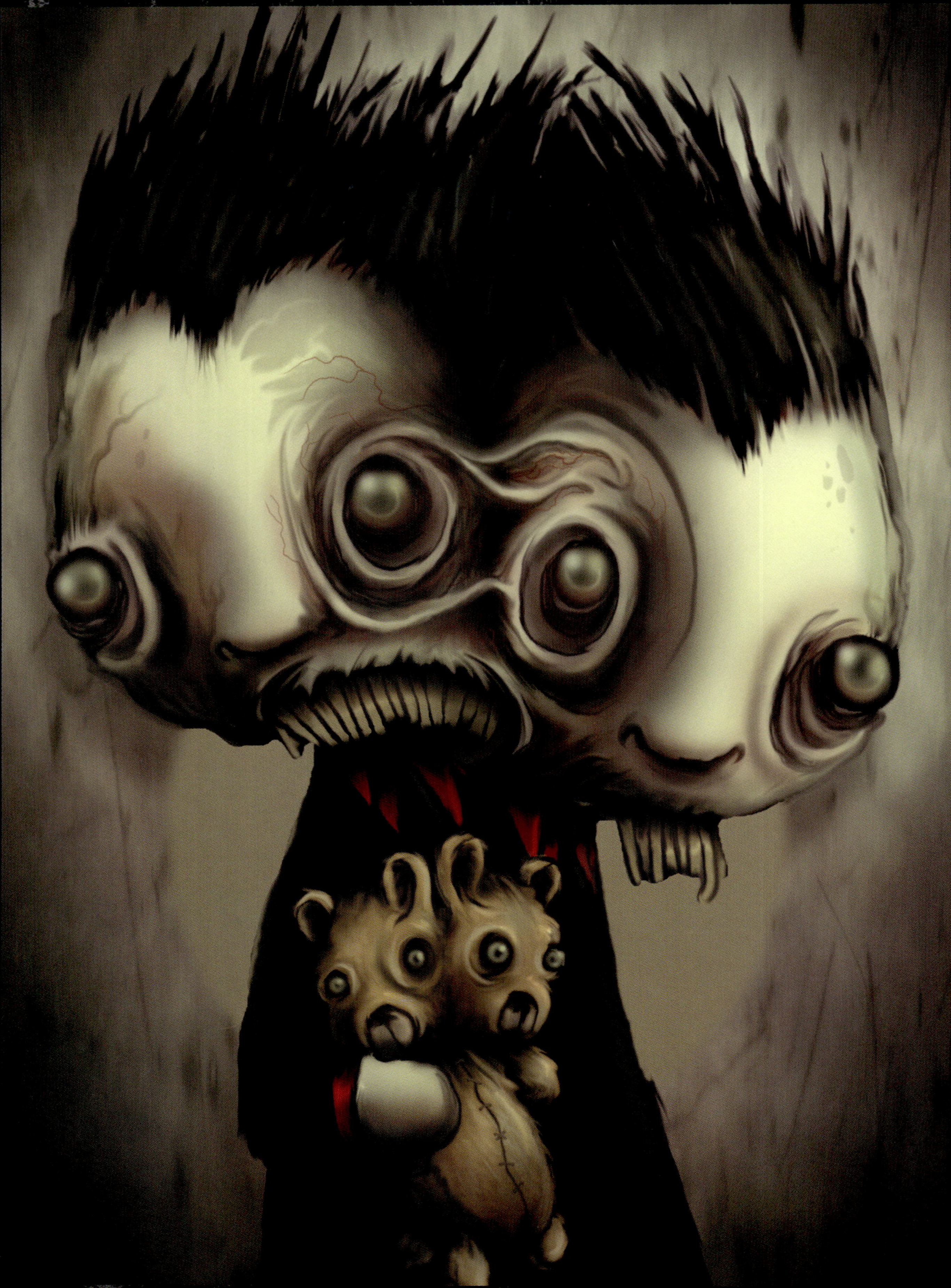

Above: "Biheaded."

Opposite: "The Couple."
Self-portrait at the time of myself and ex.

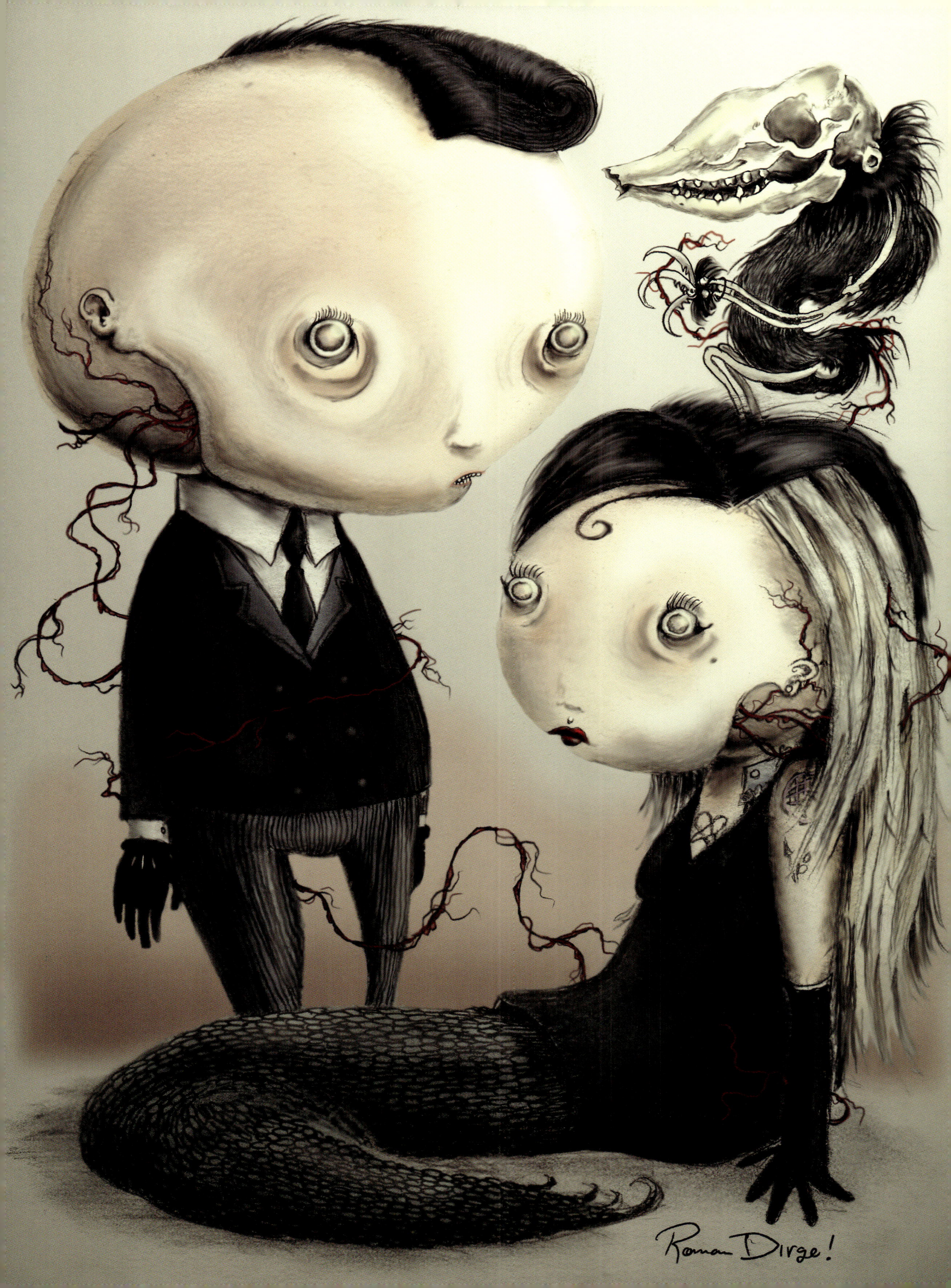
Roman Dirge!

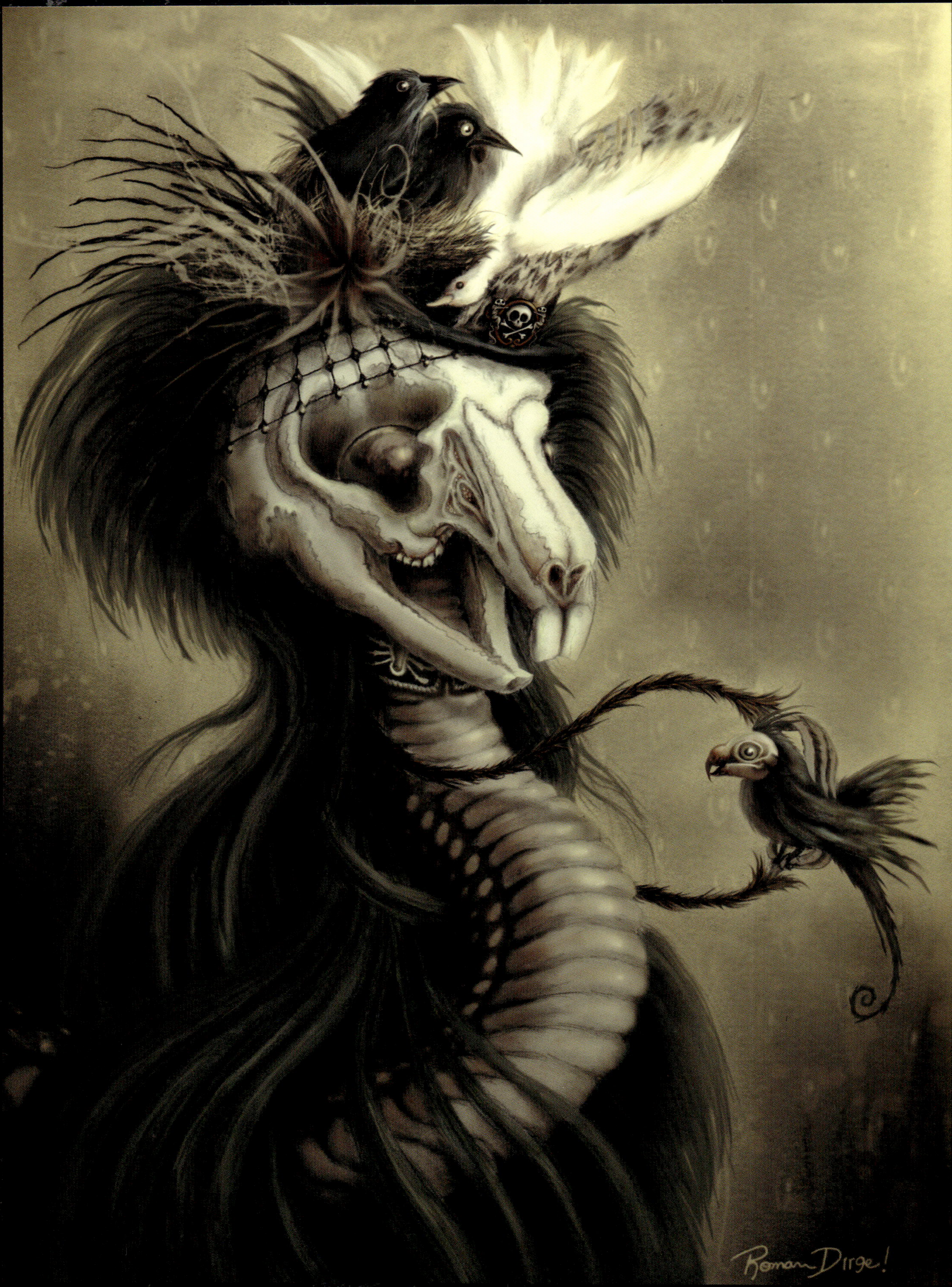

Above: "Serpenteese."
I hate birds, so I just wanted to envision the thing that would eat them.

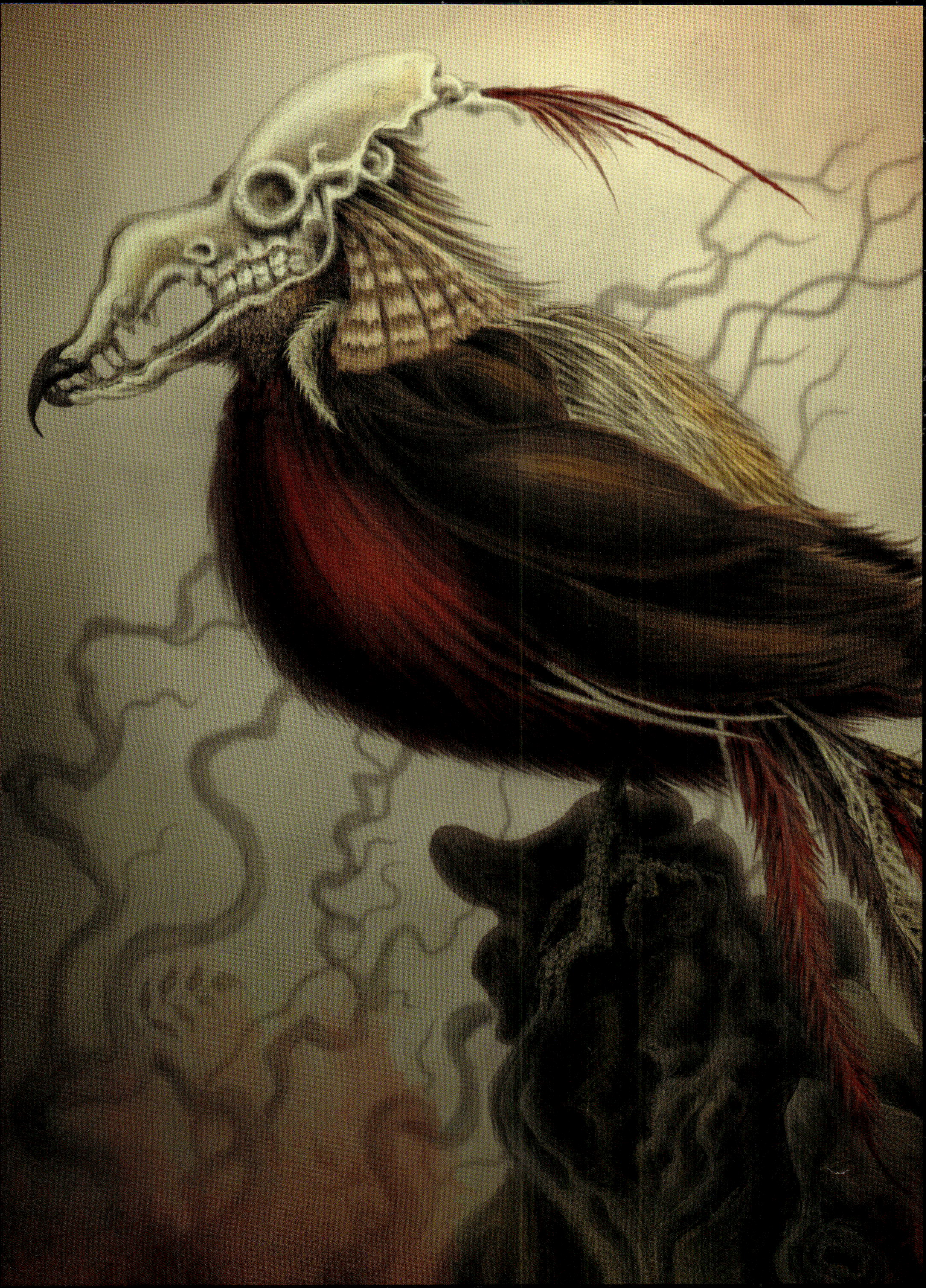

Above: "Perch."
Really wish Serpenteese would take care of business.

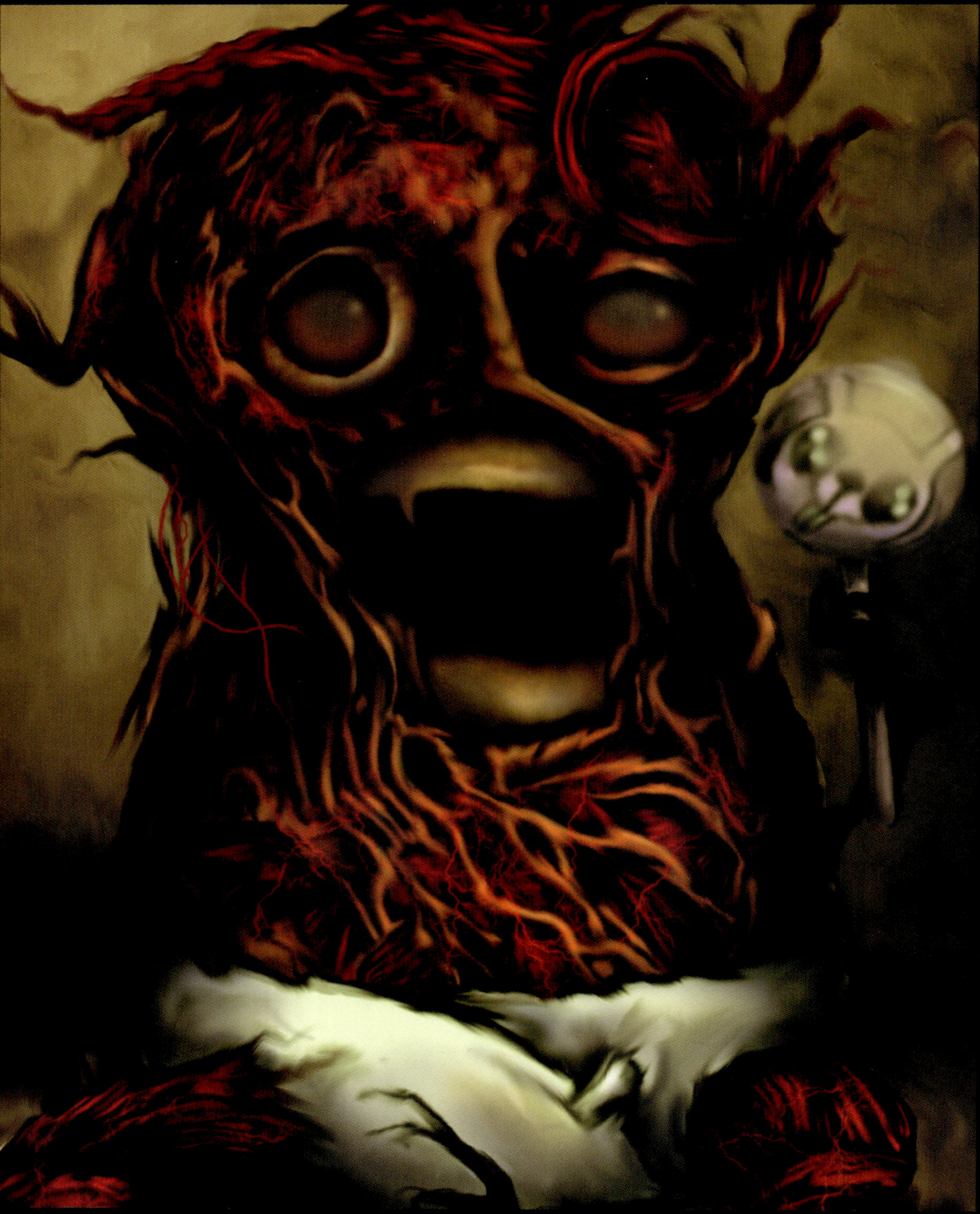

Above: "Death Rattle."
Another consistent nightmare outputted.

Opposite: "Chinese Dress."

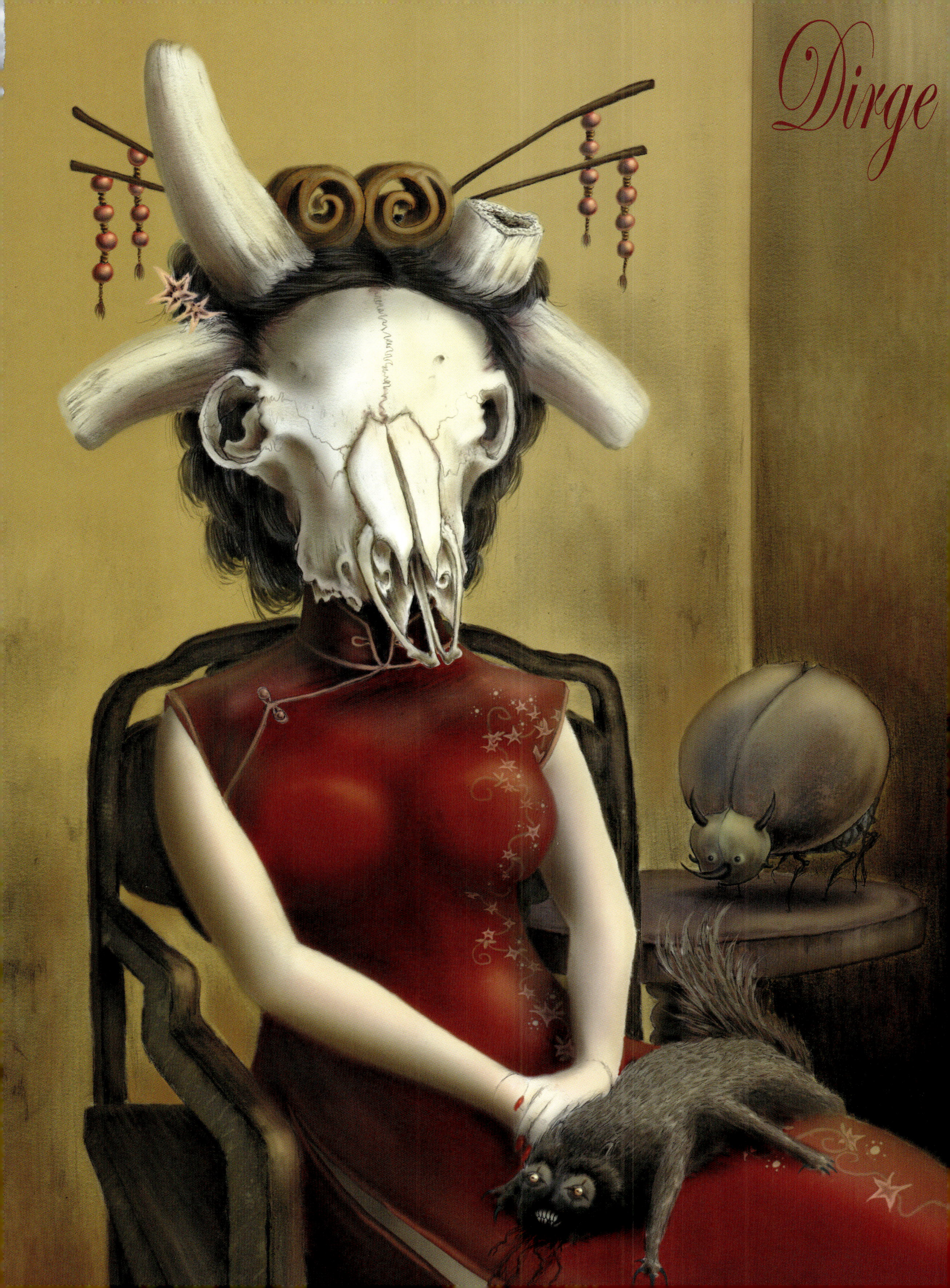

Dirge

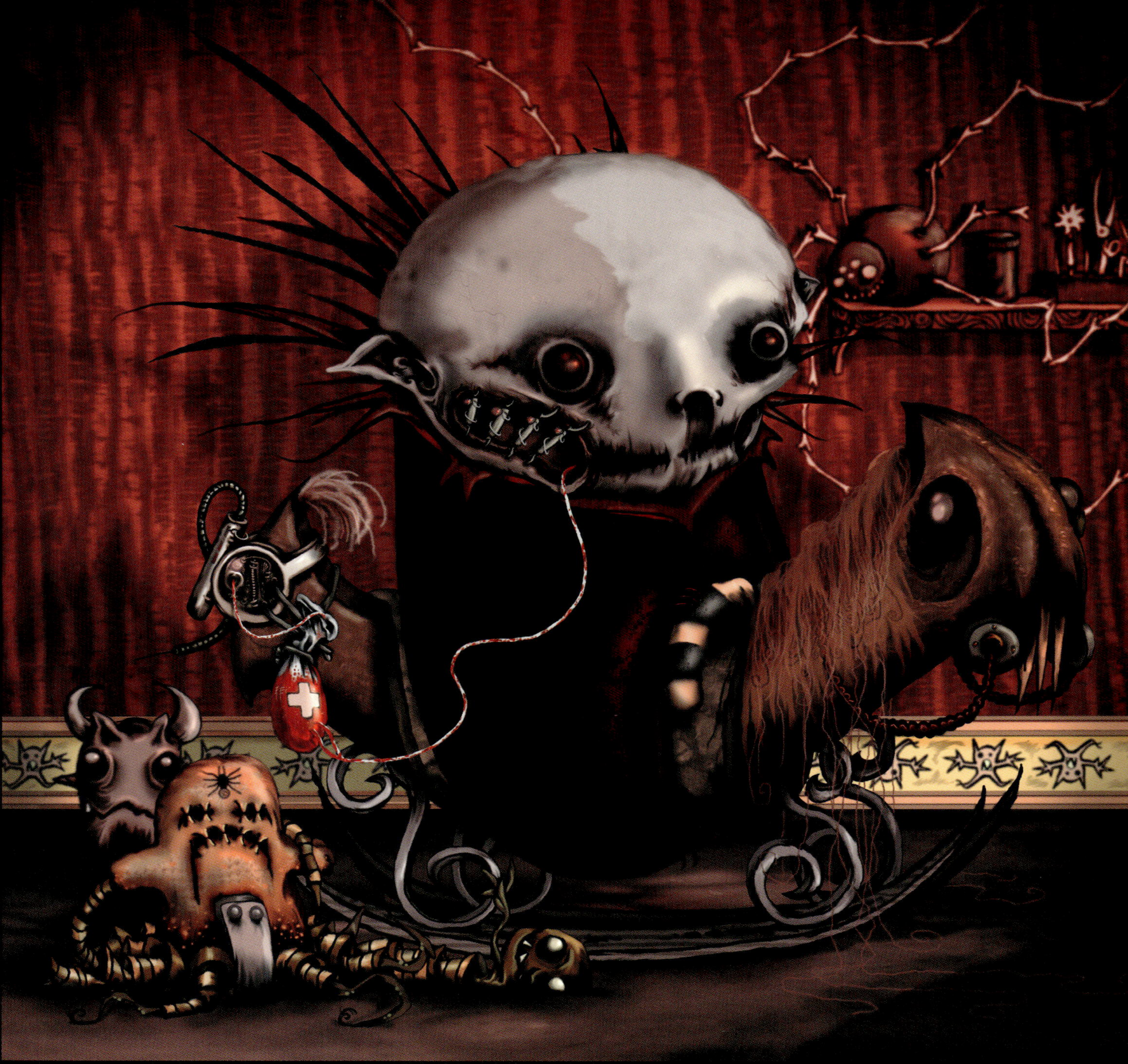

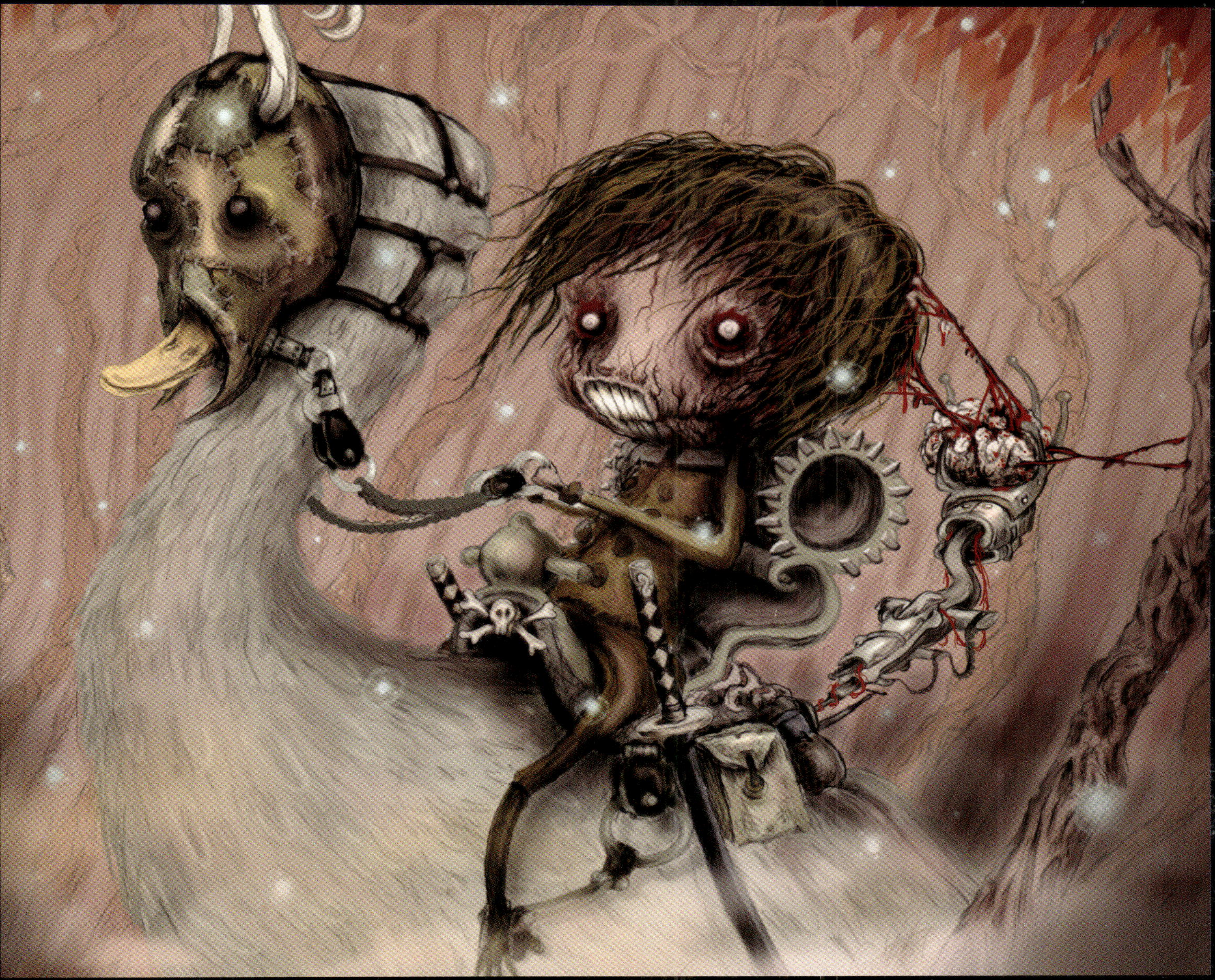

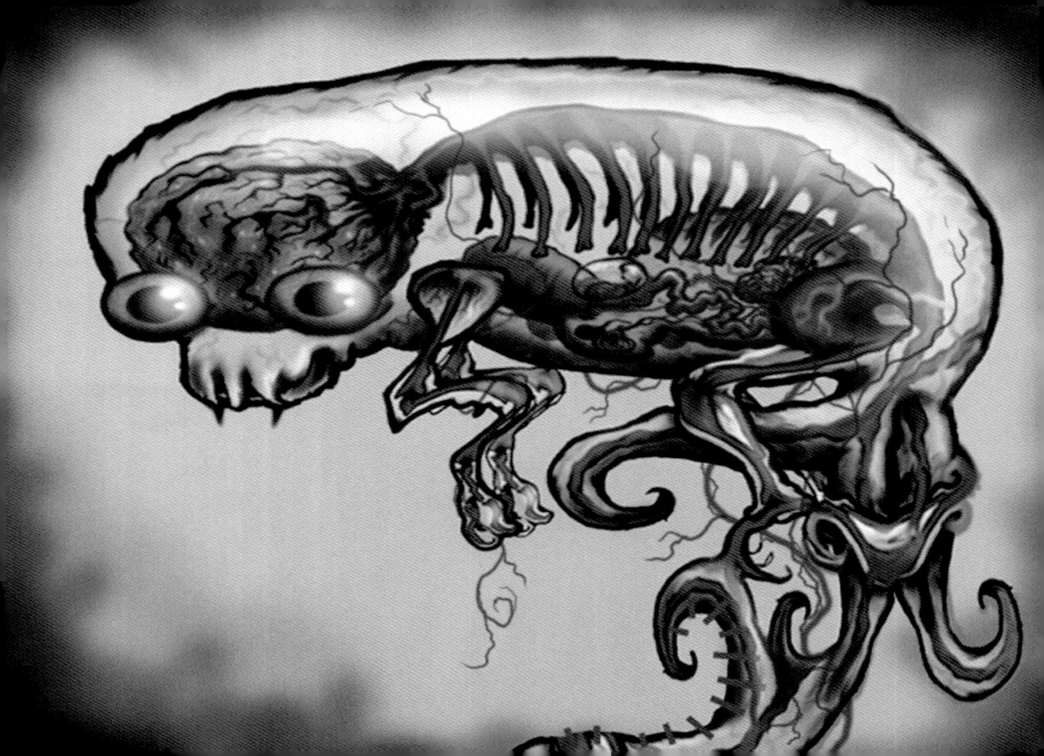

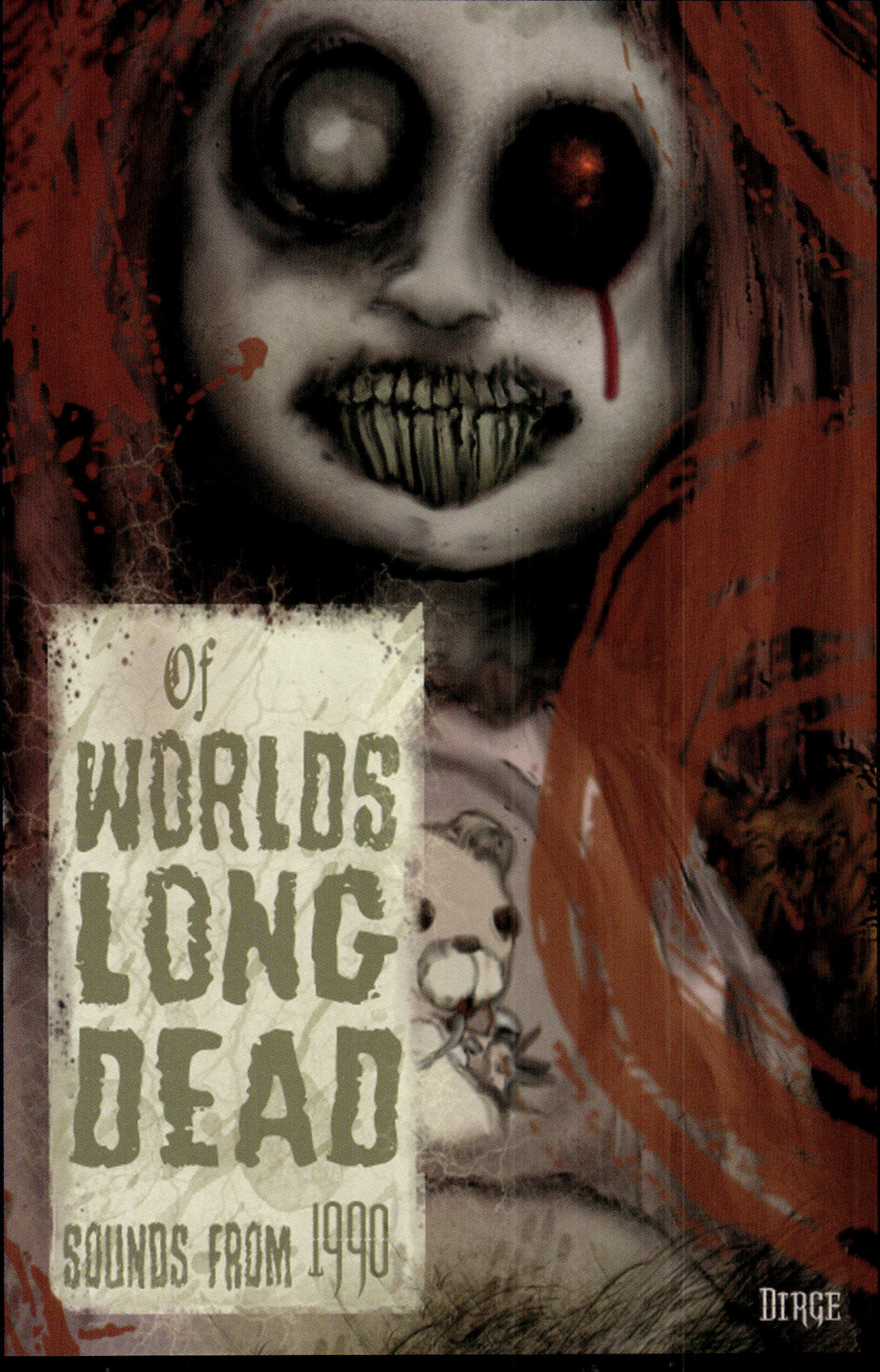
Of
WORLDS
LONG
DEAD
SOUNDS FROM 1990
DIRGE

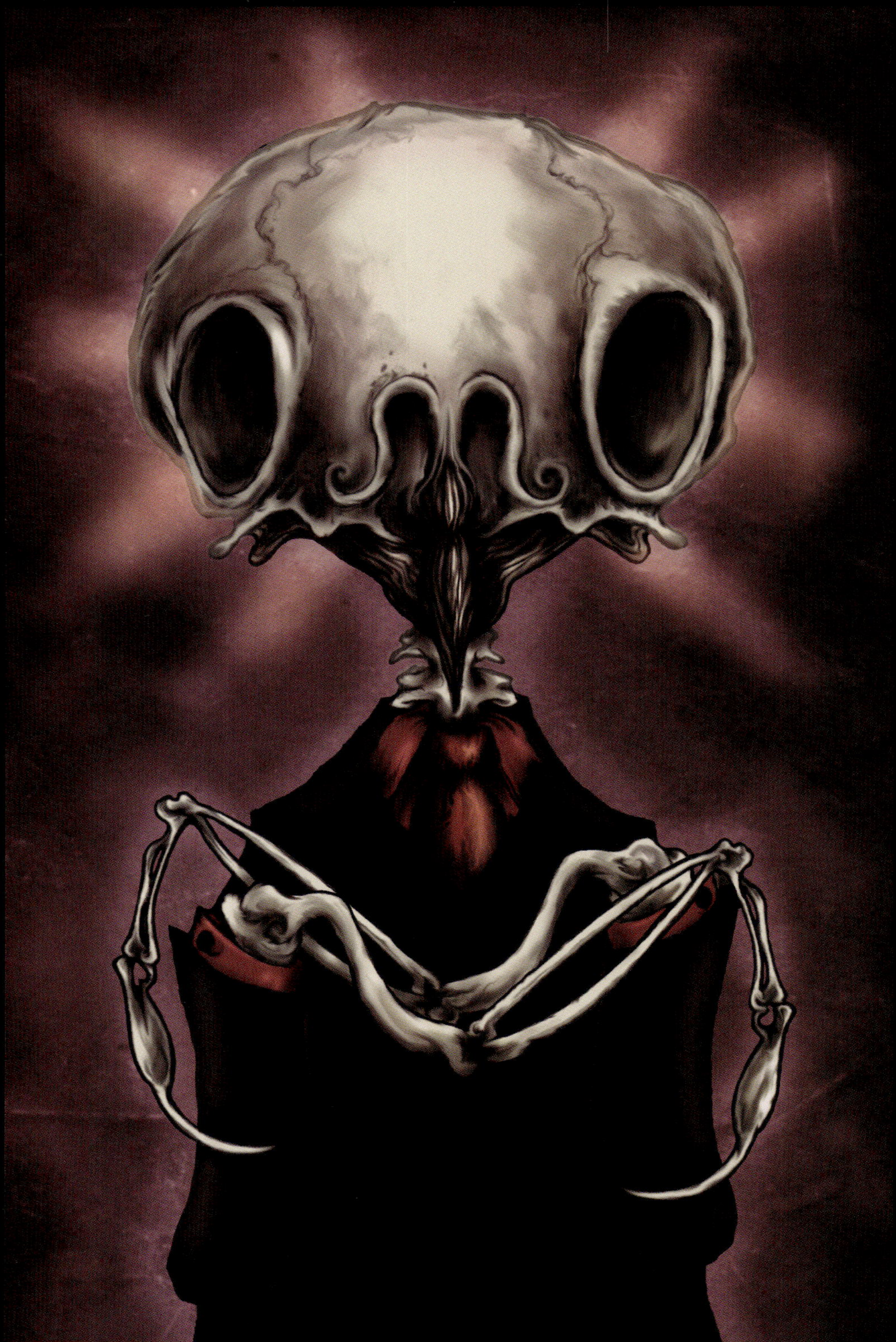

Above: "Mr. Bird."

Opposite: "Swirltongue."

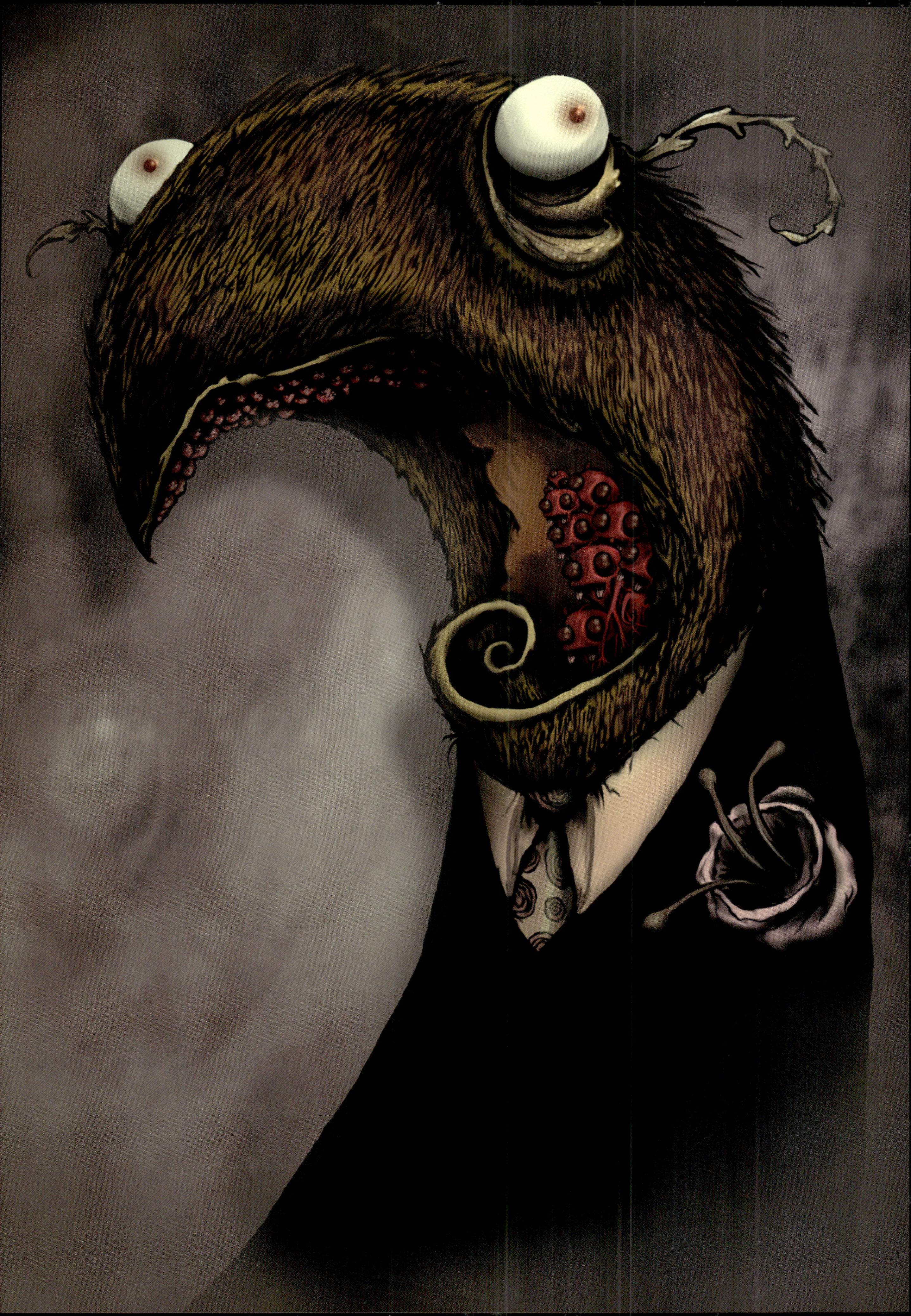

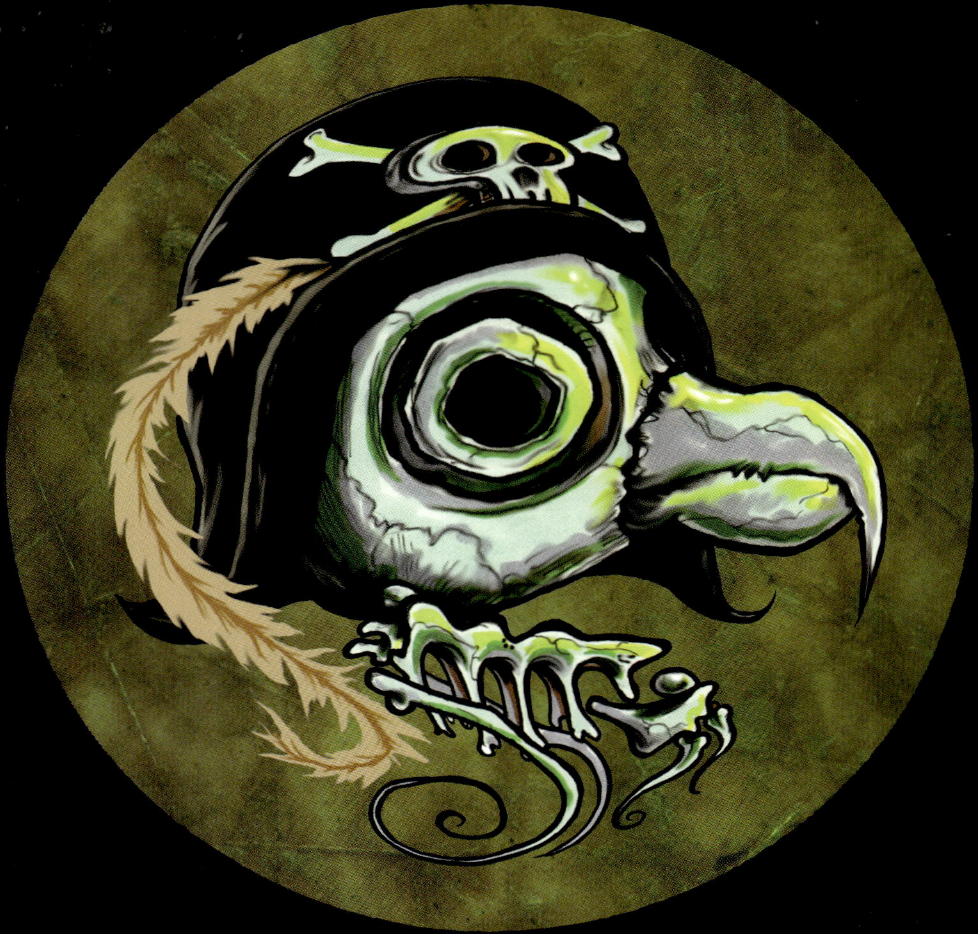

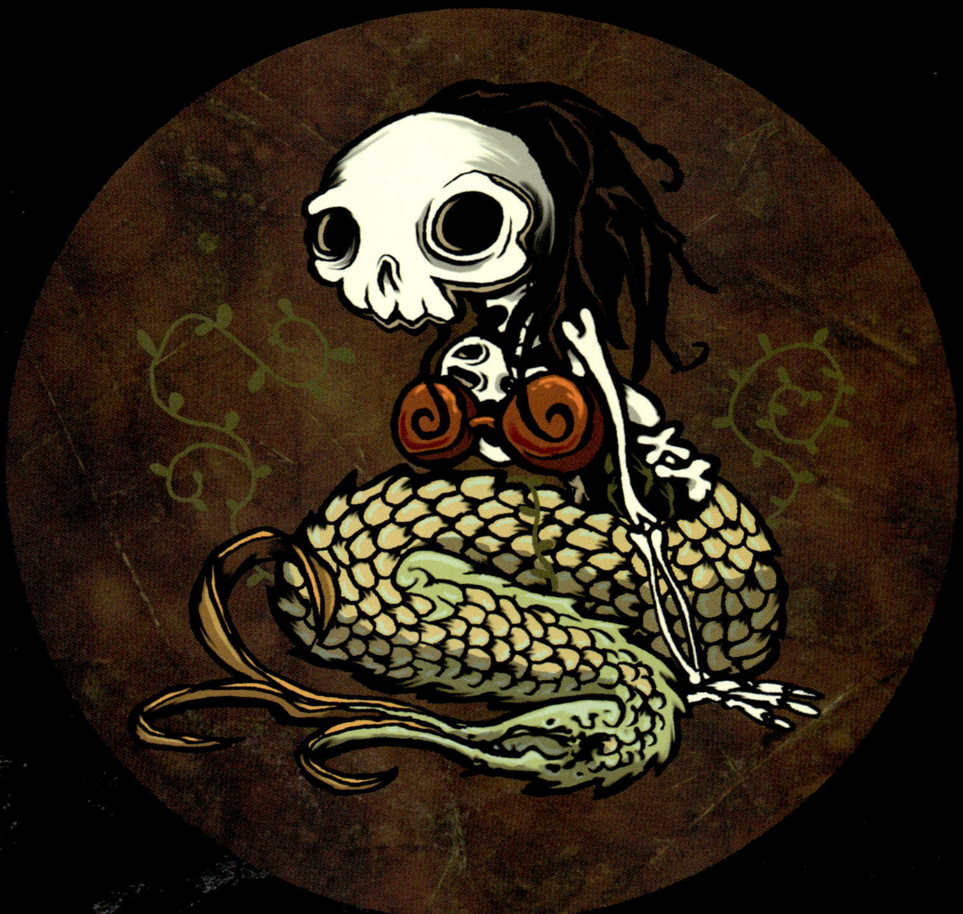

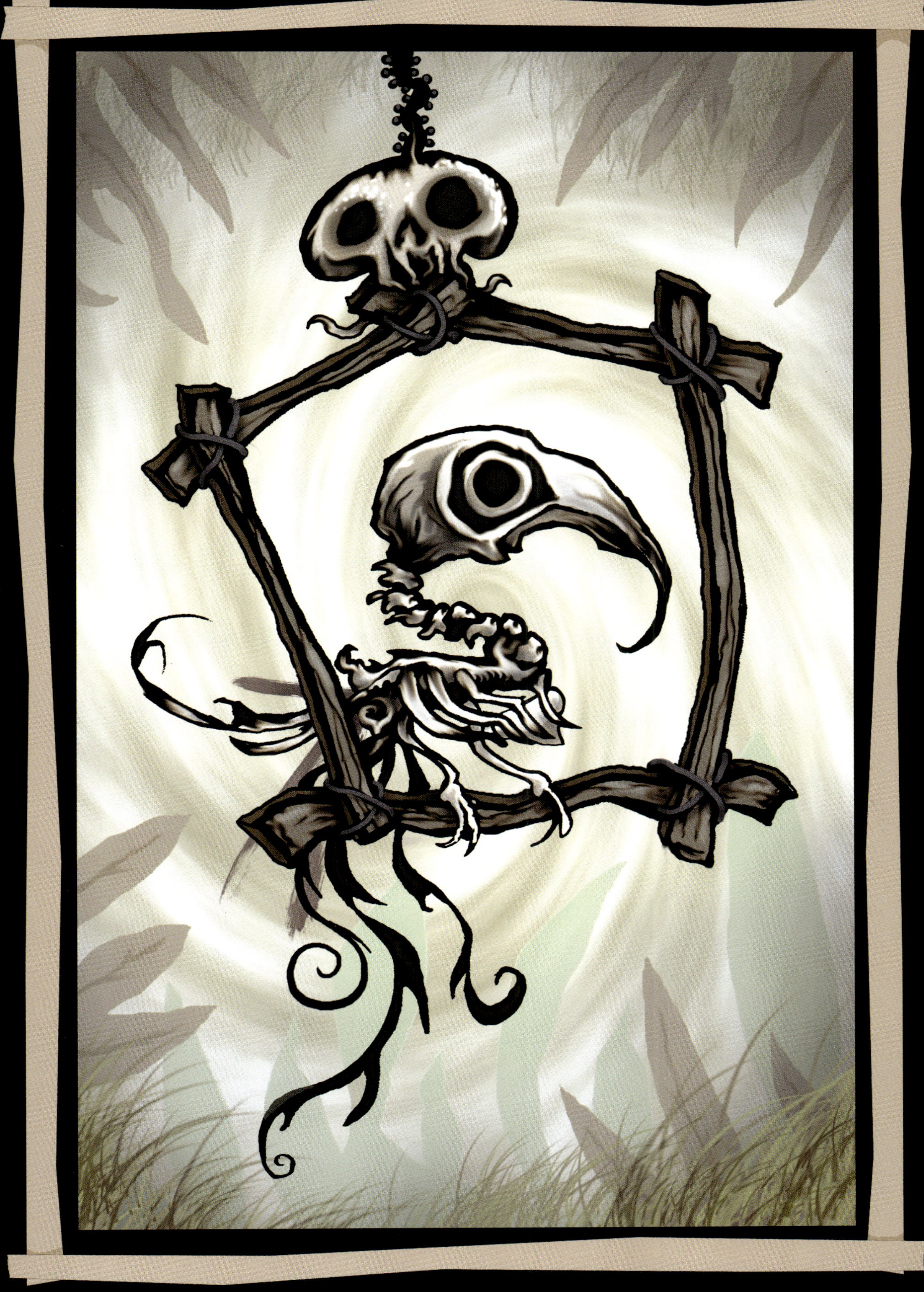

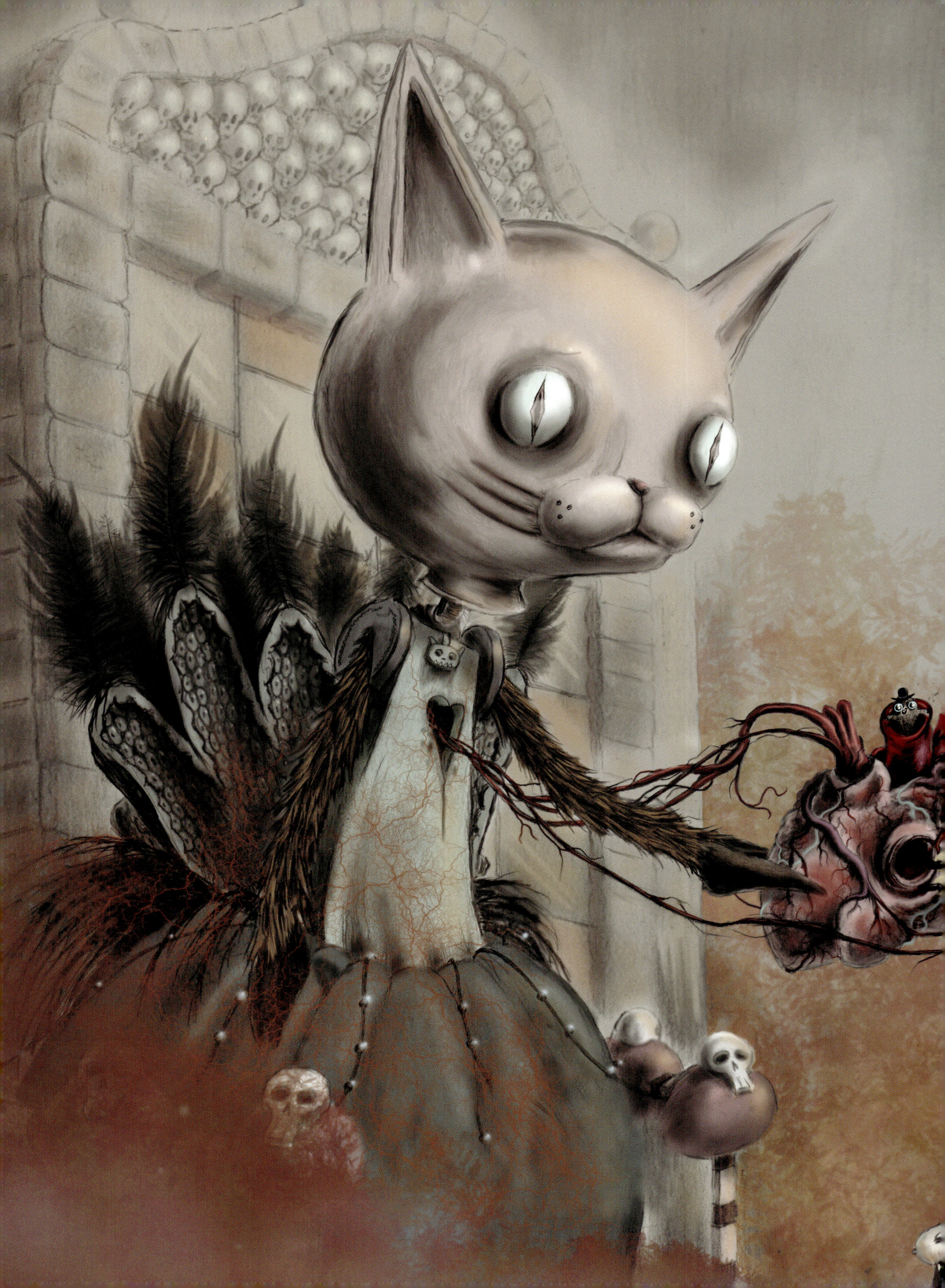

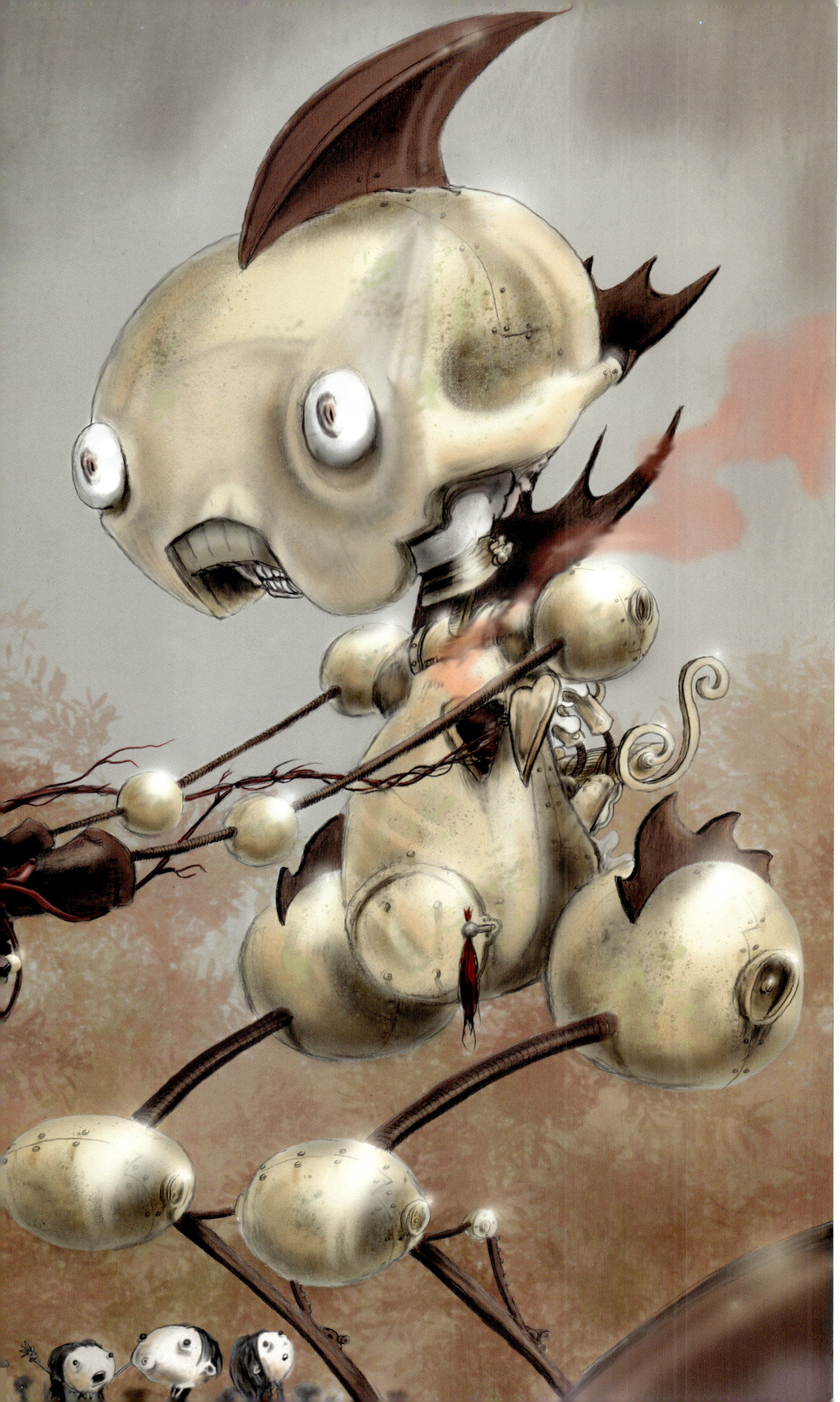

Left: "Giants."
My favorite thing about this piece is actually the little bowler hat-wearing guy that's just so happy to be in that heart.

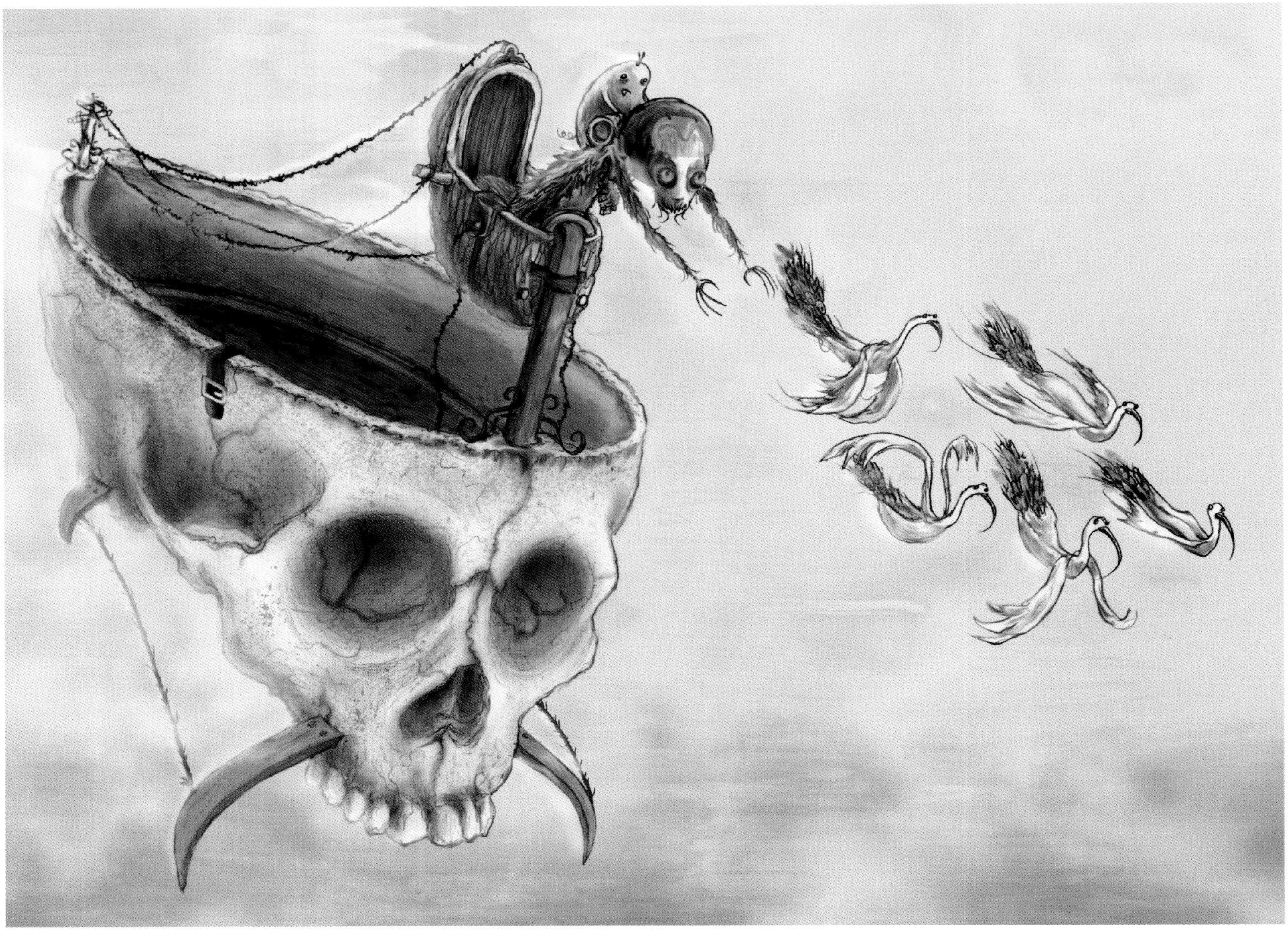

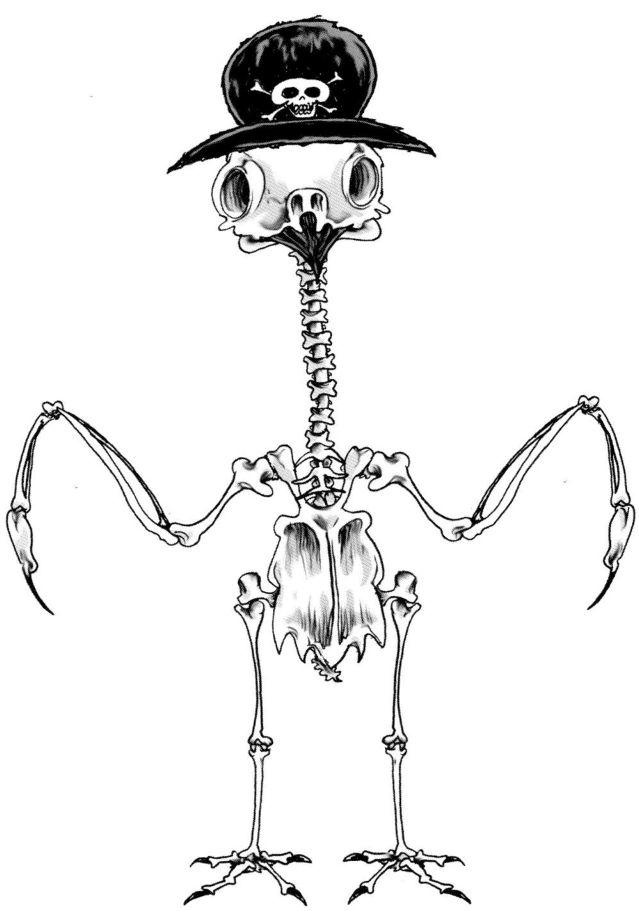

Above: "Sky Chase."

Right: "Dead Birds Tell No Squawk."

Opposite: "Cave Monster."

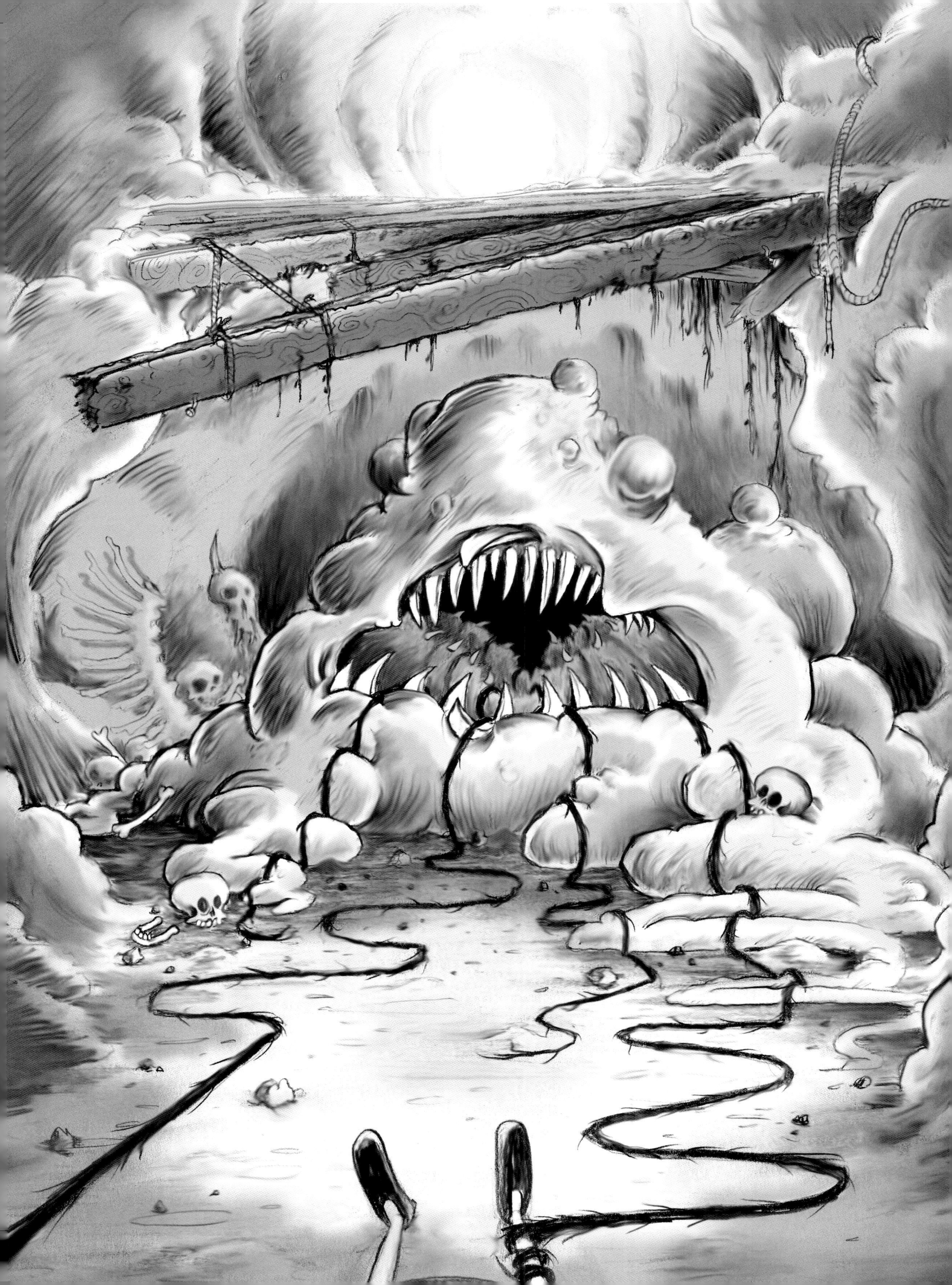

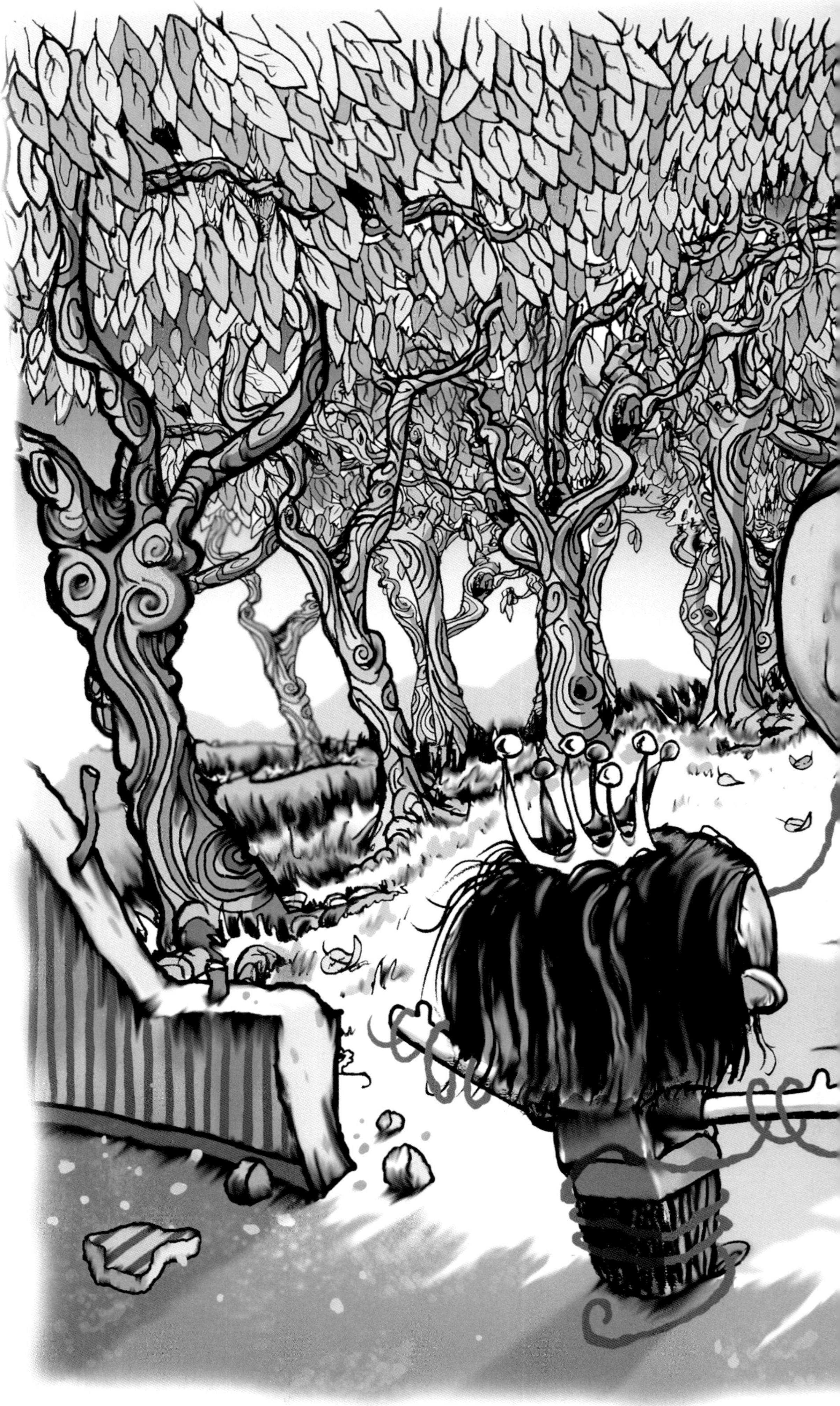

Right: "It Came On Wheels."

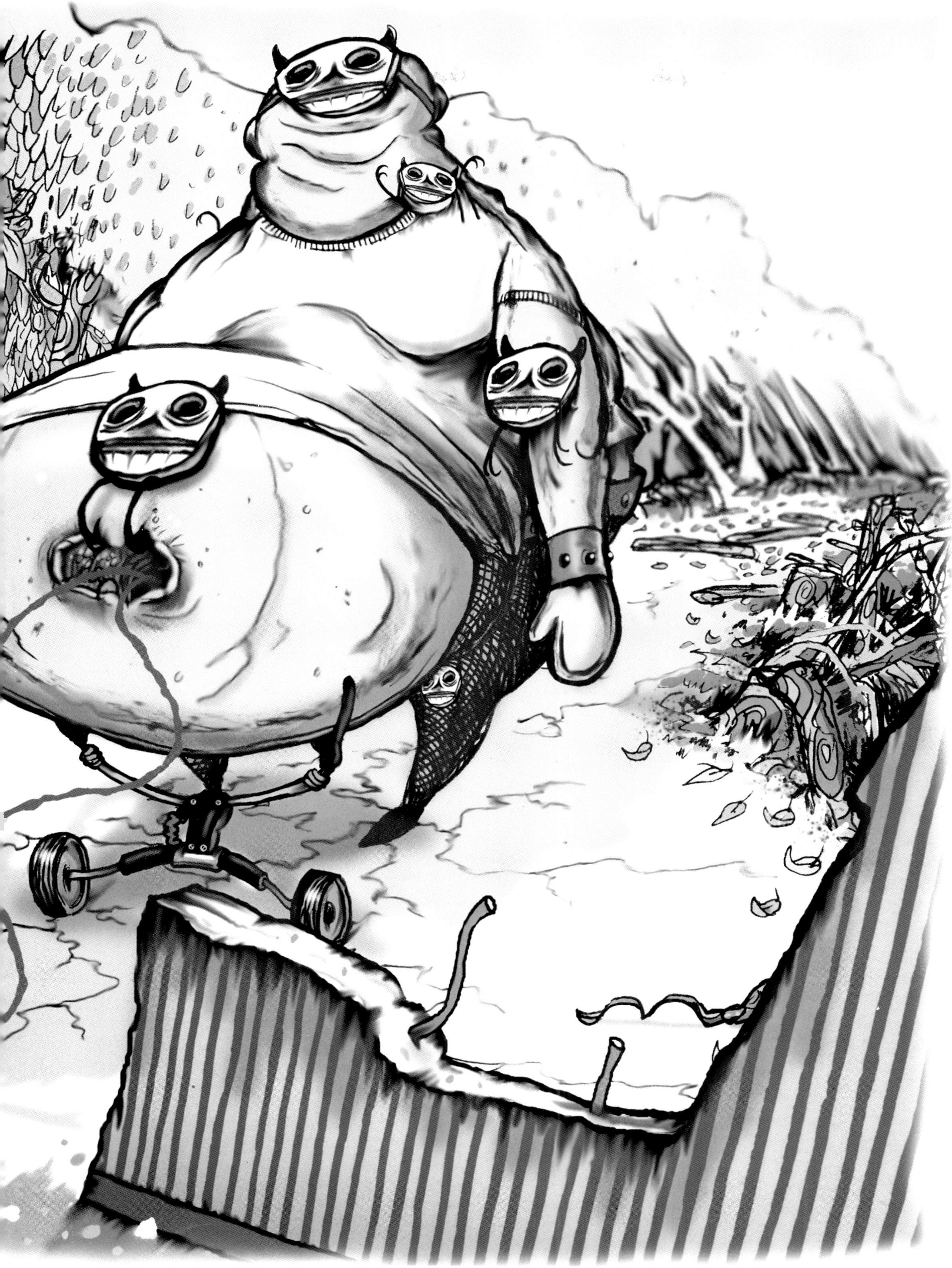

Funny Bone

Look, sometimes you just want to make silly, mindless drawings. I'm good at being mindless and I like to draw. It's a win-win, really.

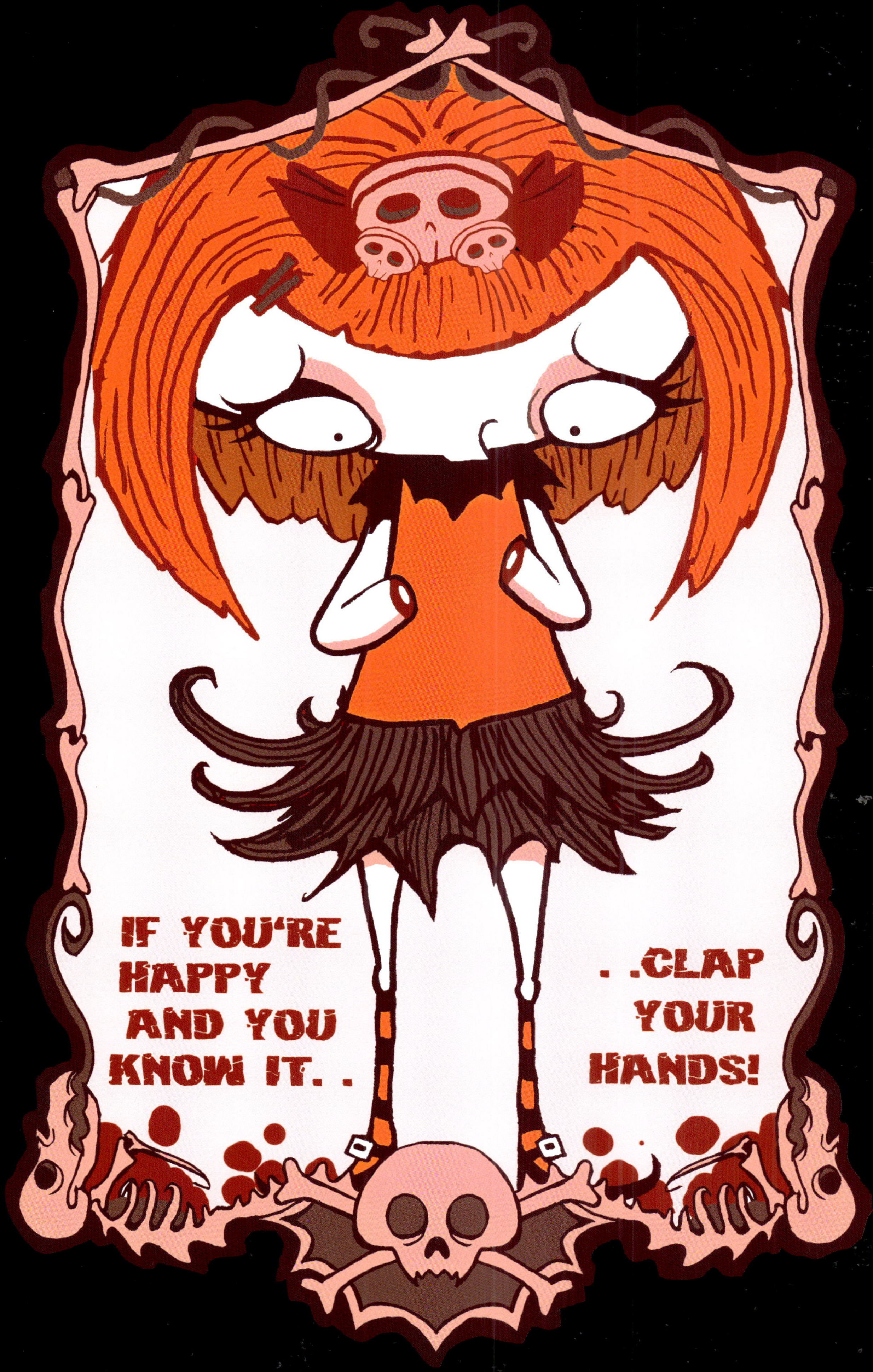
IF YOU'RE HAPPY AND YOU KNOW IT. .
. .CLAP YOUR HANDS!

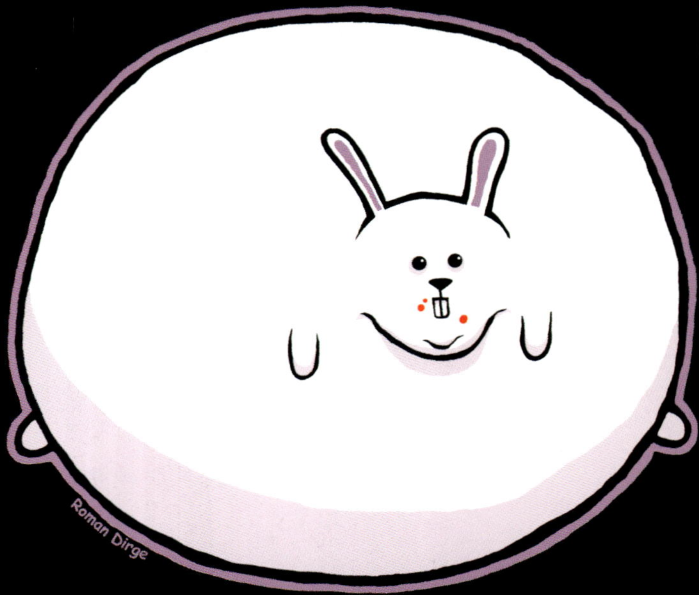

I HAD THREE BUNNIES, BUT TWO OF THEM MUST HAVE RUN AWAY OR SOMETHING.

Little Bun Bun

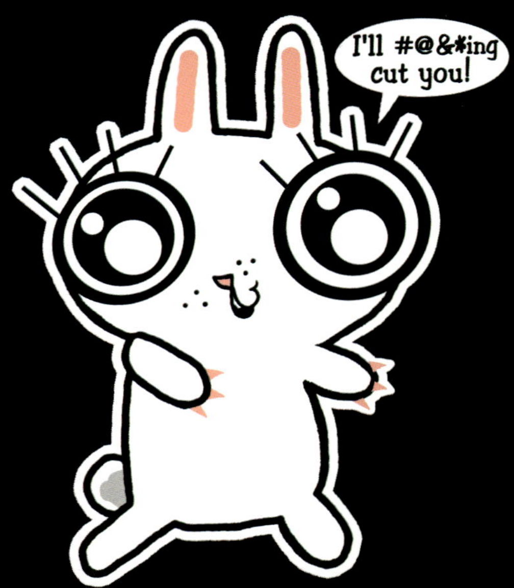

She's just a little slice of precious.

Sometimes, I just want to put on A Bunny suit and scream.

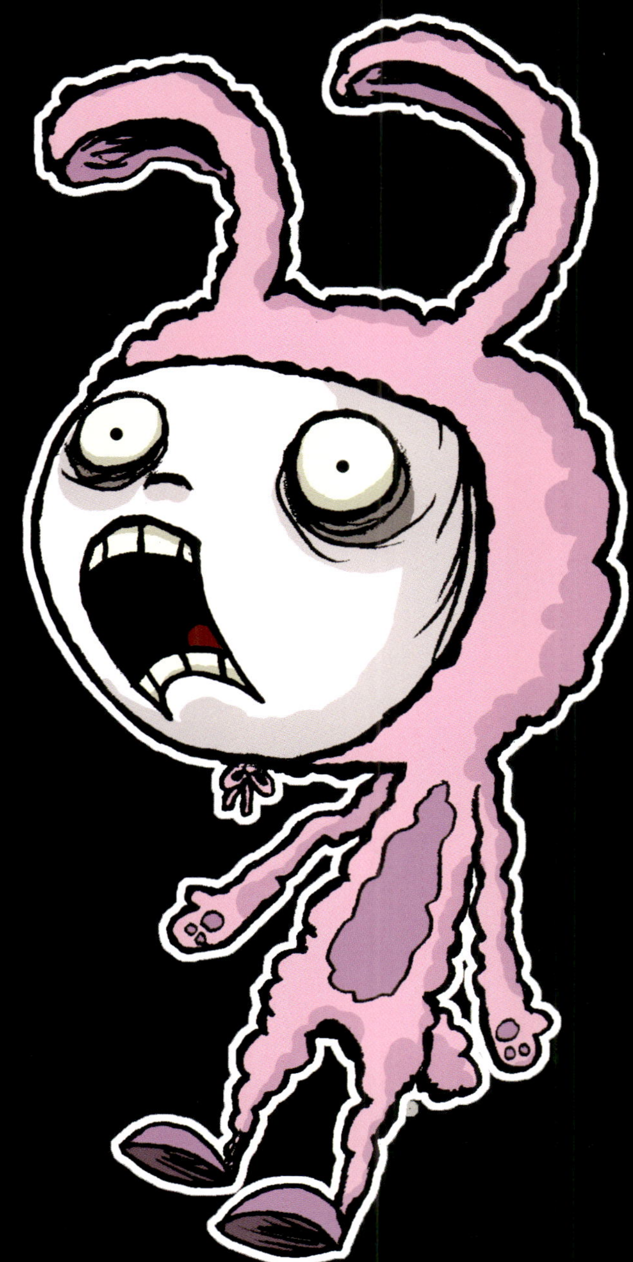

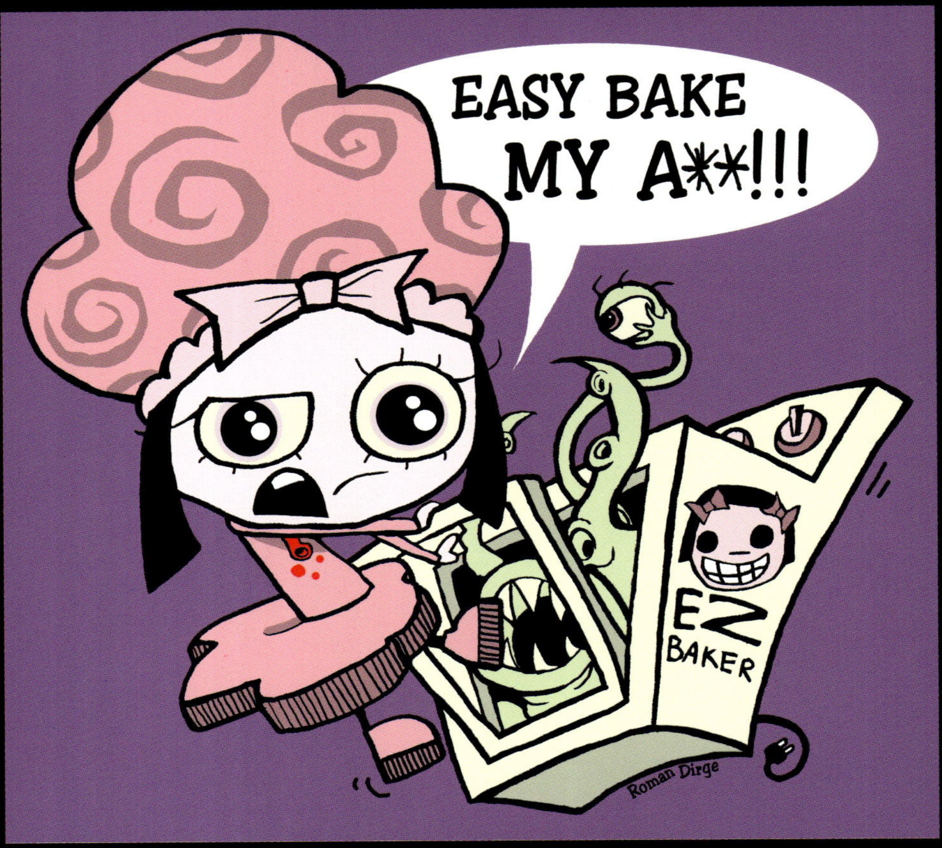

OpEn JugulAr CheesEcakE

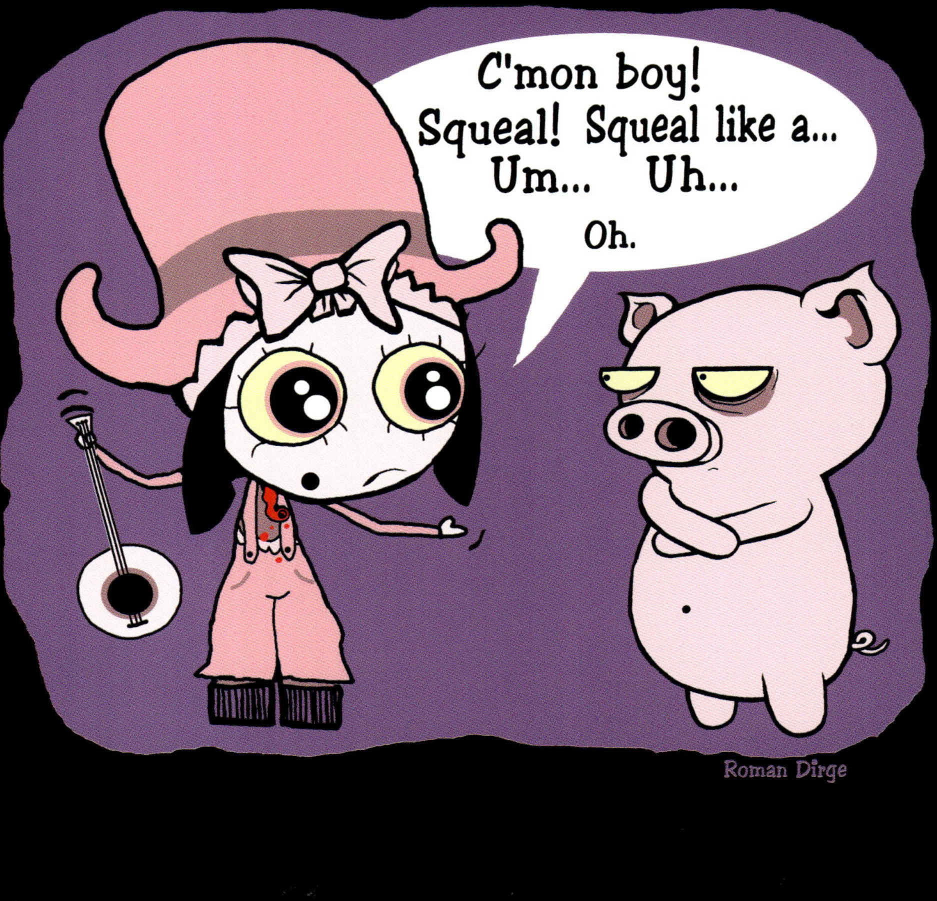

Sugar and spice and a head full of lice.

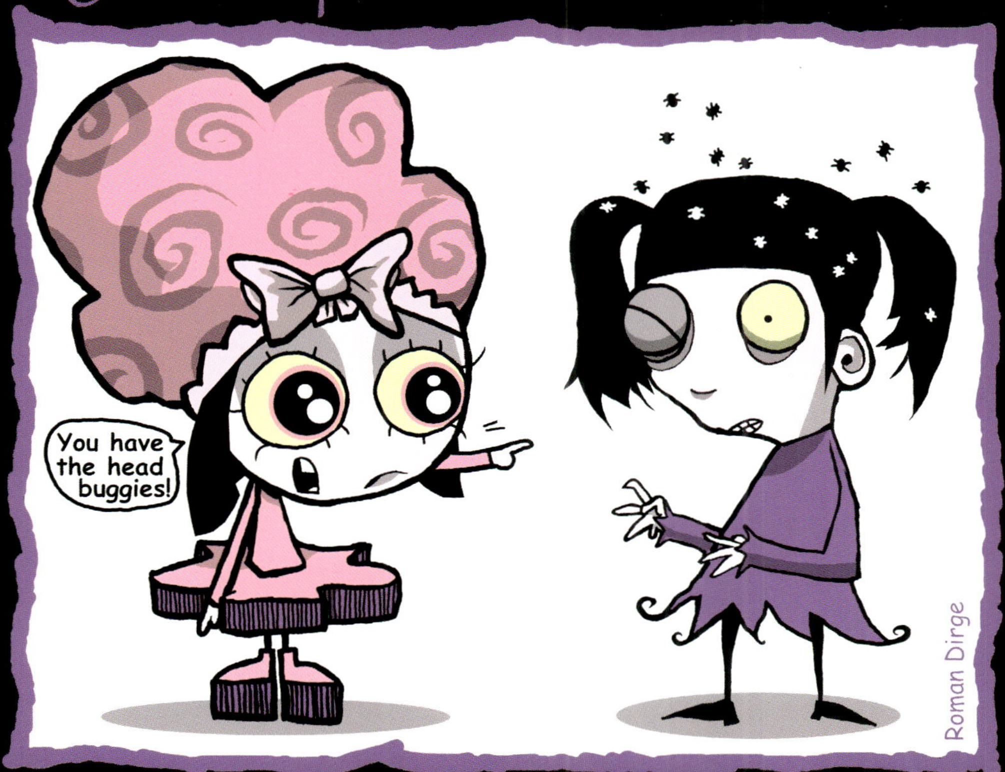

Snakes, snails and disemboweled entrails.

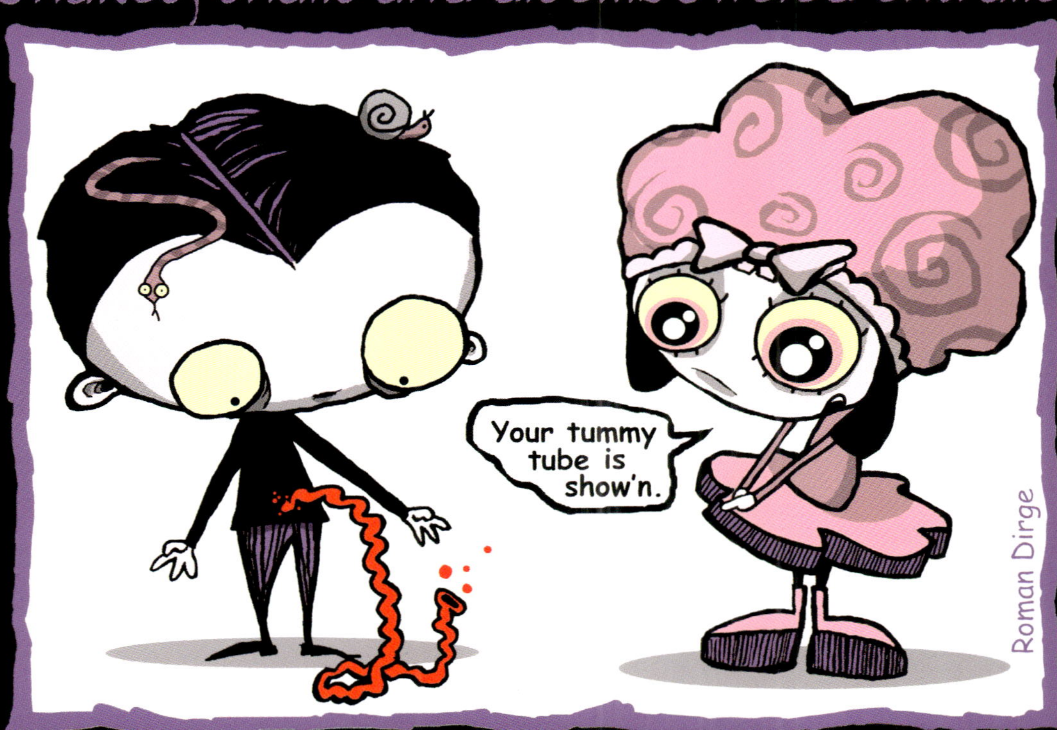

i Have the Dark Cooties

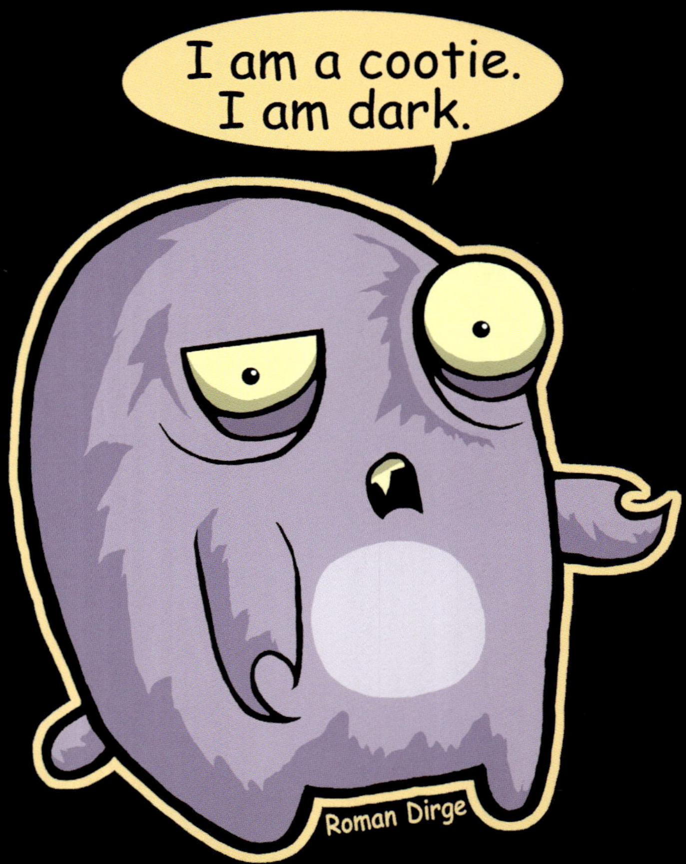

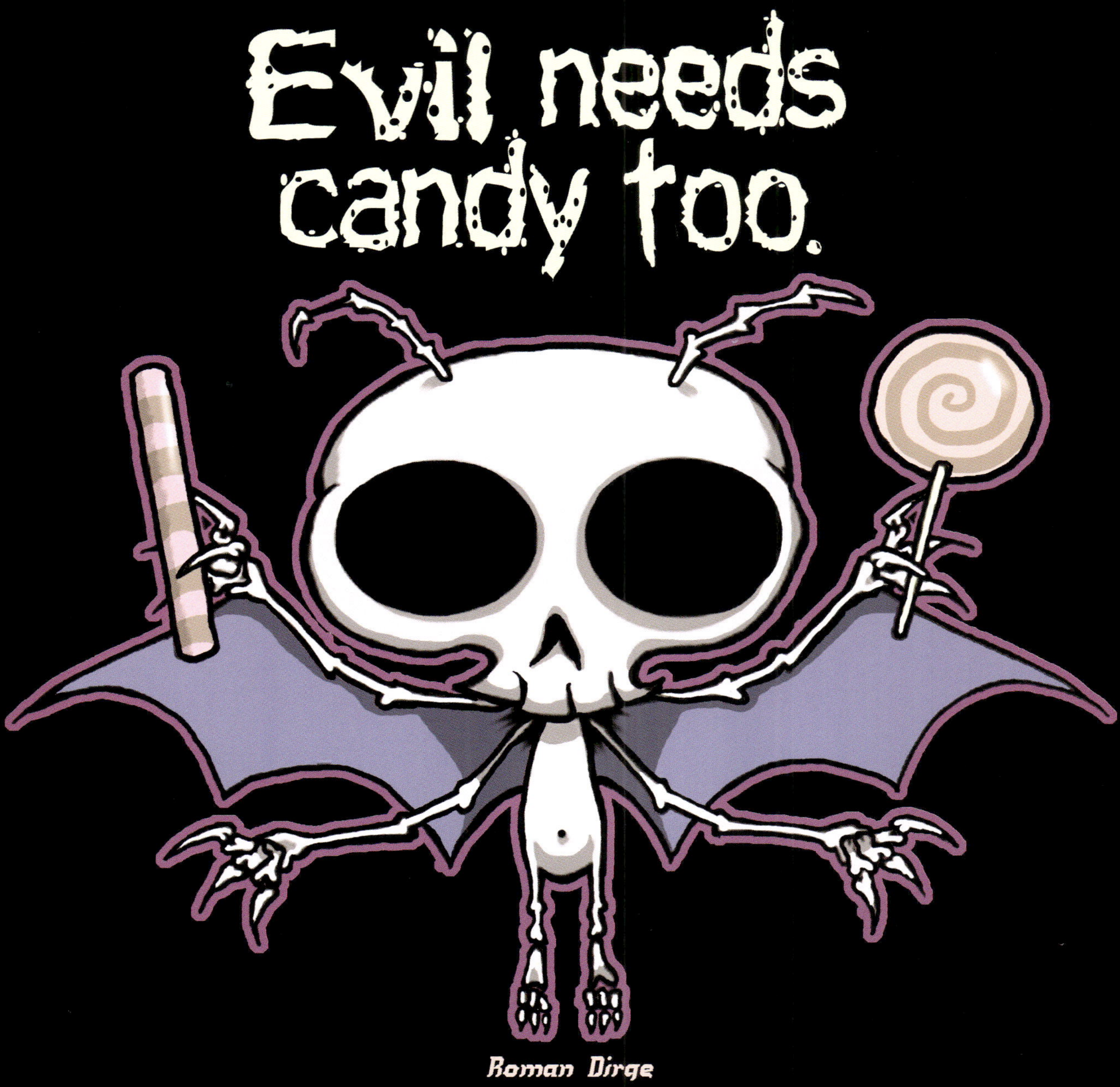
Evil needs
candy too.
Roman Dirge

If it walks like a duck
and quacks like a duck,
it's probably a duck.

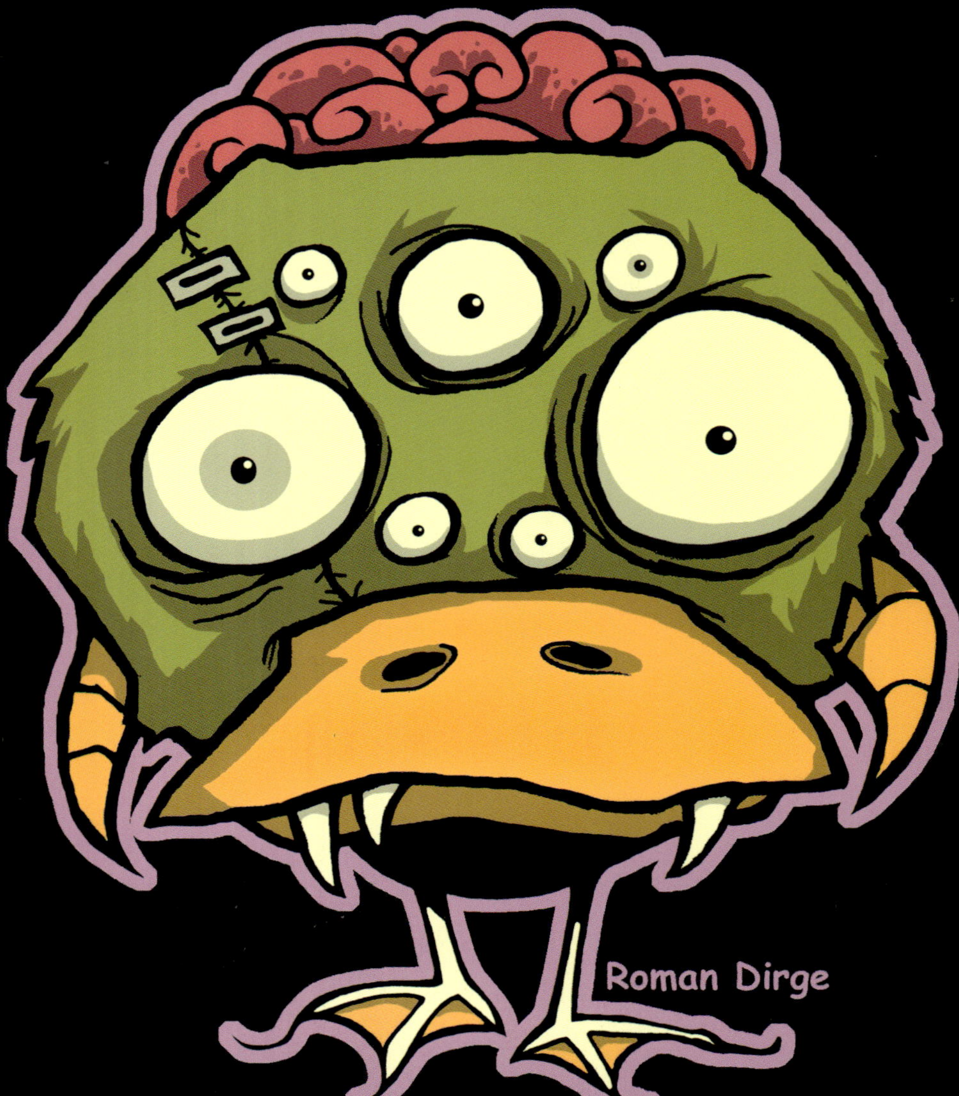

-Or it's one of those
things, in which case
you are so screwed.

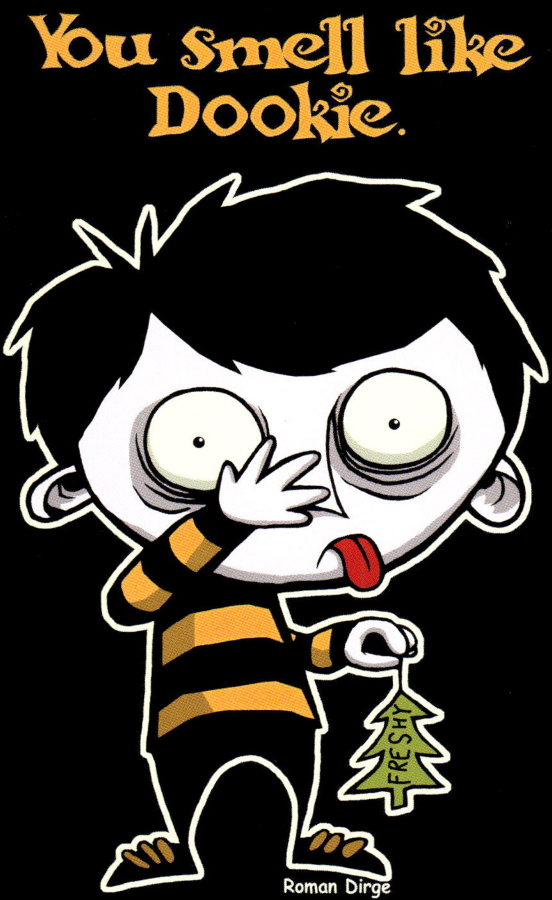
You smell like
Dookie.
Roman Dirge

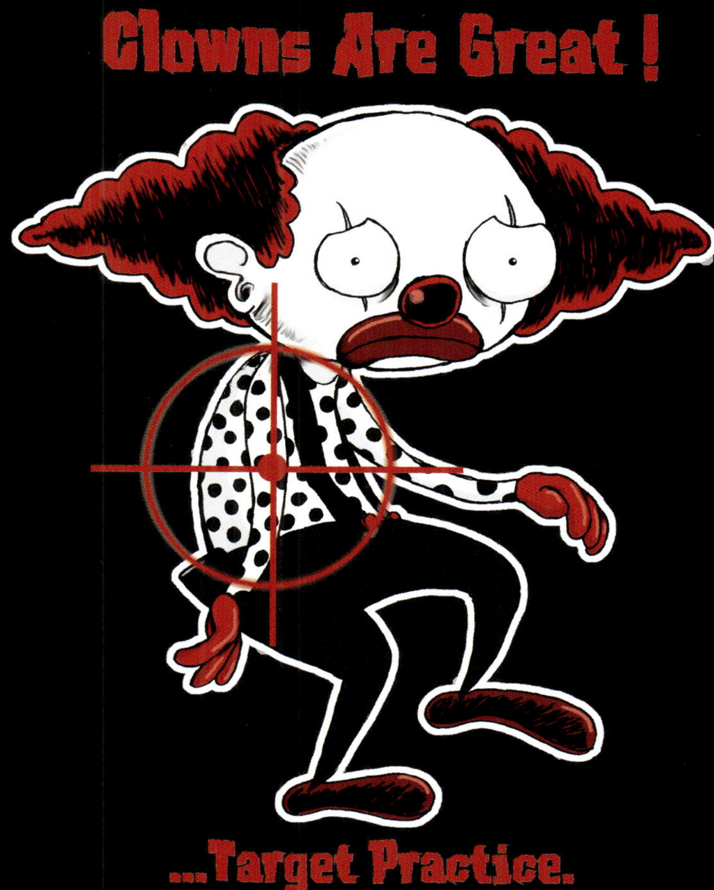
Clowns Are Great !
...Target Practice.

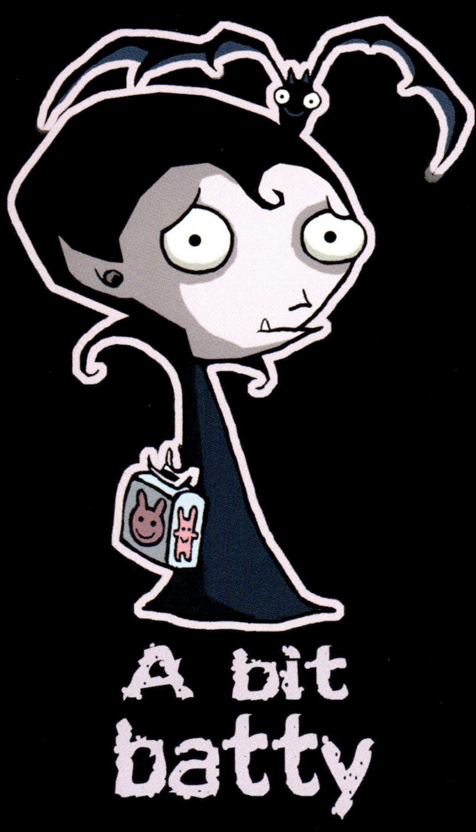
A bit
batty

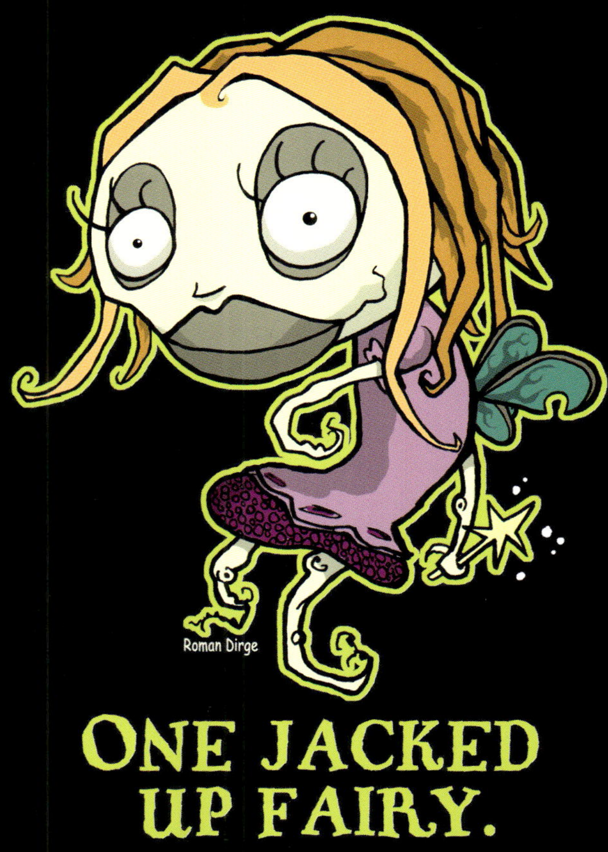
Roman Dirge
ONE JACKED
UP FAIRY.

BRIDE OF ZOMBIE BUNNY!

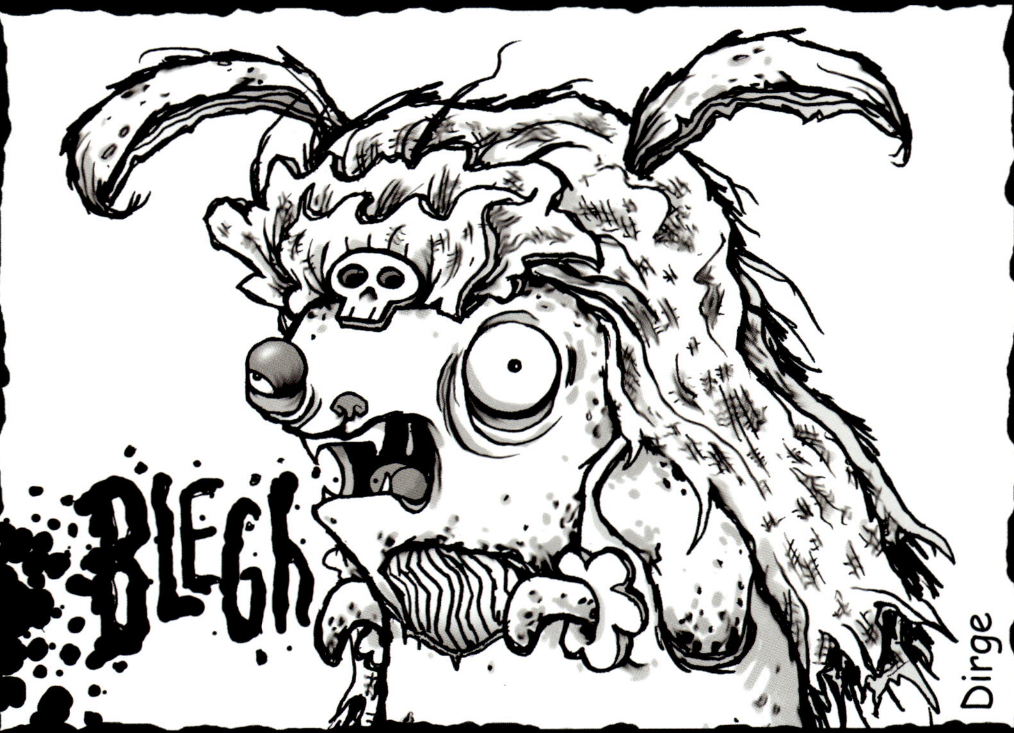

THAT'S RIGHT. SHE'S SEX IN A CAN.

ZOMBIE BUNNIES

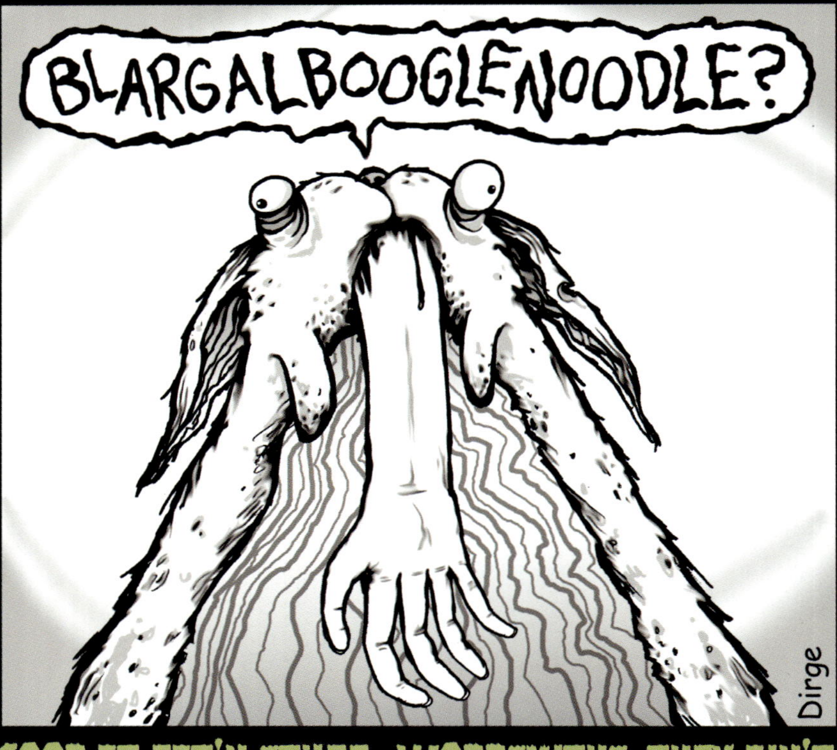

GOOD AT EAT'N STUFF. WORDSMITHS, THEY AIN'T.

PIGEONS SHOULD NOT EAT CHILI.

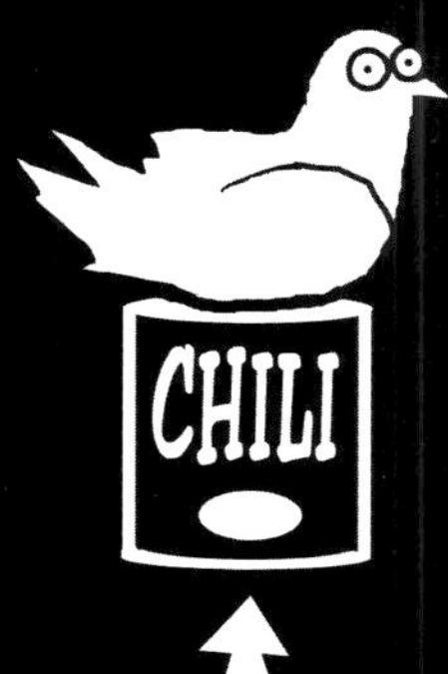

NO.

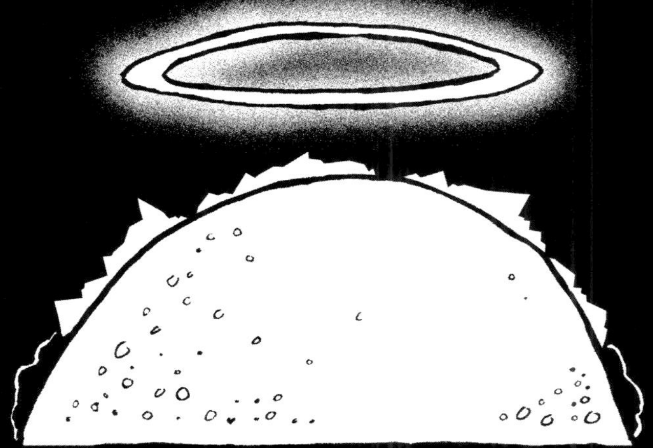

Tacos are nature's way
of giving you kisses.

WHY DOES MY CAT
KEEP YACKING UP
CAT YACK?

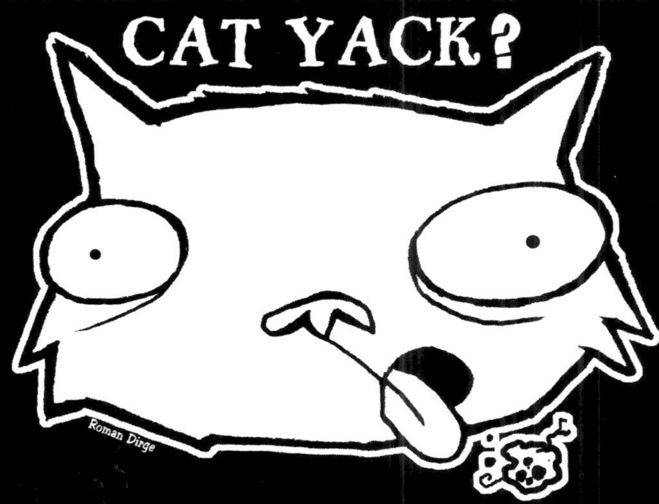

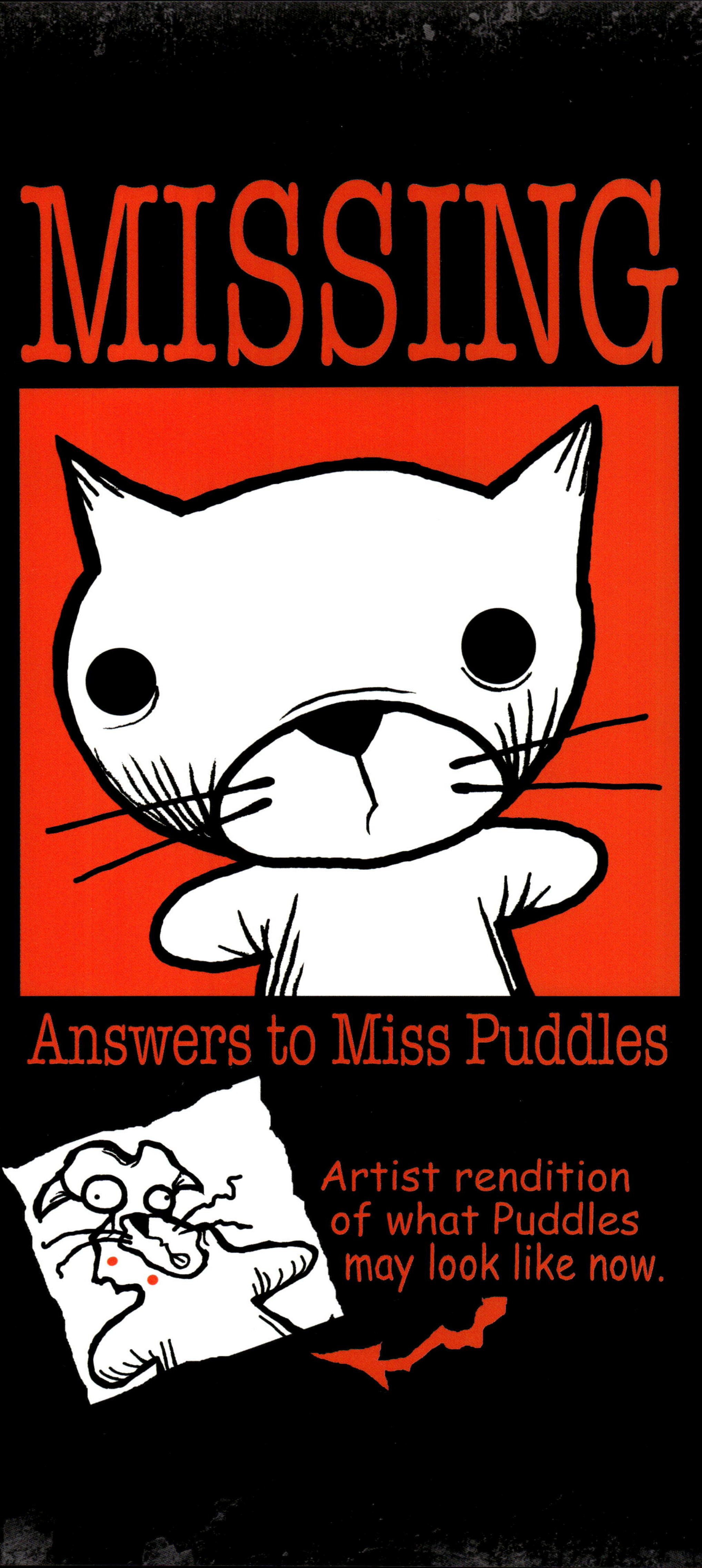
MISSING
Answers to Miss Puddles
Artist rendition
of what Puddles
may look like now.

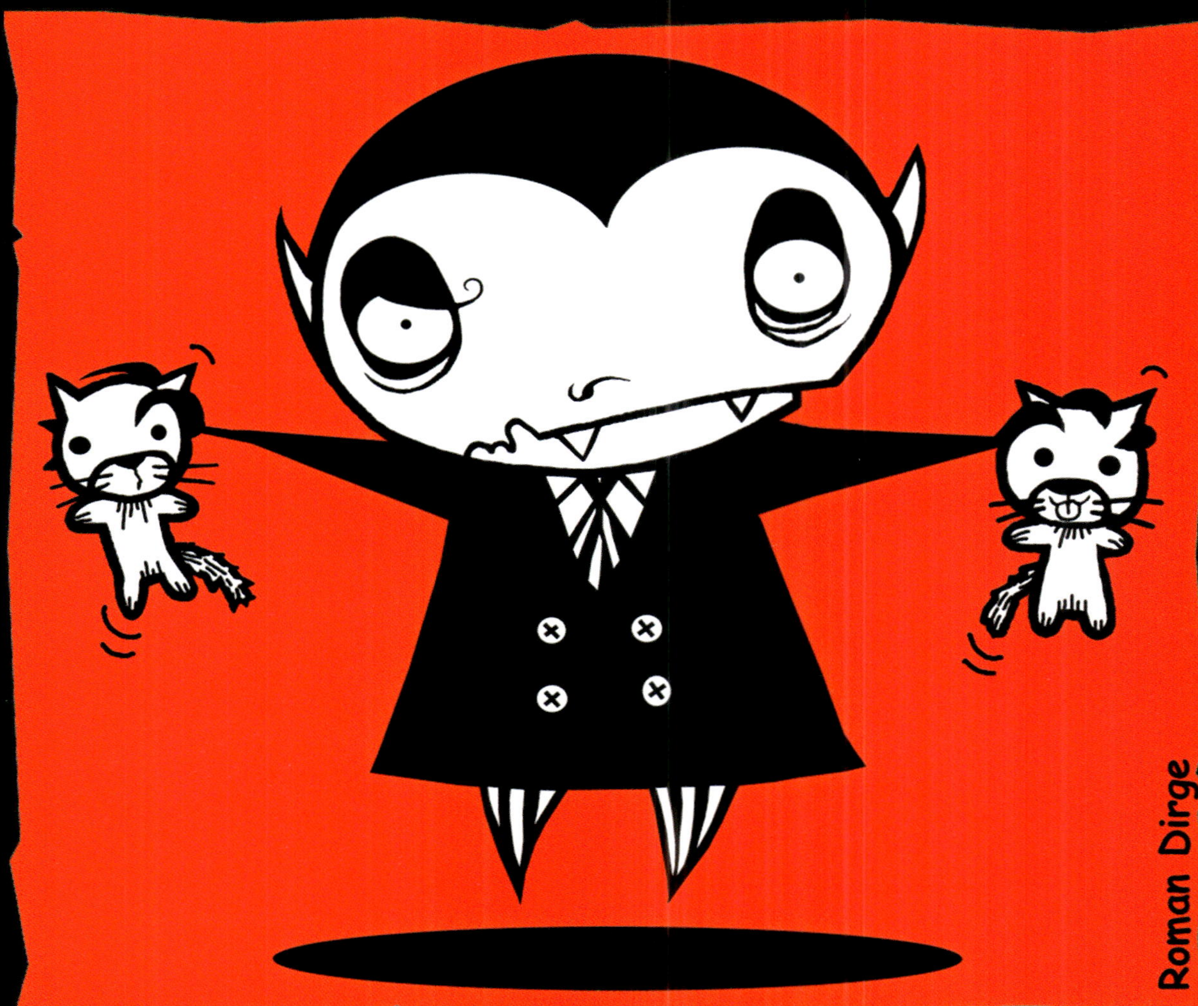

A vampire came to feed for his dark need
-but everyone had fled.
Needing blood to drink, his pride did sink
-he now bites kitties in the head.

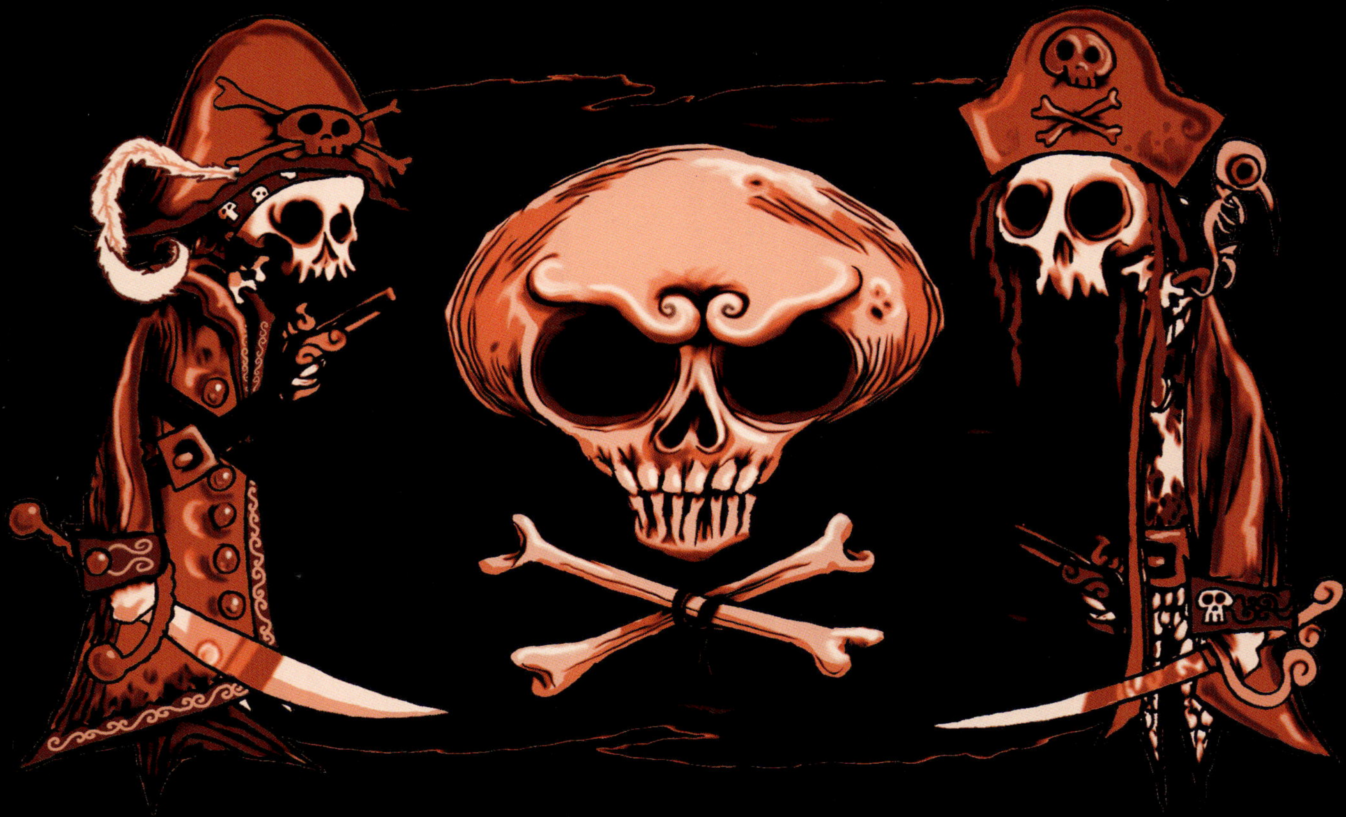

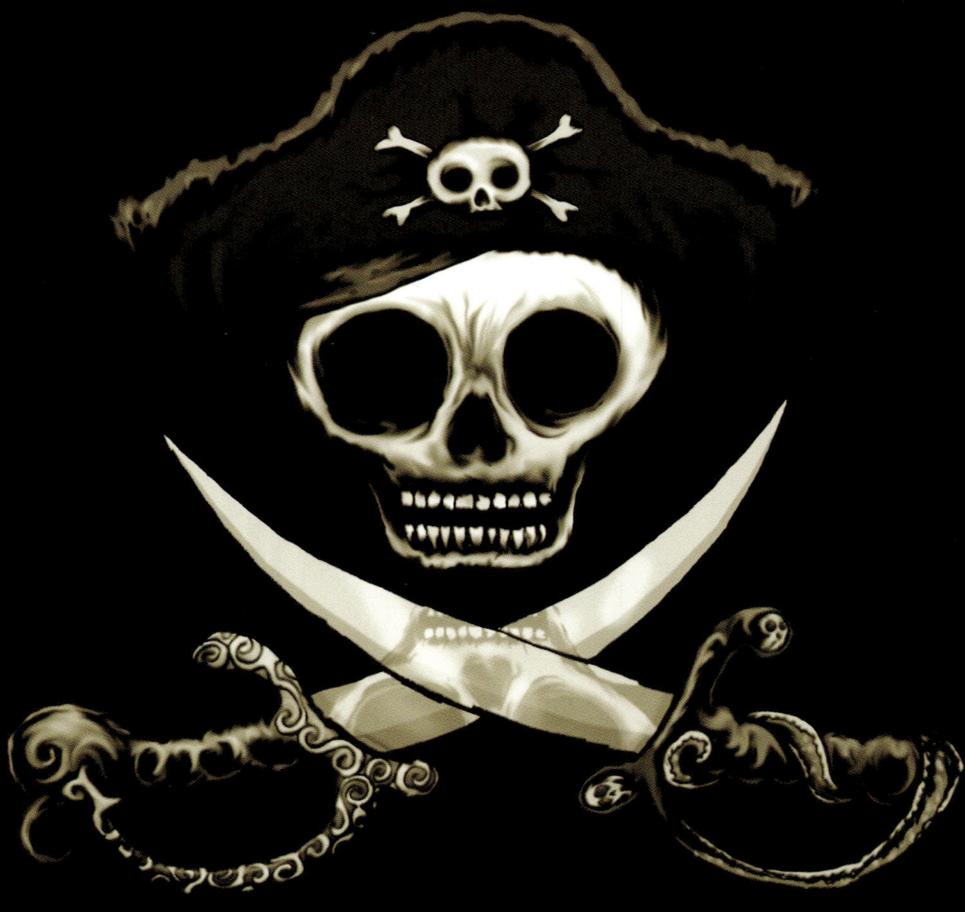

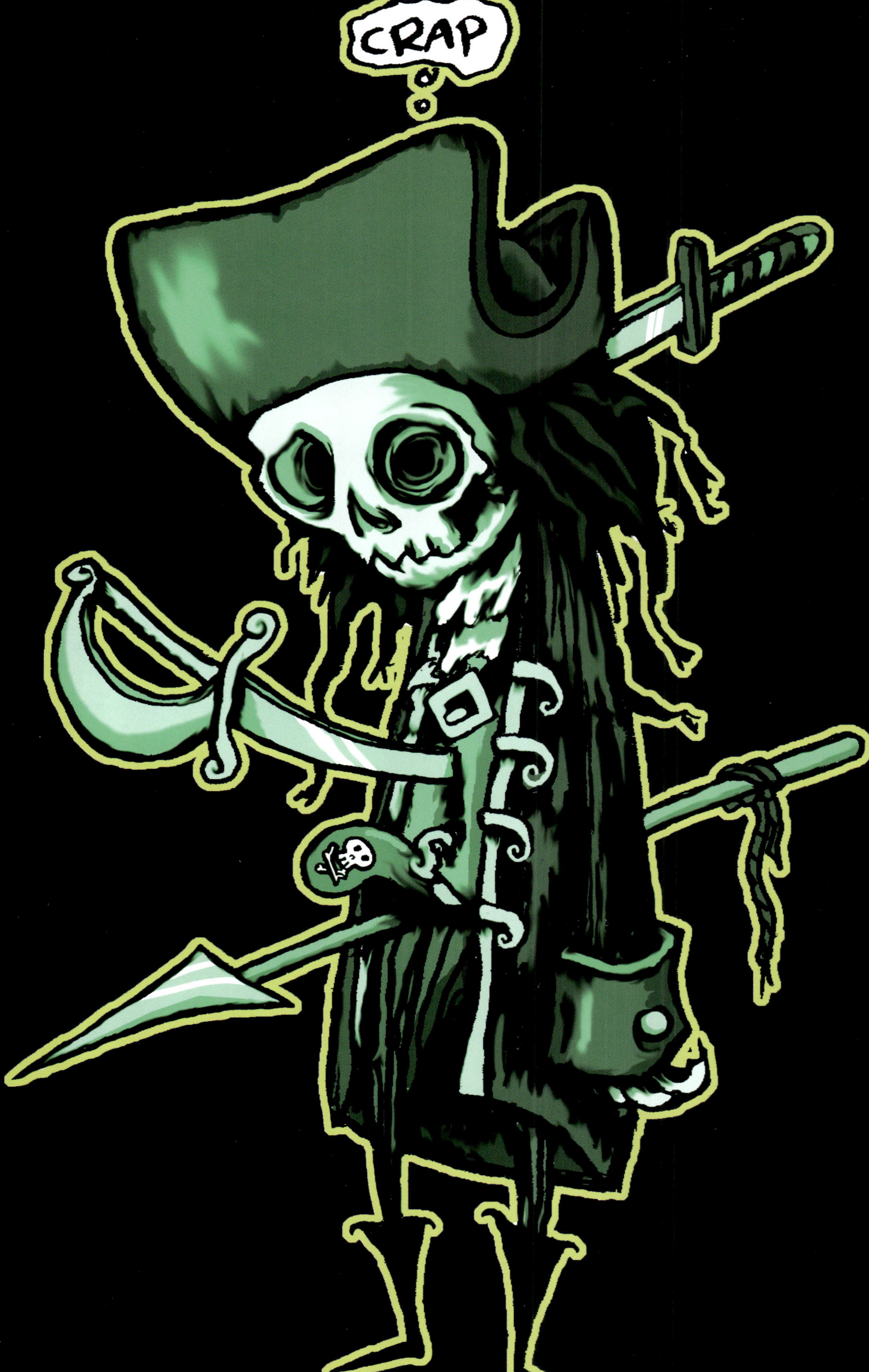
CRAP

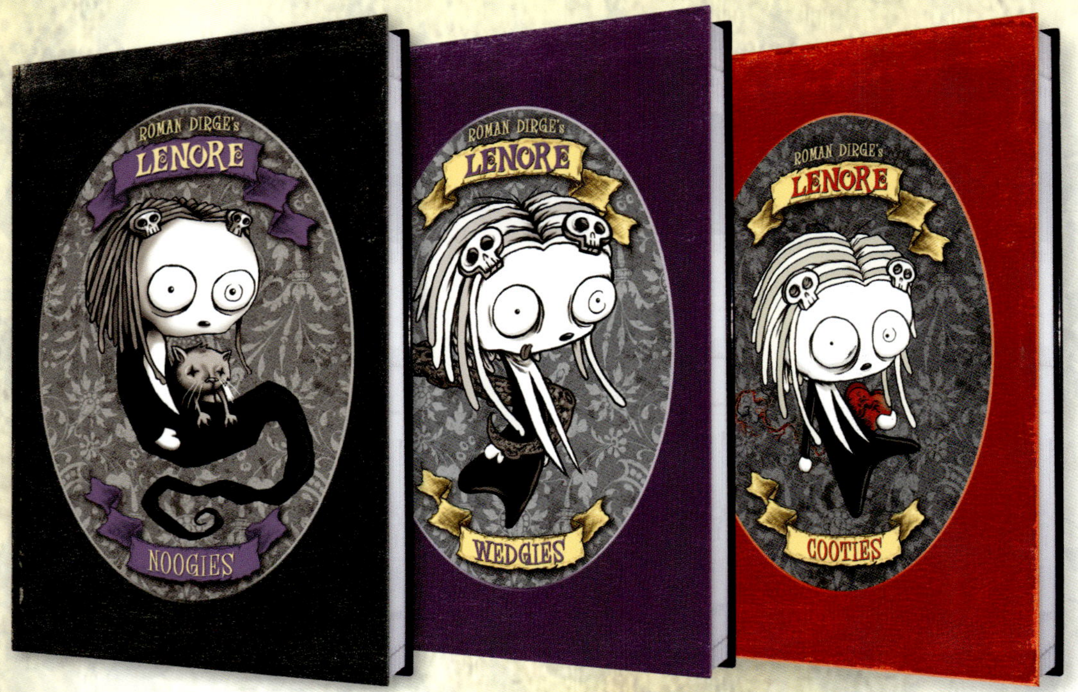

BOOKS

Return to the dark, surreal world of Lenore in these beautiful hardback editions, painstakingly re-colored by Roman Dirge.

WWW.TITANBOOKS.COM

COMICS

"Sweet and strange and slightly discomforting... An unholy union between Tim Burton and Dr. Seuss."
— *Los Angeles Times*

WWW.TITANMAGAZINES.COM/LENORE

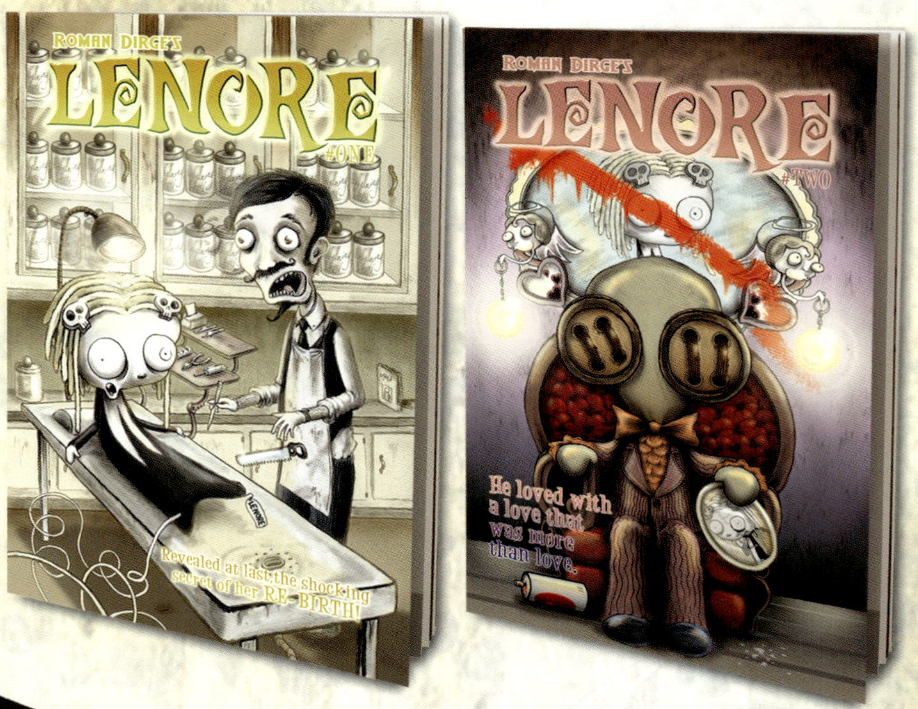

MERCHANDISE

All t-shirts are available in Men's sizes: M, L, XL and Ladies' sizes: S, M, L, XL

WWW.TITANMAGAZINES.COM/LENOREMERCHANDISE

WWW.FORBIDDENPLANET.COM

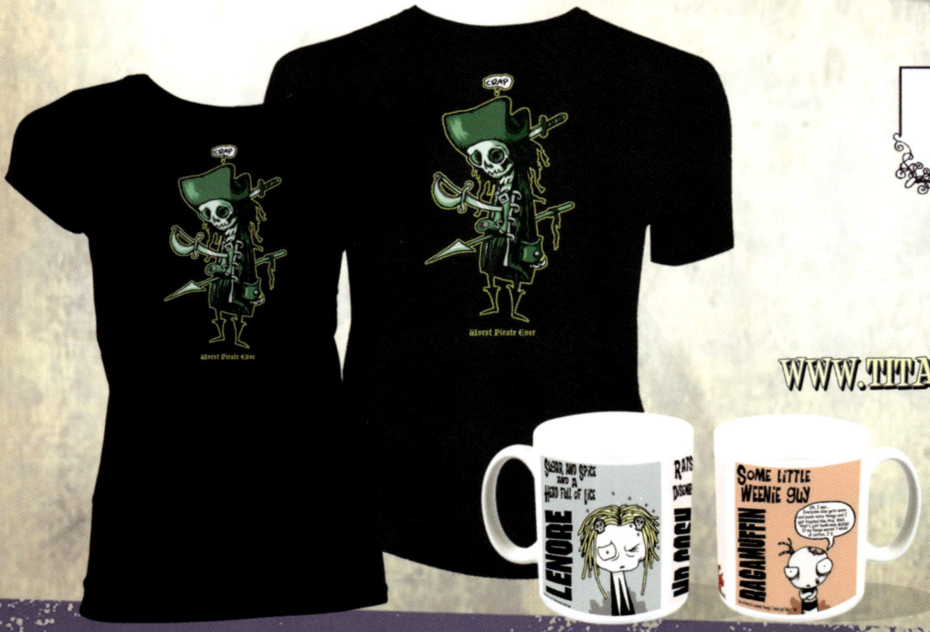

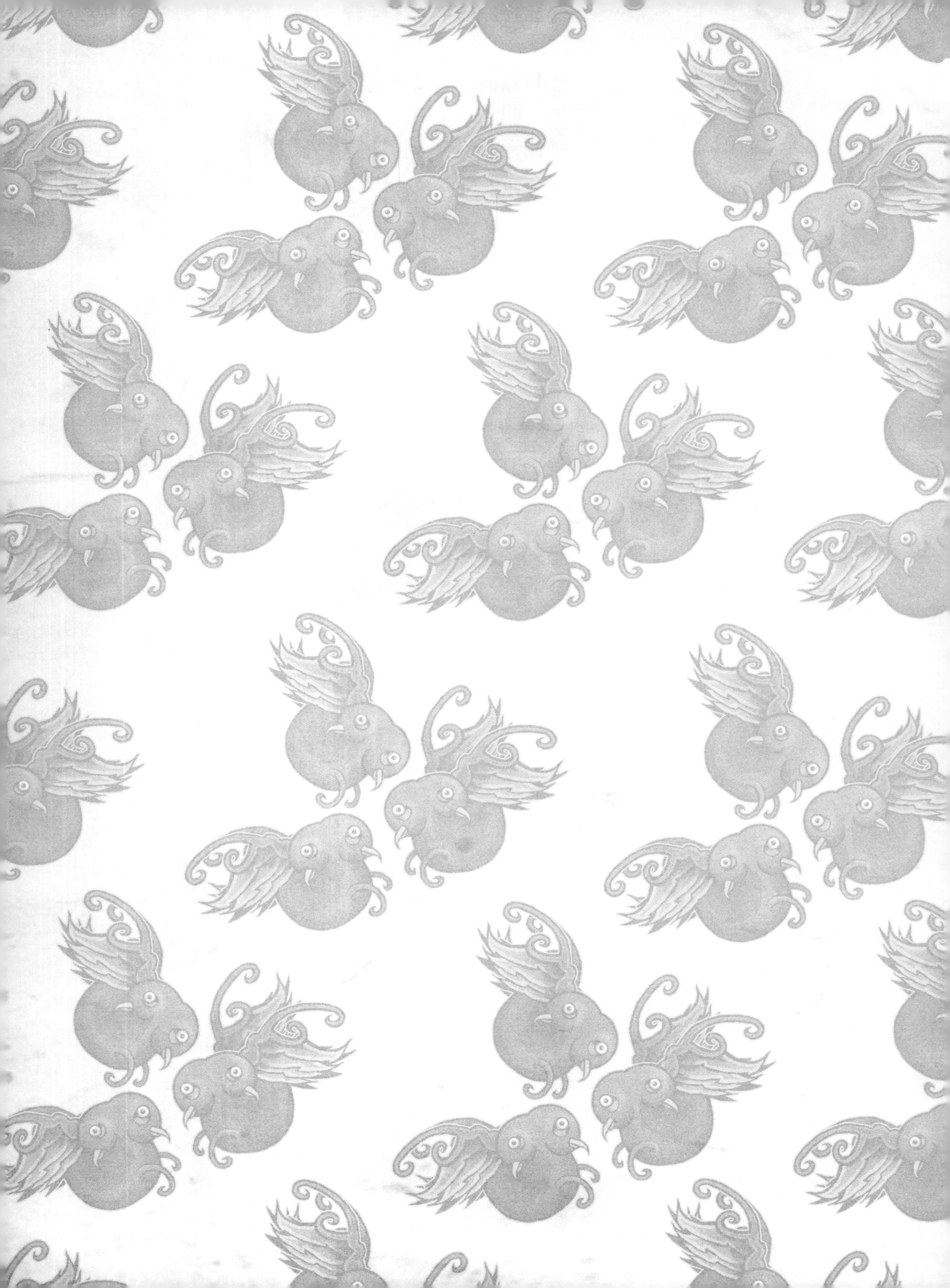